PEDAGOGIES
FOR THE
NON-POOR

Alice Frazer Evans
Robert A. Evans
William Bean Kennedy

PEDAGOGIES
FOR THE
NON-POOR

ORBIS BOOKS
Maryknoll, New York 10545

The Catholic Foreign Mission Society of America (Maryknoll) recruits and trains people for overseas missionary service. Through Orbis Books Maryknoll aims to foster the international dialogue that is essential to mission. The books published, however, reflect the opinions of their authors and are not meant to represent the official position of the society.

© 1987 by Alice Frazer Evans, Robert A. Evans, and William Bean Kennedy

Published by Orbis Books, Maryknoll, NY 10545

Manuscript editor: William H. Schlau

Library of Congress Cataloging-in-Publication Data

Evans, Alice F., 1939-
    Pedagogies for the non-poor.

    1. Church and social problems—Congresses.   2. Social
change—Study and teaching—Congresses.   3. Education,
Humanistic—Congresses.   I. Evans, Robert A., 1937-
II. Kennedy, William Bean.   III. Title
HN31.E895   1986   303.4   86-21831
ISBN 0-88344-409-7 (pbk.)

To Sally J. Scharper and Philip J. Scharper

Educators of the Non-Poor

Companions in Ministry

CONTENTS

PREFACE

"What area in the struggle for peace and justice are you most concerned about, and how are you pursuing that issue as an educator?" That question by the chairperson launched the fifteen justice advocates and scholars in the conference room into a lively four-hour session of sharing, exploring, and debating. Not surprisingly for a multiracial group of women and men with birthplaces and/or former vocational assignments on six continents, the geographical entry points varied: Nicaragua, South Africa, Lebanon, Korea, Switzerland, the USSR, and the United States. The issues were equally divergent: militarism, hunger, racism, housing, sexism, poverty, nationalism, disarmament, and so on.

Yet in the diversity of insights, interests, and energies there were at least two points of convergence. The first was a profound commitment to transformative education especially for the "non-poor"—the privileged and protected like themselves. The participants saw this as education which not only raises consciousness but also develops actions to change oppressive structures. The second was a sense of excitement about the learning and personal support generated by this kind of stimulating exchange. The project on "Pedagogies for the Non-Poor" was launched in this December 1982 meeting of the International Advisory Council of Plowshares Institute.

Agreement on the exact meaning of the term "non-poor" was a problem from the first meeting and continues in debate through Will Kennedy's discussion in chapter 10 of this volume. A working understanding of the term which will allow the reader to join the debate is that the non-poor are the middle class who as a group have low infant mortality, high life expectancy, and enough sustenance to be above the "poverty line." The commission to expand the dialogue on transformative education for the non-poor was given to a coordinating committee drawn from the Plowshares Council and included the three editors of this book. The project and this volume were a response to the challenge of developing an ongoing dialogue among the persons and groups committed to serious attempts at education for transformation.

With an initial understanding of terms, the next agenda for the committee was to develop criteria and identify effective and representative examples of liberative education. There was also a need to enlarge the number of dialogue partners and to discover a location and structure for consultation that promised to maximize the dialogue for the participants. Architects or sponsors of educational models were invited to share their program goals, designs, and research. Additional educators and theologians were invited as constructive critics to help the architects analyze and improve their work.

To our delight more promising models were nominated than would have made for a feasible first-round consultation. Applying the criteria (see "Models in Case Form," pp. 13–20, below) with a special stress on representative variety, we issued invitations. Most of those asked responded enthusiastically, thus confirming the suspicion that projects aimed at liberative education often work in relative isolation. Representatives of the projects proved eager to share with and get feedback and fresh ideas from others involved in similar activities. Seeking a format that appeared compatible with what Paulo Freire calls a "problem posing" approach to education, the editors worked with the architects to develop case descriptions of their work. The cases were circulated to all participants for study prior to the consultation. At least two commentators were selected for each case, one primarily theological and the other primarily educational in expertise. Their commentaries were also part of the preparatory documentation for the initial meeting. It is ironic that many participants knew each other by their projects or writings but had not met personally. Perhaps more important, they had seldom had an opportunity to share their own critical analyses of the models, to compare research, and to explore alternatives for improvement.

For two reasons the planners set up the consultation in California and immediately prior to the meetings of two interested professional organizations, the Association of Professors and Researchers in Religious Education (APRRE) and the Religious Education Association (REA). The latter organization, founded in 1903, has long been the major interfaith agency seeking to work in the theory and practice of religious education. It publishes the journal *Religious Education* and in its biennial international conferences honors major educational figures whose contributions have been significant for the field of religious education. For its 1983 international conference, held in Anaheim, California, the REA board had decided to present the William Rainey Harper Award to Paulo and Elza Freire of Brazil, whose writings and influence have been significant for the field.

Thus, the first reason for the choice of the time and place of the consultation was that the California location made it possible for Paulo Freire, who had influenced several of the architects and critics, to participate in a two-day consultation preceding these professional meetings. Second, the two conferences provided an excellent opportunity to extend the dialogue through arrangements to offer workshops on two of the models and include commentary by Paulo Freire.

Claremont School of Theology offered to host the consultation, and Professors Allen and Mary Elizabeth Moore graciously coordinated the arrangements at their institution. Thirty persons were present to contribute to the ongoing dialogue. Unfortunately, Elza Freire was unable to attend, but Paulo was fully engaged in exploring the idea of whether it is possible to develop.

pedagogies for the non-poor characterized by justice. The discussions at the consultation as well as the related workshops at APRRE and REA were taped for later analysis and use. Paulo Freire's distinctive contribution to this dialogical process is included in this volume in the edited version of his remarks prepared by a friend and former colleague (see chap. 9) and in a related article containing edited parts of his comments upon receiving the Harper Award (see *Religious Education* 79, no. 4, Fall 1984, pp. 511–22).

Philip J. Scharper, the late Editor-in-Chief of Orbis Books, a member of Plowshares Institute's International Advisory Council, and a former president of REA, played an important role in this project from the outset. Not only was he a strong supporter of the dialogical process, but he was convinced that the subject of pedagogies on peace and justice for the non-poor was an issue of liberation. Under Philip's leadership Orbis Books was the first of a consortium of donors that provided basic support for this effort in transformative education. Following the consultation, the three editors, again with the help of Philip Scharper, shaped the format of this book. The case studies and the commentaries were revised and refined in light of the discussions and in consultation with the architects and critics, who had become in some instances cocreators of new projects. With Philip's early encouragement during the three years of the project, the editors reflected, debated, and did additional research. Therefore, they added introductory and reflective chapters in an effort to put this material in context and to provide interpretive help for our readers and new dialogue partners. When there were delays in the manuscript due to Plowshares's projects to support struggles for liberation in Nicaragua or South Africa, Philip's seemingly inexhaustible patience was a gift of grace.

We recognize, however, that Philip Scharper seldom worked alone. Sally, his wife and companion of thirty-six years, was both helpmate and accomplished author in her own right. Both Philip and Sally, as those who saw our brothers and sisters in the Third World as instructors in life and faith, modeled a commitment to justice. Through patience and perseverance they brought to the attention of the First World the enormous contributions of theology developed in the Third World. For Philip and Sally's special contributions to the pedagogy of the non-poor, we dedicate this book in celebration of their ministry as prophetic and compassionate teachers.

On behalf of Plowshares Institute and its International Advisory Council we wish to thank Philip Scharper, Stephen B. Scharper, and William H. Schlau of Orbis Books, and all those who contributed to this volume:

To the participants in this dialogical project whose experience and commitment ground this effort in First World reality and who risked the vulnerability of sharing their projects and their hopes with a society and a church wary of change. A list of contributors appears at the end of this book.

To the donors who enhanced and sustained this dialogue and made difficult decisions about limited funds:

Church World Service, Office of Global Education
Edward Hazen Foundation
Episcopal Church, U.S.A.
New World Foundation
Orbis Books
Presbyterian Hunger Program
United Methodist Church, Board of Discipleship

To our colleagues and hosts at Claremont, the leaders and members of the APRRE and REA, and other educators who aided the project.

To Union Theological Seminary for secretarial help in typing the Freire tapes.

To the staff of Plowshares, Nancy C. Hajek, case coauthor, and Joan B. Dorman, who sacrificed weekends to give priority to manuscript preparation.

Finally, we thank in advance our readers who are invited to join us in this important quest for more effective models of transformative education for the non-poor. We trust you will accept the challenge to be engaged not just in a dialogue, but in active support of a teaching mission that seeks personal and structural transformation for justice.

ALICE FRAZER EVANS
ROBERT A. EVANS
WILLIAM BEAN KENNEDY

PEDAGOGIES FOR THE NON-POOR

INTRODUCTION

INVITATION TO DIALOGUE

Welcome to a dialogue about transformative education! Architects of eight different models offer case studies for your reflection. More than twice that many educators and theologians have written commentaries on those cases for the discussion with you. Paulo Freire participated in the conversation and invites you into the dialogue with him. We three editors have framed the case studies, commentaries, and Freire's remarks with our analyses and introductions to the two parts. In the present Introduction and the introduction to Part 1 that follows we first offer a sketch of the historical and present contexts to get you located, then give you some suggestions about the plan of the book, and finally lead you into the first model. Welcome to the dialogue.

HISTORICAL CONTEXT

Following the Great Depression of the 1930s and World War II, the United States and Canada, among other First World nations, experienced a revival of religious interest and activity that extended throughout the 1950s. That period led into what Sydney E. Ahlstrom, writing of the United States, called "The Turbulent Sixties," with that decade's confusion: "Rich natural resources, technological marvels, vast productive power, great ideals, expanding universities, and flourishing churches seem to have resulted only in a country wracked by fear, violence, racism, war, and moral hypocrisy. [A] sense of national failure and dislocation became apparent [to many]" (*A Religious History of the American People*, New Haven, Yale University Press, 1972, p. 1087). One element of that trend was what Ahlstrom called "a deep shift in the presuppositional substructures of the American mind" (ibid.). He describes the features of that shift:

1. A growing commitment to a naturalism or "secularism" and corresponding doubts about the supernatural and the sacral
2. A creeping (or galloping) awareness of vast contradictions in American life between profession and performance, the ideal and the actual

1

3. Increasing doubt as to the capacity of present-day ecclesiastical, political, social, and educational institutions to rectify the country's deep-seated woes [ibid.].

Robert T. Handy emphasizes the increasing "consciousness of the multiple problems of North American life—for example, racism, rural and urban poverty, pollution of the environment, inadequate medical care, inflation, crime rates" (*A History of the Churches in the United States and Canada*, New York, Oxford University Press, 1976, p. 416). The churches responded to that situation in a wide variety of ways, among which were newly focused ethical studies and urban mission activities like community organizing.

Many of the related educational efforts emphasized cognitive activity aimed at "attitude changes" on the assumption that a change in consciousness would lead to action for related changes in society. Although still committed primarily to the nurture of children and traditional Bible study for adults, church educational agencies began to produce "action-related" materials on such problems as racism and rural and urban poverty. These modest efforts fitted into patterns of schooling as they had developed in Western culture. Critics easily caricatured them as being passive, "sitting still" learning, not leading to any effective action. Despite the best efforts of those working on such programs, there was an admitted gap between the actual results of such educational activity and their hopes for significant change in society.

On the other hand, church-related "social action" programs stressed direct challenges to established power structures that were targeted as forces perpetuating injustices. Those programs emphasized "social analysis" and focused their mobilization efforts on situations of great need, often dramatic need, like the civil rights struggle. Saul Alinsky and the Urban Training Center in Chicago typified such approaches. Education-oriented persons tended to see them as too activist, lacking in their programs the deeper, long-range growth in understanding that would result in sustained change and development of new structures to replace the old. And, despite the best efforts of the social activists, one victory in the skirmishes seemed to lead only to the need for another. Like the action-oriented educators they found their hopes for major societal changes frustrated by the strength and complexity of what they considered the unjust structures of society.

During those hectic years of optimism and relatively easy funding, both types of efforts could afford the luxury of working in isolation from one another, even of seeing each other as competitors for church support. All such efforts had to face the fragmentation of the movements for change. In 1972 Paulo Freire was engaged in four workshops across the United States, in each of which the needs and styles of the separatist black, Hispanic, Native-American, and feminist caucuses prevented any serious common analysis or mobilization. In the final debriefing he told the evaluating group that they were naive, that while their minorities fought each other, the minority of the powerful "slept well." Over the next few years both activist and educational-program leaders began to realize that their separate strategies for change needed reappraisal and further development.

This analysis is oversimplified, for all along groups were working hard to combine action and reflection in more effective ways to change the situations that were dehumanizing people. Since the midseventies more and more organizations have been struggling to put together the raising of critical consciousness with effective action for change. With the slowing of economic growth, the drying up of financial support, and the public swing toward more conservative politics, many recognized the need for better theory about how to educate and mobilize people for liberation from their oppression. Educators began to work more carefully on "action-reflection" learning and "praxis-oriented" education strategies, and activists began to emphasize more the reflection component of their organizational activity in order to mobilize more effectively for long-range change.

During those years of reappraisal the experience of Latin Americans in their struggles for liberation became known and helpful to many of these groups. The writings of Paulo Freire, in particular, offered fresh stimulation and help in analyzing the problems and developing strategic action. Freire's sharp critique of "banking education" and his goal of "conscientization" with its essential action dimension challenged educators to struggle against the limitations of their inherited rigid patterns of curriculum and classroom instruction. (See Henry A. Giroux's excellent summary of Freire's work in his introduction to Paulo Freire, *The Politics of Education: Culture, Power and Liberation*, South Hadley, Mass., Bergin and Garvey, 1985.) Freire's efforts to develop critical consciousness about oppression from within the experiences of the oppressed and his strong emphasis that the oppressed were the experts on their problems helped others understand more clearly why some of the programs in North America and elsewhere in the First World had not worked better. With the appearance in English of *Pedagogy of the Oppressed* (New York, Herder and Herder, 1970) and two major articles in *Harvard Educational Review* (40, no. 2, May 1970, and 40, no. 3, August 1970), his educational thinking stimulated many persons and groups to deepen their questions about the relationship of education and action. Freire's emphasis on "problematizing education" challenged the passivity of many programs and the absence or limited scope of social analysis in others.

Meanwhile, movements against world hunger, environmental exploitation, poverty, and nuclear arms were all searching for ways to analyze their particular concerns in a global context. "Free enterprise," Marxist, and other types of analysis of the world economic order offered theoretical ways to understand what was happening. Freire's clear but low-visibility commitment to the church—the church at its best, to be sure—and his open self-identification as an educator helped break down some of the stereotypes that had contributed to the fragmentation of the movements. His basic point that the oppressed knew their oppression best and therefore owned their own learning about it helped contribute to a modesty on the part of many self-identified "change-agents" that freed them for more collegial and constructive effort. In many areas of the First World a major need seemed to be for a "political literacy" to overcome the naiveté about social structures that plagued attempts to change the situation.

Efforts toward consciousness-raising, conscientization, and praxis-learning appeared in more and more places. The new Doctor of Ministry programs in theological education attempted to ground pastoral learning in pastoral practice. A considerable scholarly interest in the relation of theory and practice began to emerge in theological and philosophical literature. (For a good review of such activity see Matthew L. Lamb, *Solidarity with Victims: Toward a Theology of Social Transformation*, New York, Crossroad, 1982.) Urban training centers developed programs to bring together action and reflection. Many black, Hispanic, Native-American, feminist, and gay-lesbian organizations tried to adapt Freire-type education to their own ends.

Freire's influence proved exciting, and movements in many parts of the First World worked to develop similar processes of education for liberation in their own settings. But it has proved difficult to translate or apply Freire's analysis to the situation in the First World. Doing so calls for some general analysis of the present context and some understanding of differences and similarities between Latin America and the First World regarding their cultural, social, and politico-economic situations.

THE PRESENT CONTEXT

Differences

1. *Class Distinction.* In the First World it seems more difficult to use "class" as a descriptive category than it is in the Brazilian setting where Freire developed his analysis. There the simple description of "oppressed" and "oppressor" fitted adequately enough for those terms to be useful in his analysis of education. In Canada, the United States, and many other First World nations, however, the perception of a huge, relatively undifferentiated "middle class" obscures and confuses that distinction. In a helpful analysis Gregory Baum suggests that in North America "what we have is a complex intermeshing of technocratic depersonalization and immobility, economic domination and exploitation, racial exclusion and inferiorization, and other forms including the subjugation of women" (*Religion and Alienation: A Theological Reading of Sociology*, New York, Paulist Press, 1975, pp. 218–19f.). Furthermore, the production and perpetuation of the above-mentioned perception—with its obscurity and confusion—by the ideological interpretations of the media compound the problems of helping people "see" the distinctions that do exist. Analysts of television, like Todd Gitlin, suggest that "the most popular shows are those that succeed in speaking simultaneously to audiences that diverge in social class, race, gender, region, and ideology: and this because of the mass market imperative of network television" ("Television's Screens: Hegemony in Transition," in Michael Apple, ed., *Cultural and Economic Reproduction in*

Education: Essays on Class, Ideology and the State, London, Routledge and Kegan Paul, 1982, p. 219). Such "massification" blurs the distinctive differences among classes. The result, although there is obviously a large underclass of people living in misery and oppression, is that First World educators and activists committed to liberation face a different problem than Freire in their analysis. In the United States the recent downward slide of the "middle class" under the Reagan administration and the growth and increasing visibility of a poverty class may open up new opportunities for raising class consciousness, but the different definitions and perceptions about class in North America and Latin America still cause problems.

Paulo Freire's *Pedagogy of the Oppressed* focused on the poor or lower classes of northeast Brazil and elsewhere in Latin America. In contrast to Freire's focus, the present book concentrates on the "non-poor," those who are relatively well-fed, who are listed above the poverty line, and who would be classified in the broad "middle class" of the First World. Further discussion of this definition occurs in several places below, especially in chapter 10.

2. *Marxist Analysis.* A difference between Latin America and the United States in particular is the relative absence of study of Marxist analysis in the United States. In most other parts of the world, including the so-called free world, university studies include as a matter of course more or less serious study of Marx and the analytical instruments connected with Marxism in economics, history, and other subjects. The effects of the Cold War and McCarthyism have compounded the xenophobic fear of Marxism in the United States, and, therefore, references even to the language of Marxism easily lead to marginalization of those who employ and advocate such analysis and to their exclusion from tenured spots in universities. Questions about the massive global politico-economic structures of capitalism are in turn marginalized and kept out of any significant discourse in the political arena. Where such analysis is used, it often has to be disguised. One result is that even "true-blue American" critics of capitalism lack power to influence the unconverted. Despite a history of worker-oriented encyclicals, recent papal and other authoritarian attempts to prevent or marginalize Marxist interpretation in Latin American Catholic circles are making the situation there more like the one in the North. Many church people, including educators and activists, are reluctant to tackle some of the basic analyses that are important, if not necessary, to the kind of social change most of the liberation efforts anticipate. Furthermore, the Soviet Union, Poland, and most other socialist states do not serve as ideal or even attractive models.

3. *Racism and Sexism.* In North America and some other areas of the First World, the issues of racism and sexism dominate the liberation agenda more than class. Most analysts of either sexism or racism see the overall problem as three-way, involving class in an unclear and unstable triangle of interrelated forces. The difficulties of relating liberation efforts focused on sexism and racism to one another as well as to class analysis are fomented by the ways the three are interpreted as separated from each other, so that those working on the

frontline against sexism and racism find it hard to work together on strategies or to understand how class enters into and affects their analyses and their actions. In more sophisticated circles the problem often gets caught up in the ongoing discussion of the relation of economics to culture, of the relation of base to superstructure, and of autonomous or semi-autonomous forces influencing human beings and societies. In this atmosphere it is tempting to adopt competing "my oppression is worse than yours" antagonisms that put further obstacles in the way of coalition-building. To those in the First World it looks simpler in Latin America, where the prevailing and pervasive problem is recognized as the socio-economic class structure.

In *Religion and Alienation* Gregory Baum discusses the differences between North American and Latin American situations and the related differences in theological approach and social analysis:

> The raising of consciousness in the complex situation of North America means the acknowledgment of the multiple forms of exploitation. . . .
>
> Critical theology in North America is, therefore, different from the liberation theologies of Latin America. What is different is the combination of factors in the analysis of social evil, . . . the form which the political commitment takes, . . . [and] the new imagination drawn from diverse historical experiences [pp. 219–20].

We can point to specific groups such as Sojourners in Washington, D.C., or to the gradual but impressive buildup of international opposition to South African apartheid as examples of political activity based on "analysis of social evil" and such "new imagination."

4. *Literacy vs. "Political Literacy."* In the First World, where at least the measurable literacy rate is relatively high, the approach to liberating conscientization through literacy training does not seem to be as useful as in most Latin American countries. Access to information in print and electronic media is more widespread in the nations of the North, but the control of those channels of communication is nevertheless dominated by the centers of power. For example, the U.S. federal government banned use of Canadian films on acid rain in the United States, but how many persons in the United States are aware of that control? Largely for economic reasons, major U.S. publishers of school textbooks have succumbed to pressure from a minority of conservative voices demanding omission of sexual references in literary classic such as Shakespeare's *Romeo and Juliet* and the deletion of the word "evolution" from the glossary of science texts.

Control of knowledge and information remains powerful. Although the ultimate difference between Latin America and North Atlantic countries may not be as wide as it appears at first, using print literacy as a major doorway into critical consciousness and political mobilization does not seem to be as useful in the First World as it is in Latin America. In Canada, the United States, and other First World nations more attention needs to be paid to "literacy" with new electronic media and the related "political literacy" that would foster critical awareness of the ideological forces at work in those societies.

5. *Centralized Control of Culture.* With economic analysis made more difficult in the First World, liberation efforts made on the basis of cultural analysis assume more importance. The centralization of control over media and educational curricula may provide obstacles to liberation in some ways as strong as do the military authorities in some Latin American countries. Where coercion is made less necessary by the power of influencing through "ideological apparatuses," as Louis Althusser points out (see his essay "Ideological State Apparatuses," in *Lenin and Philosophy and Other Essays*, New York, Monthly Review Press, 1971), the power of ideology spread through cultural processes becomes pivotal. So while access to information appears and may be more open, access to power remains tightly controlled. Manipulation of both "high" and "low" (i.e., popular) culture prevents easy breakthroughs on the part of people's understanding or action toward liberation. For example, most daily newspapers, news magazines, and national television broadcasters in the United States consistently describe political and military opponents of U.S.-supported regimes (e.g., in Chile, El Salvador, or the Philippines) as "terrorists" or "leftist guerrillas." However, military opponents of those governments out of favor with the United States (e.g., Nicaragua or Angola) are called "freedom fighters." The cumulative effect of such labeling subtly builds a point of view in us all. Why, ask Africans struggling for their independence, should their revolutionary heroes be called "guerrillas" when George Washington and the heroes of independence in the United States are glorified as freedom fighters against the colonial power of England? How would the British have labeled Washington and his fellow fighters? The ideological power of reproduction of the status quo perhaps takes somewhat different forms in North America than it does in Latin America, but increasingly this difference may be narrowing as the same forces control the communication processes in both continents.

These differences may be somewhat oversimplified and can easily be overstated. But to the degree that they and other possible differences between the two situations do exist, those differences complicate the process of using Freire's work to guide First World efforts toward liberative education. It is therefore helpful to keep such differences in mind.

Similarities

1. *Similarities/Differences.* Each of the above differences is more a matter of degree than of absolute difference. For instance, in regard to centralized control of culture, the same domination of North American media by a limited group of transnational corporations is also evident in Latin America (see Ariel Dorfman, *The Empire's Old Clothes: What the Lone Ranger, Babar, and Other Innocent Heroes Do to Our Minds*, New York, Pantheon Books, 1983). U.S. television programs dominate program time in most countries of the world,

and North Atlantic news services such as Associated Press and Reuters control a large proportion of distribution and interpretation of news around the world. The increasing domination of global communications by the powerful companies that control satellite systems probably means that the similarities will be more evident in years to come.

2. *Economic Decline.* Both Latin America and many areas of the First World share the general decline of prosperity evident in Canada and the United States as well as in Brazil. The international banking system seems to be in serious trouble, and drastic steps are being taken domestically and internationally to avoid major defaults. As a result the problems of inflation and sustaining growth are felt in both the First and Third Worlds. When consent gained by influencing people's interpretation of the situation becomes harder and harder in the face of declining standards of living for most people, more blatant coercion and subversive activities come into play.

One result may be an opening up of the situation to more radical analyses and efforts toward change, despite the growing coercive activity of governments. Police brutality in South Africa and Chile has reinforced the perception that violence calls forth more violence. As the covering up of the pressures and the economic decline becomes more porous and visible, more and more people may see more clearly from their suffering why and how they are being oppressed. In such a context groups and organizations devoted to education and action for transformation may have some fresh opportunities for social and structural analysis in the coming years.

3. *Small Group Movements.* Many of the models in this book come from small, local groups of people who set out modestly to change oppressive situations. Most of the groups are connected to larger networks of support. In Latin America the ecclesial base communities have become widely known as circles of sharing, analyzing, and acting. Perhaps a major similarity is the countercultural, minority characteristic of such liberation efforts. If so, then the discussions of cases in this book may be helpful to ongoing comparison of various efforts toward education for transformation, despite the differences noted above.

4. *Free Space.* "Free space" refers to settings and organizational opportunities for the work of resistance against the reproductive mechanisms by which the dominant structures of power and ideology operate in every society. Free space for action-education projects exists in Latin America and the North Atlantic nations, but the context sets limits on the kind of advantage that can be taken of opportunities. In Latin America the ecclesial base communities, or Freire's culture circles, suggest one important opening. In North American classrooms teachers have many opportunities to raise critical questions about the system. In the United States, Margaret Kuhn and the Gray Panthers have shown how the elderly can become organized and politically powerful, and welfare recipients, blacks, Native-Americans, and others are finding ways to make the system work against itself. The models in this book can be viewed as examples which take advantage of free space.

With the similarities and differences between Freire's Latin American context and the First World context as a backdrop, this book attempts to make connections among present conditions, social and structural analysis, and specific models of transformative education.

PLAN OF THE BOOK

Following this Introduction are the two major parts of the book.

Part 1 includes the major data of the models in the form of eight case studies. A brief introductory chapter by Alice Frazer Evans describes the reasons for their choice and the case form in which they have been written. A note about the significance, the nature, and the anticipated audience precedes each case. Each model has been constructed as a case and has been edited with the cooperation of its "architects," the persons who have developed the projects. Each case has a "Program Overview"—a brief explanatory self-description of the sponsoring organization. Immediately following each case there is a "Teaching Note" which contains suggestions for teaching the case, discussion questions, and a list of additional resources for further study. The "Teaching Note" is followed by the commentaries written by educators and theologians about each case.

Part 2 includes reflections on the cases, the commentaries, and education for transformation. The first reflection comes from the comments made by Paulo Freire in the consultation when the cases were first discussed and in the follow-up meetings of the Association of Professors and Researchers in Religious Education and the Religious Education Association when selected cases were presented. The final two chapters by editors William Bean Kennedy and Robert A. Evans represent their attempts to theorize about the models and the general nature and processes of transformative education in the light of the preceding materials and discussion. They identify and analyze new patterns and guidelines for transformative education.

The book may be read in several useful ways:

—by plunging directly into the case studies, reflecting on the clues they offer which may be helpful in the reader's own situation;

—by reading and discussing the cases in groups where diversity of experience enriches the understanding of everyone;

—by beginning with Paulo Freire's conversational article and dialoguing with him so that readers are moved to establish and clarify the ground for their work;

—by reading straight through, beginning with this Introduction and Alice Evans's introduction to models in case form, the latter offering a perspective on the process that brought the cases into the discussion;

—by dipping into the theoretical reflections by Evans and Kennedy at the end to whet interest in the analytical framework and questions relevant to the models.

The major purpose of the book is to promote and advance dialogue about education for transformation. There are dozens of other models similar to those in this book that could have been included. The eight in this book are offered only as a first "come-on" to others to engage in the discussion. This volume should encourage more sharing and mutual analysis of such efforts. The case architects, commentators, editors, and participants in the consultation are serious about corresponding with persons interested in the work of the contributors to this volume. They all urge continuing critique and suggestions in a larger conversation.

The editors entered upon this venture because we are convinced that the causes to which we are committed need more serious strategic development as various liberating education and mobilization efforts continue. The clues and questions, as well as the components and dynamic of transformation, may provide a basis for re-evaluating and modifying the educational projects in which we participate. We hope this book will become an initial instrument for enriched interchange and continued building of coalitions that we believe are needed.

PART ONE

MODELS OF TRANSFORMATIVE EDUCATION

ALICE FRAZER EVANS

MODELS IN CASE FORM

Early in the planning stage of this project on transformative education, the editors and project directors were faced with the challenge of selecting, from the vast array of movements, educational programs which would fit into the dialogue. To focus the search we adopted certain criteria. These were that each model

—should state its pedagogical goals with relative clarity;
—should be researched seriously or be open to research and evaluation;
—should be potentially replicable in congregations or other communities;
—should be generative of other programs;
—should show evidence of some kind of empowering, liberative education and show signs of behavioral as well as attitudinal change;
—should, collectively with the other models, contribute to an overall offering of a representative variety of approaches and focal points while at the same time addressing fundamental issues of global justice.

Using these criteria, eight models were chosen.

The second major challenge was to present the models in a form which would be consistent with the theme of "education as liberation." The editors would agree with Paulo Freire that "liberating education consists in acts of cognition, not transference of information" (*Pedagogy of the Oppressed,* New York, Herder and Herder, 1972, p. 67).

Employing some of Freire's terminology, we sought to counteract as much as possible a "banking" approach to the presentation of the models. Banking is an understanding of education as a process in which a teacher "deposits" information into a student, an "empty vessel," who "receives, memorizes, and repeats" (ibid., pp. 57-74). A straight narrative description of the models would imply that an astute observer, a teacher, could convey to others, the students, the essence of each educational program. A narrative description of the models would also tend to communicate an image of static, completed programs. To the contrary, each of the models chosen was clearly "in process," with the primary architects open to constructive critique of their designs.

Besides involving acts of cognition, liberating education also involves genuine dialogue between student and teacher with the realization that they are partners educating one another. The goal is the development of "critical consciousness" and "creative power" leading to humane transformation of one's world rather than passive adaptation to that world (ibid., p. 62). The goal of the dialogue facilitated in this book is that "students" (readers and dialogue-partners with the models) will become engaged with the models in a way that frees them to apply new insights and learnings to their own unique experiences with transformative education.

For these reasons we sought a "problem-posing" approach to the models, one which would challenge project architects, commentators, and reader/ participants to be in dialogue about the essence of each approach and to recognize the role of creative reflection for "knowing" and understanding (as opposed to "memorizing") each model. Though it is not without limitations, we found the case approach had potential for a liberating and responsible presentation of the models.

There are numerous types of "cases" used in contemporary education. These range from a hypothetical problem, to a one-page "critical incident" or "verbatim" which reports a specific actual incident, to a four-hundred-page case history describing in detail an event or situation. The type of case employed in this project is modeled after those used by the Harvard Law and Business Schools and the Association for Case Teaching: that is, each case consists of selected information from an actual situation that raises specific issues or problems that require a response or decision on the part of one or more persons in the case. The problem should be substantive enough and so balanced in its approach that reasonable people would disagree about the most effective or appropriate response. As a pedagogical tool the case calls for a response not only from the case characters but from those studying the case.

CASES FOR GROUP DISCUSSION

Though cases can be extremely useful for inducing reflection by an individual reader, they are specifically designed for group discussion. Any of the eight models in the book might be used in retreat settings, classrooms, community gatherings, or with any group seeking to gain new perspectives on transformative education. The case setting calls on participants to listen to one another, to challenge their own and others' perceptions, and to build on one another's insights. There is tremendous potential in a good case discussion for developing sensitivity and building trust in a group of colearners. One of the most exciting results of this project to date has been the enthusiastic response of those project staff members who have analyzed their own and others' cases and have initiated modifications in their programs. This open sharing also affirms a level of trust in the ability of those invited to be dialogue partners.

As this is a distinctive educational approach, it might be helpful to list several suggestions for guiding a case discussion that have been proposed by experienced case teachers.

Preparation

It is possible to hand out copies of the shorter cases in this volume (e.g., "Bread for the World" or "Plant Closures Project") and ask discussion participants to read them immediately prior to discussion. However, the quality of most case discussions is heightened by careful advance reading. A case leader might suggest that participants read through a case at least twice, identify the principal case characters, possibly develop a "time line" to indicate significant dates or events, list the issues which appear to surface, and think through a number of creative alternatives to the dilemma posed. Small groups meeting to prepare ideas about a case prior to a larger group discussion can also be extremely beneficial to the total learning experience. This type of detailed and structured analysis of a case is equally valuable for the individual reader. A structured process for "entering" each case provides a base that may be challenged, expanded, or affirmed by the commentaries which follow each model.

Teaching the Case

As stated above, the role of a case leader does not follow a traditional model of the teacher as a dispenser of knowledge or information. The primary functions of a case leader are to facilitate meaningful dialogue among the participants, to highlight insights they mutually discover, and to assist in summarizing the learnings from the discussion. As a facilitator, the case leader is responsible for clear goals and objectives for each discussion session and for guiding the quality and rhythm of the discussion. Many who have worked with cases suggest that the most crucial factor for a rewarding case experience is the leader's style; openness, affirmation, and sensitivity to the group create the climate in which genuine dialogue can occur. Second in importance is that the case leader thoroughly master the case facts and develop a discussion plan or teaching note.

Teaching Notes

Following each case is a list of questions and topics for readers or discussion participants to consider. The goal is to draw participants into dialogue with one another and with the architects or staff members of each model. This process is at the heart of problem-posing education. The questions and topics offered for consideration have been suggested by the case authors to focus discussion around central issues raised by each model. The broad variety of types and tones of these discussion notes reflects the variety of styles and approaches of the models' architects and case authors. However, there are several central questions which may be applied to all of the models. These may seem to go well beyond the "presenting problem" of each case, but response to these questions may be essential to the development of effective and justifiable alternatives to that problem.

—How and why do people change? What ideological assumptions does the model make about the nature of transformation?
—What are the stated goals of the program? Are there unstated goals?
—What are the barriers to those goals being reached (e.g., institutional, cultural, economic, political, or personal barriers)?
—What forces provide support for reaching those goals?
—What are the weaknesses and the strengths of the program as an educational model?
—How does the program measure success or failure?

There are no right answers either to the questions above or to the presenting problem of each case. This means that the problems posed are genuinely open to a number of creative alternatives. (This approach is in contrast to a "closed" problem-*solving* approach, in which the right answer or solution can be found in the back [or at the heart] of the book. These are usually answers which the teacher already knows.) In a banking approach students are receptive *objects* of the teacher's wisdom and insight. In contrast, the case approach calls for participants to become active *subjects* in the learning process, to consider various responses, and to analyze the values which inform their decisions.

Most case leaders prepare in advance a "teaching note" with suggestions for the general direction of the discussion as well as clear, transitional questions to move from one topic to the next. The most engaging way to "enter" a case is often by identifying the case characters and raising questions about their attitudes or approaches. In the course of the discussion other general topics to be covered might be the issues, alternatives, and rationale for each alternative, and the possible resolution available both to the case characters and to the participants.

The questions and topics for discussion which follow each model and the general questions noted above are intended only as aids to a leader's creative imagination.

Case Discussion

Experienced case leaders report that recording the essence of participants' contributions on newsprint or a chalkboard gives order and direction to the discussion. A skilled instructor is able to help participants show the relation among contributions. The leader should be willing to probe respondents for additional clarification of points.

Honest conflict of opinion is often a characteristic of these dialogues and can be quite constructive in a case discussion. The case leader may need to assume the role of referee and urge participants to listen to one another and to interpret the reasoning behind their conclusions. It is often helpful to put debating participants in direct dialogue by asking, for example, "Susan, given your earlier position, how would you respond to Antonio's view?" The leader's role as mediator is also significant, especially as a discussion nears conclusion. It is helpful to encourage a group to build on one another's suggestions. One constructive process for closing a case discussion is to ask participants to share their insights from the discussion. Of particular relevance to a discussion of the cases in this volume would be to ask how any learnings about a particular educational model might apply directly to projects in which members of the group are involved.

Additional Teaching Techniques

Two additional techniques are often employed by case leaders.

1. *Voting.* A discussion may be focused and intensified by calling for participants to vote on a controversial issue. For example, in a discussion of "Parenting for Peace and Justice" one might ask, "If you were a part of this community, would you vote for or against the group's direct support of the Sanctuary Movement?" Most case leaders record the vote on the board. The dynamics of case teaching reveal that once persons have taken a stand, they assume greater "ownership" of the decision and are eager to defend or interpret their choice. Voting provides an impetus for participants to offer the implicit reasons and assumptions that stand behind a given decision. It can also be a test of the group's response, especially if one or two outspoken participants have taken a strong stand on one particular side of an issue. For example, if a goal of the session on the parenting case is to develop a set of "next steps" for the parenting group, or for any group involved in conflict, then the processing of a vote on Sanctuary may be an excellent way to help participants become aware of the intensity of feelings surrounding an issue such as civil disobedience and consequently be more realistic about the "next steps" they suggest.

2. *Role-playing.* Another way to heighten existential involvement in a case is to ask participants imaginatively to assume roles of persons in the case for a specified period of the discussion. In a group role-play or simulation experience, the leader might ask the entire group, for example, to become members of the peacemakers in "Peacemaking in a Local Parish" and respond to Susan Edwards's questions about future directions. When individuals are requested to assume roles before a group—for example, that of Pastor Ed Harrington speaking to the session members of his church in "Plant Closures Project"— experienced case leaders have found that rather than making assignments or asking for volunteers, it is better directly to ask participants who have given evidence in the discussion that they can identify with the characters and understand the issues. It is often most helpful for individuals in a role-play to move into chairs visible to the entire group. The personal integrity of those who

assume individual roles is then guarded following a five-minute role-play by allowing them space to "de-role." This is done by asking them, for example, how they felt during the conversation and by asking them to return to their original seats. Then the group may be called on to share learnings from the experience.

Notwithstanding the preceding hints and principles for case teaching, the editors wish to acknowledge that a good case discussion is not ultimately dependent on a trained professional teacher or on a learned group of participants. A gifted leader is one who listens well, encourages participants to do the same, and genuinely trusts the wisdom, insights, and personal experiences of the group. To benefit significantly from the cases a reader needs to be willing to wrestle honestly with the issues of the models, embodied in case form, and willing to evaluate with an open mind the insights of the commentators.

DISTINCTIVE FACTORS OF THE CASE FORM

There are two other distinctive factors of the particular case form used to present the models in this book. First, though the names of the persons in most cases have been disguised to protect the privacy of those involved, each of the cases describes an actual situation. For the architects, staff, or directors of the models, this approach is much riskier than a controlled narrative description of their program. The case exposes to the reader the conflicts, questions, and genuine dilemmas which confront each organization. Yet it is this open sharing which may hold the greatest potential for constructive change and growth for the programs being analyzed and for those seeking understanding.

The reality of the cases and the story-telling quality of style are intended to invite readers to suspend their disbelief and enter the case situation as much as possible. By "experiencing" a meeting of the Bread for the World community, by considering recommendations for the Gospel Agenda in a Global Context project, or by "joining" a parish peacemaking group, readers are invited to go beyond the rational perception of ideas and become acquainted with the people who live out these ideas. This imaginative connection offers the opportunity to test the application of understanding, analysis, and alternatives.

Second, each case represents a photographic snapshot of a point in time. The program architects or directors were asked to select a particular period in the life of the program or organization when they were faced with a problem which raised significant issues. For example, Women's Theological Center in Boston, now well established, faced critical decisions in its formative years which would affect the future directions of the organization. Staff members felt that the dilemmas they faced at that time revealed the challenges as well as the potential of their program. In the same way, the case on the Christian Theological Seminary's Chrysalis Program focuses on a critical historical point in the development of that model. "Plant Closures Project" exposes to the reader not only the continuing problems faced by unemployed workers but also the strength of ideological barriers the project faced surrounding one particular plant closure in the past. In contrast, the presenting problems of "Parenting for Peace and Justice" and "Traveling for Transformation" were unresolved at the time of writing. The goal for all of the cases was to raise those issues which are central to the challenges each model faces and the unique educational approaches each model takes.

In order to allow readers to pursue the most current issues and directions of each model, the addresses, phone numbers, and names of program contact-persons (as of 1986) are supplied in the "Program Overview" which was submitted by each organization and which precedes each case model. In the same vein, a brief list of additional resources follows each case. Staff members of the programs suggested resources which readers could pursue in order to clarify the goals and directions of a program, to locate parallel programs, or to study works which influenced the ideological assumptions of a program.

LIMITATIONS OF THE CASE APPROACH

Even with these safeguards and procedures for updating, the case approach is not without limitations. Any written material must go through the personal filter of the writer. The case form used in this book calls for a selection of data, not an all-inclusive case history. The editors and case authors sought to widen the perspective on each case by having others involved in the programs carefully read and review the accuracy of the material selected as well as evaluate the significance of the material chosen or not chosen to be included in the case. The crucial test for each case was: Does it convey the essential issues with which the program deals? Each case passed this test, but the limitation of each author's perspective still stands.

A second drawback is that the success of this form of education and presentation of material is ultimately dependent on the participation of readers and those discussing the models. This can be quite disconcerting, even threatening, for those who are used to a process in which they are handed a complete analysis from a silver lectern. For most of us tutored in an educational system which fosters, even if unintentionally, uncritical acceptance of the teacher's wisdom and authority, passive reception of information is the comfortable norm. However, this is also the pattern of the uncritical acceptance of the world as it is, and is a form of education which can dim the vision of the world as it could be.

In order to lead readers and ourselves into a more critical analysis and comprehension of the models, two or more commentaries follow each case. Some of the commentaries are contradictory while others are complementary. They reflect widely differing perspectives on transformative education and reaffirm the concept that there are no right answers to the case problems. The differences in style, length, and tone of the commentaries also reflect the variety of styles and approaches of the authors. The commentators are dialogue partners not only with the model architects but with the reader as well. The intent of the commentaries is to stimulate discussion and to liberate readers to develop their own creative and distinctive analyses. This leaves the "real" work with our readers. We can only urge them to accept the challenge.

Finally, a case discussion can consume much more time and emotional energy than the direct communication of information. (In the same way an actual experience is usually much more "costly" in terms of time and energy.) Those studying the models must assess the relative value of time, energy, and levels of comprehension for liberating education.

The case approach is not an educational panacea and must be seen as only one of many effective educational instruments. The editors have sought to respond to those limitations in methodology that have been identified in this and the preceding introduction. We have not removed them. We hope, however, that the case approach used to present the models will lead to constructive, liberating engagement with the exciting concepts they encompass.

The editors assume that many of our readers are presently involved in various forms of transformative education for the non-poor. We hope that constructive analysis of the case models can lead those engaged in the development of educational models to risk holding their own programs up to the light of dialogue, to rethink the programs' assumptions and objectives, to identify the barriers to change, and to clarify the steps to more effective transformative education. The process of analysis and dialogue should be one of constructive critique, undertaken on the assumption that genuinely transformative programs are never finished, static entities. Creative educational models are always in process, asking questions, open to change.

The goal for persons and groups is much the same. Genuinely liberating education involves us as colearners, always in process, open to the promise and potential of a more humane world and the discovery of our part in the realization of that vision.

CHAPTER 1

PEACEMAKING
IN A LOCAL PARISH

This model is distinctive as a peacemaking strategy because it developed "from the bottom up," in a congregation, rather than "from the top down," from a national headquarters. The case describes how an urban parish began a peacemaking group, how the group gradually developed its theological base and its program activities, and how it expanded into the larger church and societal context in ways that led to a crisis for the group leader. The case is filled with stimulating insights into why and how people move into peacemaking activities. It also articulates a theoretical understanding of peacemaking.

The model builds on a challenging sequence of local initiatives and resistance to national bureaucratic programming. Its focus on the "inward-outward" tension in a group's development offers helpful guidance about how to combine the spiritual and the activist dimensions of peacemaking efforts.

This model will be useful to persons and groups committed to peace and disarmament, and to all those who are searching for a variety of ways by which people can become engaged and mobilized to do something about the threat of war and nuclear destruction. It offers help and hope for local church leaders who see the value of working to get and keep the whole congregation involved rather than fostering an isolated action-group. The strategic movement beyond the local church opens up reflection about the limitations of centralized organization for transformative activity. The model highlights the value of local creativity, local initiatives, and individual contributions.

Program Overview

Our vehicle for peacemaking, like the vehicle for faithfulness in Latin America, is a great secret of the church through the ages: the small group. We know that in a small group of ten to fifteen persons enough mutual trust, fellowship, and openness to the Holy Spirit can be nurtured to allow ordinary individuals and churches to take extraordinary steps in action and in faith— even toward something as large and frustrating as nuclear disarmament.

We are particularly influenced by the World Peacemakers at the Church of the Savior in Washington, D.C., in their bringing together the journey inward and the journey outward. We have learned that these two journeys cannot be separated.

Our journey inward involves us in :

1. regular Bible study in the small group and in special programs offered for our whole church;
2. regular worship and prayer as a small group and a regular peacemaking aspect in every Sunday worship service at our church;
3. attempts to share our experiences of violence, hostility, and fear, as well as grace, forgiveness, and peace;
4. self-education about the nuclear arms race and its economic, military, and spiritual implications;
5. opportunities for fun, fellowship, and deeper friendships.

Our journey outward involves us in:

1. sponsoring several actions or activities per year in which all members of our church are encouraged to take a step in peacemaking, e.g., church viewing and discussion of a movie, annual peacemaking offerings, bus trips to demonstrations, and lobbying efforts in Washington, D.C.;
2. preparing and leading worship services to interpret to the whole congregation what our inward and outward journeys have taught us;
3. sponsoring a peace education center in the balcony of our sanctuary which works in these areas:
   a. coordinating six hundred volunteers from other Presbyterian churches with a goal of involving our entire presbytery in peacemaking;
   b. coordinating four hundred volunteers from our neighborhood to promote the nuclear freeze and the adequate funding of human needs through such activities as education, outreach, political action, and

fundraising. (We have also had some success in bringing a more reflective or spiritual journey to our very secular neighborhood.);

c. starting, sustaining, steering, and funding the nuclear weapons freeze campaign while undertaking several specific projects for the national freeze campaign;

d. publishing a small journal, *The Peacemonger Press,* which is received by two thousand Presbyterians nationally and which offers suggestions and resources for peacemaking in congregations from the point of view of the congregation;

e. finding opportunities for outreach, evangelism, and consultation with local and national organizations;

4. divestiture of stocks that the church holds in companies that produce nuclear weapons.

Though the inward and outward journeys can take many forms, some general lessons we have learned are: (1) our goal is not to do peacemaking "on behalf of" or "instead of" the church as a whole, but to involve the whole church as individuals and as an institution—that is, not to see "how much we can get away with," but how to involve and inspire the whole church; (2) we must keep faith in Christ as the central reason for and guide in peacemaking, and work on the assumption that, because of God's grace, *each* person has gifts for peacemaking. Our hope is to reach out to the presence of God in each person and to draw it out so that each of us may grow in faith and in the ability to take leadership in our own lives and in our actions on behalf of life itself.

For further information, contact: The Rev. Jan Orr-Harter; West-Park Presbyterian Church; 165 West 86th Street; New York, NY 10024.

Case Study
Peacemaking in a Local Parish

Susan Edwards slowly turned the pages of the "peacemaking journal" she had kept for the past five years. During that time she had been instrumental in organizing the U.S. Nuclear Freeze Movement and in developing peacemaking groups across the United States. But her home congregation, where it had all begun, was foremost in her mind. She was keenly aware of her present frustration with the small, faithful Peacemakers group at Covenant Presbyterian Church. What does it take to sustain the commitment to peacemaking action and reflection? When over a period of several years a movement that began as many small groups becomes large, what becomes of the role of the small groups?

THE CALL

Susan readily acknowledged the similarity among the peacemaking of Covenant Church, the basic concept of liberation theology, and the educational approach Paulo Freire designed for the poor in Brazil (see *Pedagogy of the Oppressed,* New York, Herder and Herder, 1970). She realized that variations of Freire's concepts were leading individuals in the United States to take concrete action toward world peace. Small lay groups studying, praying, and acting together in the United States were similar to the ecclesial base communities in Latin America. Susan had envisioned a national network of religious groups in the United States "journeying inward" by finding ways to involve the whole church in peacemaking. Susan smiled as she looked down at one of her early notations:

> I wonder what would happen if every church and synagogue in the United States had such a group working and praying together. The government would call it a plot, because they couldn't think of any other way to account for the work of the Holy Spirit.

Susan had first come to Covenant Presbyterian, an urban church of 250 members, as a seminary fieldwork intern. Just prior to her arrival in the fall of

---

1978, the chairperson of the Covenant board of trustees had brought to the church session a "Call to Faithfulness" from *Sojourners* magazine. Christians were asked to sign the call to signify their commitment to nuclear disarmament. After discussion, the session agreed to circulate the call after worship for several Sundays. Everyone was surprised when it was signed by over fifty people.

Soon after that, when Susan came to work at the church part-time with a specific focus on peacemaking, she spoke with a number of people who had signed the call. Many said they had "worried for a long time" about the future of the world, but they had "never shared that as a church."

FIRST MEETING

Working with the adult fellowship group, Susan helped organize a potluck supper to "talk about war and peace, about disarmament, about false security and real security." Over a dozen people came. These included Tom, a trustee and elder; Alice, a young librarian and elder; Dan, a mental institution outpatient who quoted scripture after scripture; Anna, who had prayed every night for eighty years for peace; Claudia, another librarian, and her husband, Jim; Connie, a candidate for ordination; Herman, a Vietnam veteran; Carol, the president of the women's association; Gayle and Cliff, longtime members of the church; Almena, a mother of children in the church school; and Bob, the pastor of the church, and his wife, Evelyn. It was a diverse group racially, economically, and theologically.

Susan reread her journal entry for that first meeting:

With everyone a little nervous, we blessed the supper and sang a song. To introduce ourselves, we went around the dinner table, telling our names and something that made us feel secure. Claudia talked about the security of locking her door after getting home at night. Others talked about their jobs, their family, or the church as a source of security. Some were not able to think of any source of security. After discussing this, we read a liturgy together and viewed *The Last Slide Show*. Produced with a grant from the United Presbyterian Church U.S.A., the slide show tells about a planet that built nuclear weapons and moved directly toward nuclear war, but then stopped and reversed itself toward peace and survival. This opened a long discussion about which we feared most—armament or disarmament. The group liked meeting together and agreed to meet again in two weeks. We sang "Breathe On Me, Breath of God," cleaned up the dishes, and wished each other good night.

PARALLELS TO LIBERATION THEOLOGY

Susan was convinced that many concerned with disarmament, such as the potluck supper group, were originally motivated less from a notion of Christian charity and the needs of others than from a reflection on their *own* needs, fears, and concern for the future. In her theological studies Susan began to draw parallels between this pattern and liberation theology. In her journal she had recorded a description of liberation theology as "what some of the poorest and least powerful people in the world do when they examine their own oppression, begin to act for political and economic freedom, and reflect on this action in light of the gospel." In peacemaking and disarmament she saw North Americans as both oppressors and oppressed. Paraphrasing Robert McAfee Brown's thesis in *Theology in a New Key: Responding to Liberation Themes* (Philadelphia, Westminster, 1978), Susan felt that peacemaking was a North American version of liberation theology. Her assessment was based on the understanding that peacemaking is:

1. the aspiration of people who live under the threat of nuclear war every day of their lives to get free from that threat;
2. an understanding of history in which we realize that we can take a conscious responsibility for our own destiny, not leaving it solely in the hands of the government or nuclear industry, and not assuming nuclear war to be inevitable. This recognition that there are possibilities for disarmament and survival and that God empowers us to work for peace is crucial;
3. a transformation made possible through encounter with Jesus Christ, who liberates us from death and for life. This involves recognition, however, that violence is not just private, inward, and personal, but also is the death wish to which our whole society has been subjected.

Susan realized that most North American Christians support the nuclear arms race with their votes, taxes, and, in millions of cases, careers. So the task for peacemakers is actually to change the majority, the peacemakers included. Susan was convinced that this change or conversion, which begins with seeing things from a new perspective, is the transformation that liberation theology demands. She looked at her journal and read: "Through this slow and often painful process, we can examine our experience in the nuclear age, its impact on our jobs, our families, and our souls. Peacemaking begins with our own experience."

Susan turned the pages to her notes on the second meeting of the Covenant peacemaking group:

Tonight a smaller group gathered in the church basement to talk about our own lives in the nuclear age. Before supper, Connie led us in some exercises to huff and puff and work out some of our feelings of aggression. Eighty-year-old Anna did them best of all. A little embarrassed, we rested and laughed and then sang together. Bob Arnold had brought a liturgy on peace, so we read it out loud. As we sat around the Sunday school tables to eat, I suggested a way for us to look at our lives by creating "name tags" for ourselves. We would look through a stack of old magazines for pictures, words, and ads that could be pasted together to form a collage about the impact of war and peace on our own stories. With scissors and glue and brightly-colored paper in the middle of the table, we set out. After twenty minutes of working quietly, we went around our circle explaining the name tags. Anna started—she showed us beautiful meadows with airplanes in them. Anna had been a child in Germany during World War I. Gayle showed pictures of balloons and airplanes. She told about growing up in Seattle and living under regular air raid drills warning of attack. Bob Davidson showed a progression from working for civil rights to working against the Vietnam War to becoming concerned about nuclear weapons. Bob Arnold made a symbolic collage of a modern mind—a clock ticking away under a bottle of fine whiskey and some gold coins. Connie pictured her childhood in Los Alamos, next-door to the first bomb tests. Herman talked of Vietnam and his own confusion about the war. After several others had shared, I suggested that we display the collages after church on Sunday and was met with unanimous opposition. Not that much sharing!

Though it was late, we talked at length about the news of the suicides in Guyana. We had all been keeping our feelings to ourselves for days—now it all came out. Suicide is so difficult to picture, but more difficult to forget. We talked about mass suicide and nuclear weapons. Were we so different from Guyana in our plans for death? Someone said that she didn't want to believe that, but secretly feared it. Someone else said that he had brought a commentary from the newspaper on the suicides, and we closed by reading parts of it. The feeling was quiet, sad, but very close—we were close to each other in that little room, stuck away from subways and suicides yet thinking of them even there. We sang "Shalom" in our small circle, and walked Anna home.

BARRIERS TO PEACEMAKING

During the next months and then years Susan worked with the group, which decided to call itself the Peacemakers, as well as with other members in the congregation. She continued to find parallels between Freire's analysis and her perception of the barriers to peacemaking.

Freire identifies a process called "massification" by which people are manipulated into an uncritical, manageable "glob" by the use of myths created by powerful social forces. In addition, Freire sees the mass of people as convinced that their situation is the will of God. When Susan recalled numerous conversations in which people had said "We're going to blow ourselves up and there's absolutely nothing we can do about it," or "Military spending is good for the economy," or "Those in government know more than we do," or "God only asks us to save souls," she saw people who, in Freire's words, are "reluctant to resist and [who] totally lack confidence in themselves. They have a diffuse, magical belief in the invulnerability and power of the oppressor" *(Pedagogy,* p. 50).

Susan recognized a need to address this reluctance by helping the group members see themselves as "oppressed" and by learning facts about defense spending, such as the proportional loss of machinists' union jobs with every increase in military spending. She wrote, "We must recognize the arms race as a human action if we are to see the arms race as an object to be transformed by human actions."

Through her work with the Covenant congregation and with other area congregations, Susan identified additional barriers to peacemaking. She became increasingly aware of the power of fear as a basis for national policy. She realized that fear of the Soviets "makes it impossible for us to ever be satisfied with any sort of security." Susan found that confession and honest discussion of fear *as fear,* within a supportive community, were two of the most powerful ways to free people to respond in new ways.

A turning point for the group occurred around the barrier Susan had identified as "grief." Following the Soviet invasion of Afghanistan, a parishioner walked out of church in the midst of Susan's call to confession. Susan had called the congregation to acknowledge the possibility that the United States had contributed to the Soviet decision "through our recent moves to escalate military spending . . . and the decision to place first-strike weapons in Western Europe." A few days later the parishioner raised a number of questions about possible Soviet influence on the church through Susan. The Peacemakers discussed their role; one of the group responded to the parishioner by writing a long letter answering all her questions in what Susan felt was a loving, pastoral way. He closed the letter with a personal statement about why he was a peacemaker.

Susan saw the parishioner as a staunch patriot and defender of "the American dream" of peace and protection through military superiority. Citing Robert Raines's essay "Grief and the American Dream," Susan wrote in her journal:

> As we grapple with the hard fact that there is no defense against nuclear weapons, "we experience an anger at the faltering dream and anger at those who announce its faltering." In order to be able to let go of this dream we must be able to grieve. We need to affirm the person and the lost dream. Like the prophets, our task as peacemakers is to help our country let go of a dream of false security. But we must also envision and create new possibilities for security or patriotism or peace—a new or reinterpreted dream beyond the false dream of security through nuclear weapons.

BIBLICAL AUTHORITY

Following her internship Susan was called to Covenant Church as an assistant pastor, again with a primary focus on congregational and community efforts in peacemaking. She continued to meet bimonthly with the Peacemakers, and those meetings helped reaffirm central tool for peacemaking. The group often followed Walter Wink's approach to Bible study as described in his *Transforming Bible Study* (Nashville, Abingdon Press, 1980). Susan again consulted her journal:

Last night during our Bible study we were discussing Jesus saying "Watch!" and we realized we were watching for the wrong things. We were watching for the disasters to come. We never knew he meant for us to watch for something else. This was the moment of conversion, of envisioning a potential future laid out by the prophets. When Jeremiah holds out that vision, he becomes an energizer. Our group is coming to a vision—watching not so much for a nuclear war as for God's hand in our lives and in our world at this point in world history.

Susan found that different members in the group were finding their vision of peace rooted in different concepts, different reasons or authorities for peacemaking:

Alice, for instance, told us early on that Genesis 1 was the basis of her peacemaking. She has elaborated on this to show us that the call to be stewards of creation conflicts with the stockpiling of nuclear weapons. For Alice, stewardship of creation is the authority for peacemaking.

Others in the group have raised the issue of idolatry or faith in false gods. Bob, for instance, has approached peacemaking as a sign of where he vests his security. He believes that when we build nuclear weapons, we show everyone that our security is based on something besides God. Faithfulness to God alone is Bob's authority for peacemaking.

Many of us, while undecided about how to achieve disarmament, are deeply moved by the biblical vision of shalom. We have a dream of "everyone 'neath their vine and fig tree," living in peace and without fear. We can see the lion and the lamb lying down together, and we know that that peace is what God wants for us. This vision of God's shalom is our authority for peacemaking.

In the midst of this diversity, the Peacemakers seemed unified in their understanding that the final authority for peacemaking was in the teaching and example of Jesus Christ. The group members wrestled with what it meant in concrete terms to forgive and be forgiven, to love their enemies, to acknowledge victory over death, and to care for one another.

MOVE TO ACTION

The Peacemakers reaffirmed for Susan the importance of the opportunity in their meetings to share their insights and to learn to trust one another. She also discovered the enabling power of the group's support for her as she moved her peacemaking efforts into ever-wider circles. Both Susan and Alice had been elected commissioners to the Presbyterian General Assembly. They were highly instrumental in developing a peacemaking covenant signed by over five hundred commissioners.

As a national peacemaking network was being developed, Susan and two other members of Covenant's Peacemakers worked with a peacemaking task force in their presbytery. They also worked with other denominations and local congregations on short-term, intensive peacemaking workshops.

During her third year at Covenant, Susan directed much of her energy toward the goal of a nuclear freeze. Not only emotional support for her work but significant development of the concept came through her reflection and "visioning" with the Peacemakers. Susan found a journal entry that recorded that insight:

> Unfortunately the world doesn't understand the full vision. Suddenly we can believe in universal peace with justice. The Senate, however, cannot understand universal peace with justice. So we have to come up with a "middle axiom," some way of getting across the message of the gospel in language our historical context can understand and act on. For me that middle axiom is the nuclear freeze. It's not the Kingdom of God, it's not the whole vision, but it's a faithful step toward it. In Latin America the "middle axiom" is land reform. We're wrong if we think that's their long-range vision, but it's a vehicle for helping their historical context have a larger vision.

Different forms of the vision were taken up by the Covenant Peacemakers as they, too, began to move toward corporate action. Susan recalled the hesitancy with which the group joined in its first demonstration. A journal entry about a key meeting in the process states:

> Perhaps our best meeting yet. We met in the session room with low lights and wine from Alice. We had a lot of business and announcements to cover; I told them about the session's decision to fund the Peace Education Center and they were glad. But when I reminded them about the "Swords into Plowshares" demonstration on Armed Services Day, I could feel the fear in the room. Slowly we started our discussion about two short Thomas Merton articles that we had read. Very quickly our discussion returned to the demonstration issue—everyone had read in the newspaper about the recent Holy Week demonstrations in Washington. Claudia wanted to know why anyone would throw human blood on the Pentagon and White House. Someone else asked whose blood it was. Connie said that she thought the blood was a clear and powerful symbol—that the blood belongs on the White House and Pentagon. Alice was the most disgusted of all; she said it wouldn't have been so bad if they had used red paint—but blood, ugh!
>
> I told them about the demonstration I had attended at the Trident base in Connecticut. It had been very different from the blood pouring. On the day

of the "christening" of the Trident submarine, thousands had come dressed in black to stand silently in a line on both sides of the street as military officials and local families paraded into the shipyard to see Mrs. Carter break the bottle over the hull. I thought it was a very effective and helpful action. I had never been to a demonstration before that.

We began to talk about different kinds of protest, and I asked them to share any stories of demonstrations that they had attended. Only Bob and Evelyn had ever been to a demonstration—and their stories really shone. Bob told about bus trips with Martin Luther King, Jr., about playing pool with Andrew Young and being overfed by Southern churchwomen. Evelyn told about taking her young children to marches against the Vietnam War. Their stories were reflective, funny, and exaggerated. The other peacemakers listened with increasing ease, laughter, and questions—they wanted to know more and more. We talked about the Merton articles that we had read and about his insistence that protest be born of hope and fellowship rather than despair and frustration.

Then Elizabeth, who had been quiet, said: "Well, we've got to make up our minds about this demonstration thing." She actually led the discussion that ended with our decision to attend the Armed Services Day demonstration as a group experiment. We would do it together, reserve judgment, witness with all our hearts, and then reflect upon the experience afterwards. We were so comforted by this decision to review the experiment after doing it! We even decided that we would plan a liturgy to do at the demonstration. Maybe our friends at the synagogue would want to do it with us.

Somehow we ended up with a discussion of "counting on each other"— that we could count on each other at any hour of the day or night. It was such a new and intimate way for us to talk. We were happy and prayed quietly. I remember Claudia saying how glad she was that we were not like "those people who burn draft cards and throw blood."

The Peacemakers worked for two weeks sending out press releases, creating the banners, and planning the liturgy. Susan recalled the sense of celebration and peace which enveloped the group during and after the demonstration, at which they marched in solidarity with hundreds of other peacemakers. The huge white dove they had made was a fitting symbol for their little band. Susan again recorded her learnings: "We must develop strategies for peacemaking that do not cut most people out of the picture. Like Paul, our proclaiming of the gospel must take into account the worldview of each audience."

FROM EXPERIMENTATION TO INSISTENT REALISM

Susan was convinced, however, that peacemakers needed to move beyond "innovative learning," beyond experiments such as participation in a demonstration. The preface to *Pedagogy of the Oppressed* reminded her that "those who are truly oppressed do not enjoy the freedom to fail, the luxury of experimenting." The urgency, the "insistent realism," which Susan acknowledged about the nuclear arms race motivated her to deeper levels of commitment.

Under the small group's leadership, the church session established a Peace Education Center to stimulate peacemaking in Presbyterian churches and in the immediate neighborhood. Eventually the center grew to utilize four hundred volunteers in the neighborhood and six hundred in the presbytery. As the center became more financially independent, it developed its own board of directors and paid staff. The Peacemakers began to publish and distribute nationally the *Peacemonger Press,* a quarterly pamphlet about peacemaking in local churches. This clearinghouse of peacemaking programs provided annotated lists of audiovisual resources and books, suggestions for creative Bible study, and practical suggestions for peacemaking from local churches across the United States. Susan became increasingly involved in city, state, and national programs. She was aware, however, that when she was not providing as much guidance as before, the Covenant Peacemakers moved much more slowly in their action and spiritual reflection.

Susan looked down at the most recent entry in her journal, dated that evening:

> I have given less time to the group because I'm spread thin, and so much of my time is consumed by the national programs. I think the group is proud of my national role, but they don't want to be directly involved. I also want the group to take off on its own. I am trying to do more listening and less leading—not coming to every meeting with ten options of things to do. What do *they* want to do?

COVENANT PEACEMAKERS

Susan glanced back at the group's activities over the past two years. A few members had moved out of town, and other people had joined. But there was a consistent core of eleven who continued to meet on an irregular basis. Susan saw most of the projects as "one shot" activities such as inviting the congregation to go as a group to the film *Gandhi* and then attend a follow-up discussion. The group continued to share input in the Covenant Sunday worship service with their "Minute for Peace" devotional.

There was a special evening for the group on "Peacemaking and Poetry," during which they shared their own poems. During the past year one couple in the group had become involved in the presbytery projects; one member joined the neighborhood freeze movement; one served on the freeze campaign's national funding board; and another participated in a citywide project. For the most part, however, Susan felt that the vision of the group was limited to supporting each other and the church as a whole in those already existing projects and movements.

She reread part of her final journal entry:

At tonight's meeting the Peacemakers seemed to be moving toward a "Sunday school" model. They are continuing to rotate leadership and to do Bible study, but they have decided to move to a prepared curriculum. In the past, we did all of our own programming. Some even suggested tonight that they would like to read and discuss books. They seem to want to maintain the fellowship and nurturing and to focus on the inward journey. They want to hold steady and "regroup."

Susan was convinced that the Peacemakers had taken crucial steps toward active peacemaking. They had started with their own experience and needs, seeking to see the contradictions and to overcome the "culture of silence." This was the process of conscientization. They had done this through a supportive community, through learning together, through participation, through posing problems rather than starting with solutions. Susan was convinced that the inward and outward journeys could not be separated. But she wondered about the life cycle of small groups, about laziness, and about sustaining not just the action agenda but also the sense of inward journey and excitement about participating in God's peacemaking. "As the church becomes institutionally involved in peacemaking, what is the role of the small Peacemakers group?" she wondered. She knew that even such a small step as bringing to fruition the nuclear freeze would take a long time. Can a church maintain and strengthen its commitment over time?

Teaching Note

TOPICS AND QUESTIONS FOR DISCUSSION

Overall issues for consideration:

1. While most churches are accustomed to "annual" issues, to changing topics frequently, how can concern and action for peace and justice be sustained over time?

2. When working on large and long-range visions, how does a group measure growth and impact?

3. How can a small group or community share faith and action in ways that make it possible for others to become changed and to join in?

Specific questions for discussion of the case:

1. What does Susan see as obstacles to peacemaking in local congregations?

2. What steps do Susan and the Peacemakers take to address those obstacles?

3. How is this approach to peacemaking similar to Paulo Freire's pedagogical approach? Are there significant differences?

4. What factors may be involved in the Peacemakers' "moving much more slowly" when Susan is not guiding the group?

5. How might one counsel Susan about her initial question: "What does it take to sustain [a small group's] commitment to peacemaking action and reflection?"

ADDITIONAL RESOURCES

Books and Periodicals

Forsberg, Randall. *Confining the Military to Defense as a Route to Disarmament.* Brookline, Mass.: Institute for Defense and Disarmament Studies.
Handbook for World Peacemaking Groups, 1979. Write to World Peacemakers, 2852 Ontario Rd., NW, Washington, DC 20009.
The Peacemonger Press. A periodic journal of ideas and resources for peacemaking in local churches. Write to West-Park Presbyterian Church, 165 W. 86th St., New York, NY 10024.
Schell, Jonathan. *The Fate of the Earth.* New York: Avon Books, 1982.

Stassen, Glen. *The Journey into Peacemaking.* Memphis: Brotherhood Commission, Southern Baptist Convention, 1983.
Yoder, John Howard. *The Christian Witness to the State.* Newton, Kan.: Institute of Mennonite Studies, Faith and Life Press, 1964.

Organizations

Center for Defense Information, 1500 Massachusetts Ave., NW, Washington, DC 20005. A group of retired military officials who provide information about the dangers of the arms race and possible steps toward greater world security. Of special interest: *The Defense Monitor*, a monthly review of military and arms control issues.
Nuclear Weapons Freeze Clearinghouse, 3195 South Grand, St. Louis, MO 63116. Provides excellent resources on the nuclear arms race and the need for a bilateral nuclear freeze.

NOĒ GONZALES

Commentary on
Peacemaking in a Local Parish

In attempting to analyze "Peacemaking in a Local Parish," I would like to make a distinction between: (1) the medium or vehicle for social change—the small group—that predominates this case study; and (2) the overall message of the case study.

THE MEDIUM—SMALL GROUPS

Using small groups as a way of breaking down large congregational or denominational groupings helps to particularize persons' gifts, graces, and opportunities for ministry. It is very interesting that the use of small groups in churches—like the Covenant Presbyterian Church—in the First World in many instances is patterned after the Latin American ecclesial base communities.

There is no question that in Latin America the ecclesial base community is a functional model, but we must ask whether we have understood it adequately so as to be able to make the necessary adaptations for it to be planted in the soil of the First World. As a United Methodist, I would, by the way, raise similar questions about the use of the eighteenth-century Wesley class meeting as a model for small groups in the late twentieth and early twenty-first centuries.

There is an unsettling and unnerving question that grows as I stretch the parallel between small church groups in the First World and the ecclesial base communities. It has to do with motive. I have been in touch with ecclesial base communities through observation and reflection, and I know that in them the fundamental struggle is for life. That struggle has to do with hard issues of life. It is not a matter of choice or convenience. It is here that I find the sharpest cleavage between the North American and South American models of small groups. In my experience with small groups in North America and in this case study, it becomes clear that those involved have the opportunity to make a conscious choice to participate or not to participate. In such a setting, the element of *compromiso* ("commitment," but more than that—"a staking of one's life" is closer to it) is absent.

In the case study before us, there is a good deal of focus on addressing the congregation as a whole and the society as a whole, but less on building a distinct and bonding identity for the group. Thus, the group's drifting toward being distracted by its agenda and toward a discussion forum seemed logical. It is insightful that the leader of this group saw it "moving toward a Sunday school model." Where are the elements of struggling together to formulate a shared vision? Is there a common action plan with intermediate markers as the basis for evaluation and reflection? How does the model provide for convenanting for mutual support and accountability as members move and evolve on their individual journeys of faithful ministry and growth?

THE MESSAGE OF THE CASE STUDY

Turning to a discussion of the *message* of the case study, we notice that the title, "Peacemaking in a Local Parish," gives us some interesting clues. It is about a small group within a congregation. The small group raises a concern first for itself and then for the entire congregation to address. It is a world/global concern viewed from the local church focus. It seems that from its inception the model is to be institutionalized, not only within the local congregation, but within other churches in the community and within the whole denomination.

The basis for the group's identity and purpose appears to emerge from genuine efforts to address and respond to a compelling social challenge (i.e., the "Call to Faithfulness" in *Sojourners*) that elicits responses based on the individuals' needs and hopes for alternatives. Thus the motivating power for subsequent activity seems to have been helpfully lodged in the *condition* of the participants themselves, and not in the "good intentions" of a professional programmer.

The case study seems to suggest that attention was given to both the inward and outward dimensions of the participants' "journeys." There were efforts through Bible study, worship, reflection, and structured learning opportunities to clarify the links between peacemaking as an act of faithfulness and the traditions and mandates of the biblical story and teachings of Jesus. What is less clear is the relation between elements of the "inward journey," particularly Bible study, and the participants' "outward journeys" toward living out their faith in social action.

What seems missing from the case is a discussion of the individual journeys of participants as they tried in an ongoing or disciplined way to apply what they were learning to their personal situation. To what extent did the inward/outward journeys impact the participants' self-understanding and behavior in their roles as parents, spouses, homemakers, workers, students, neighbors, and citizens? Is it possible that the focus of the group was at once too broad (global issues such as nuclear disarmament) and yet too narrow (concentrating on transforming the thinking and action of a small group within a congregation)? Thus, the global focus allowed for too little sense of immediate personal accomplishment, and the constricted nature of the group did not allow the participants to feel they were involved in a sustained and constantly developing project. It seems that there was a lack of opportunity for growth in personal confidence and for acquiring the needed competence to sustain initiative and commitment over the long haul.

Given a set of almost random and somewhat extraordinary activities (e.g., support for Susan's ministry of peacemaking and the one-time engagement in active participation in a demonstration), is it possible that the life and activity of the group revolved around abstractions not seen as integral to the participants' daily life experience? While there is a helpful discussion of the need for identifying intermediate action-possibilities to propel group growth and development, there is little to suggest a step-by-step approach to disciplined and systematic work in shaping both the long-range and short-term vision and agenda needed to sustain the *developmental* activity of linking the inward journey and outward witness.

QUESTIONS FOR REFLECTION

The following is a brief list of questions which I think bear further reflection:

1. Can such groups develop a distinctive identity that allows them to proceed in their tasks regardless of acceptance by or interplay with the "whole congregation"?
2. Do issues of proximity (community/globe) and immediacy (daily life/long haul) impact the level of motivation and degree of sustainability for such a group?
3. Is the outward journey really *outward?* Don't such small, intimate groups always remain inward-looking, at times moving outside the "walls but always surrounded by an insulating, transparent "membrane"?
4. If shared aspirations open the door to new understandings, might disciplined and intermediate planning be the pathway toward *both* personal and social transformation?
5. While providing support, encouragement, and a base for the wider activity of one member is a legitimate and important function for a group, is it enough to maintain commitment and continuity for *all* group members, especially when the key member is regarded as a professional and not a peer?

JOHN QUINN

Commentary on
Peacemaking in a Local Parish

The small group model envisioned by Susan which came to reality in the Peacemakers seemed better to meet the needs of the group members than those of Susan. The group attempted to integrate the inward and outward journeys necessary for Christian peacemaking. However, individuals' journeys do not always go along at the same pace, and there seemed to be expressions of concern about the relation between Susan's and the group's expectations.

The group started with persons who had indicated an interest in and concern about peacemaking. They signed a petition, but balked at civil disobedience, and it seems Susan's expectations ran ahead of the reality of the group. The reality was that there was a recognition that the most basic reason for getting together was fear. That fear remained within the group. Susan was aware that her own pedagogical approach was concerned with releasing herself from the fear and oppression within her. It seems that at times the highest concern of members of the group was having their fear dissipated in the group.

THEOLOGICAL/EDUCATIONAL INSIGHTS

The three points made by Susan on peacemaking and liberation theology (p.26) are statements of *basic* faith understood in Tillich's sense of *courage:* the affirmation of *life* in spite of the threat of extermination. Note the understanding of faith as a *communal* event (an understanding advanced by Luther and even, to some extent, Hans Küng). These definitions are directly relevant to education for peacemaking.

Susan notes that "peacemaking begins with our own experience." The experience of many is of being worried and fearful. Philip Rieff uses that experience to critique the core of Christian life—the capacity to live for others. Christians today are called to a solidarity, a common human solidarity in Jesus and with each other that is necessary if nuclear holocaust is to be averted. This extraordinary sense of solidarity in the face of fear is seen in the reflection on the Jonestown suicides.

QUESTIONS

Susan is described as acknowledging that "the nuclear arms race motivated her to deeper levels of commitment." I would raise several questions which relate to this commitment and to the group as Christian peacemakers:

1. *Peace Movement or God.* Is the primary focus of the faith of Christian peacemakers on the peace movement or on God?

2. *Balancing the Journeys.* Susan expressed concern that the group seemed "to want to focus on the inward journey." Do we put time limits on the inward journey? Do the inward and outward journeys have to be in balance all the time? Using Sam Keen's metaphor of inhaling deeply in order to exhale more strongly, is the group taking a "deep breath"?

3. *Reflection on Group Dynamics.* Susan notes, "At tonight's meeting the Peacemakers seemed to be moving toward a 'Sunday school' model. They are continuing to rotate leadership and to do Bible study, but they have decided to move to a prepared curriculum." Is there a point when a group needs to reflect on its own behavioral dynamics? How does a group attempt to understand its avoidance/flight mechanisms? There is a need to learn to identify the often painful manifestations of growth: fear, frustration, ignorance, conflict with power and authority, and so on.

4. *Group Ownership of Agenda.* Susan "was keenly aware of her present frustration with the small, faithful Peacemakers group at Covenant Presbyterian Church." Was Susan equally aware of her agenda for the group (specifically what she envisioned it being and doing in one to three years)? Was this implied agenda checked out with the group?

ECONOMIC, POLITICAL, AND SOCIAL IMPLICATIONS

Because of its makeup, the group qua group is never likely to come to a consensus around radical action (e.g., civil disobedience) though it could support such action by individual members of the group. The group seemed to function as a *support* group, not an *action-oriented* group. The strength of the base community/support group can be an impediment to its involvement in larger political, economic, and social activity.

STRENGTHS AND WEAKNESSES OF THE MODEL

Strengths

1. The recognition of barriers to peacemaking that are internal to the group is important because we so often see barriers as being solely external. In recognizing and dealing with internal barriers, we can often raise up significant support systems; for example, the grief and lamentation urged and practiced by the prophets can be the beginning of a counter power.

2. The willingness to come up with a "middle axiom" is critical. Interestingly, Susan is comfortable with the middle axiom of the freeze but seems unaware of the group's need for a similar middle axiom—a prepared curriculum—when she leaves them.

Weaknesses

1. Freire's statement that "the oppressed do not enjoy the luxury of experimenting" is vital. When Paul VI spoke of *patience* in Bogotá, the people booed him. Parkinson's Law of Delay is, as Parkinson insists, the Law of Refusal. To tell a drowning person to "wait" is to refuse to save that person. The group seemed to have no process to deal with the contrast between Susan's urgency and the group's poetry.

2. The move to become a publisher and a clearinghouse of programs detracts from anticipated actions and spiritual reflection. It is controlled and controllable, and it reveals an emphasis on thought rather than action. Thought must follow action—not vice versa.

CHAPTER 2

PARENTING FOR
PEACE AND JUSTICE

This model combines an emphasis on the nuclear family with mobilization of local groups for support and action on peace and justice issues. It also highlights the mutual interaction between those groups and a national support organization. The model begins where people are, with their need for significant relationships beyond the immediate family and their desire to respond creatively and responsibly to the needs of the larger society. The case study focuses on the development of one particular group as it moves through elementary stages toward a more risky option for action, civil disobedience. Distinctive of this model is its modest, down-to-earth effort to develop a cohesive and effective group to make some impact on local and global issues of justice.

The commentaries affirm the practical value of the model and also raise critical questions about its structure and procedures and about the controlling power of the ideology of the nuclear family.

Organizations searching for fresh ways to get persons involved will find here clues for mobilizing families into effective groups for support and challenge. Parents and single persons looking for a good entry into significant group activity toward peace and justice will also find in this case creative suggestions for participation.

Other aspects of this model deal with church concern for parenting and peace, opportunities for intergenerational enrichment, the extended family model vis-à-vis the nuclear family model, and seminars dealing with value-formation for families and congregations.

Program Overview

I. GOALS

A. to analyze with families how they are affected by the materialism, individualism, racism, sexism, violence, and militarism in the world around them;

B. to suggest ways families can work together to affect those forces and discover alternative ways of living that are more simple and cooperative, nonviolent, multicultural, nonsexist, globally conscious, and prayerful;

C. to link families and family support groups—locally, nationally, globally—so as to deepen commitment, provide support and challenge, and expand the possibilities of effective action at home as well as in the larger world;

D. to integrate parenting for peace and justice (ppj) into existing marriage and family enrichment programs, family religious education, and peace and justice programs;

E. to train and update national, regional, and local leaders in the use of ppj resources and in their efforts to integrate those concerns into their ministry.

II. ORGANIZATION

A. *The Parenting for Peace and Justice Network* (PPJN) is currently located at the Institute for Peace and Justice in St. Louis and is a program component of the institute. However, the PPJN has its own advisory board.

B. *Advisory board* determines the priorities of the PPJN, plans the annual meeting of local coordinators and denominational representatives, and extends ppj into the programming of various family-life and social concerns agencies in North America. It meets yearly and is composed of denominational representatives, PPJN local coordinators, and other family-life and social concerns leaders.

C. *National staff* is responsible for coordinating the PPJN, especially servicing the local coordinators, conducting leadership training workshops, and implementing the other basic goals and the decisions of the advisory board.

D. *Local coordinators and teams* represent the PPJN in their area: doing ppj presentations and programs, assisting other local leaders doing ppj programs, and encouraging the use of ppj resources by other groups/programs.

III. CHAPTERS

A. Local coordinators and/or ecumenical teams represent the PPJN in some seventy-five U.S. and Canadian cities and in Manila, the Philippines.
B. In a number of these areas, local family support groups have come together to reflect and act on the various ppj issues.
C. Fifteen national (U.S.) denominations and one Canadian ecumenical agency (Ecumenical Family Ministries in Toronto) have made ppj a part of their family life, social concerns, and/or religious education programming.

For further information contact: James and Kathleen McGinnis; Parenting for Peace and Justice Network; The Institute for Peace and Justice; 4144 Lindell #400; St. Louis, MO 63108.

Case Study
Parenting for Peace and Justice

"If we're unwilling to do this, I think we need to ask how committed we really are. It's the real test—right in our own backyard—of how serious we are about standing in solidarity with our brothers and sisters who are oppressed."

"I can't agree. We ought to work harder through legislation. We haven't exhausted that avenue. I just don't think breaking the law is the right way."

"We could be directly responsible for saving the lives of other people. How can we refuse to help?"

"Peace, Nicaragua, now El Salvador. How many different issues can we take on all at once? I didn't join this group primarily for social action. It seems to me we are changing our original focus."

"I'm uncomfortable with my discomfort."

Those painfully honest comments made at a meeting of the Kansas City parenting for peace and justice group continued to run through Peter Sawyer's mind as he and his wife, Anne, drove home. As they began to discuss what had brought the committed group of eleven to the present impasse, they realized they had seen it coming for several months. In Peter's mind, offering sanctuary to refugees from El Salvador and Guatemala was a logical and responsible step for their peace and justice group to take. But as the group coordinator, he was also committed to nurture and support individual members of the community according to their level of awareness. Peter and Anne acknowledged that the group was faced with some difficult choices.

FORMATION OF THE SUPPORT GROUP

It had been two and a half years since Anne and Peter Sawyer decided they needed to come together with other families, both to find support for their peace and justice efforts and to be in contact with other parents who could share the tasks of speaking to families and groups in the Kansas City area about parenting for peace and justice. They had previously been associated with peace and justice groups that did not have a specific family orientation and with a four-family prayer and parent support group that did not have a specific focus on peace and justice issues.

This case was prepared by James B. McGinnis and Alice Frazer Evans as a basis for discussion rather than to illustrate either effective or ineffective handling of the situation. Copyright © by the Case Study Institute.

In October 1980 the Sawyers invited three couples to their home to share concerns and to consider forming a family support group that would be willing to give talks to others about parenting for peace and justice. The children of the four couples ranged from infants to college students, but the majority were in elementary school, as were the three Sawyer children. The occupations of the parents ranged from clergyperson to social worker, and from health center director to small business owner and elementary school principal. One of the couples was black; they all considered themselves middle-class North Americans.

In the past each of the four couples had been involved in community social action concerns. With the decision to form a group the couples agreed on the importance of community support and challenge to sustain any long-term commitment to work for peace and justice, whether in their own family and neighborhood or in the larger global family. The couples decided to affiliate with the national Parenting for Peace and Justice Network, a component of the Institute for Peace and Justice, located in St. Louis. They also affirmed the need to participate in a parenting for peace and justice leadership training workshop, sponsored by the network, to develop skills in making presentations and to share a common experience as a way of bringing them closer together as a group.

TRAINING WORKSHOPS

In January 1981 the four couples participated in a workshop sponsored by the Parenting for Peace and Justice Network. Here they met Karen Roberts, a day-care teacher, and her husband, Mark, a pastor, who wanted to integrate their social concerns with newly acquired responsibilities as parents of two very young children, and Walt and Betty Rogers, parents of elementary school children, who expressed similar needs and concerns. During subsequent regular meetings at which they implemented suggestions they had picked up at the training workshop, the six couples found many opportunities to grow in their understanding of how to integrate peace and justice into family life. They also began planning for a local weekend workshop for October 1981 as their first joint effort to introduce parenting for peace and justice to the Kansas City area.

Thirty-five people signed up for the weekend workshop, which had been advertised through local congregations. The workshop met in a retreat center with the six couples sharing leadership responsibilities. The program ranged from helping children deal with pressures of the 1980s to living responsibly in relation to the world. The leaders utilized several audiovisuals supplied by the Parenting for Peace and Justice Network.

The Saturday evening session on "Stewardship and Countering Materialism as Families" took place in the homes of the members of the support group. Each family hosted from three to four participants. The evening began with a simple meal followed by informal sharing of steps each family had already taken to become more aware of and responsive to the need to use less of the world's limited resources in their own daily living and to share some of the savings generated by their changes in lifestyle. The school-age children of the host family were also able to participate in these home sessions, something that members of the group were beginning to realize needed to be added to their adults-only focus.

The Sunday morning session focused on the theme of "Families Building the Global Family." The idea of buying Third World handicrafts surfaced when the group watched a slide show (*People of the Field*—from Jubilee Crafts) about Santiago Alonzo, a former political prisoner in the Philippines, and his craft of making bone pendants inscribed with the words: "Those who would give light must endure burning." The slide presentation also described the injustice and repression in the Philippines and what North Americans could do about it. Having been touched by the life of this Filipino—both his suffering and his struggle for dignity and justice—and having concrete possibilities for action, several participants wrote letters to their Congressional representatives protesting U.S. support for government-sponsored repression in the Philippines, in addition to ordering from Jubilee Crafts some of Santiago's pendants as Christmas gifts.

WORKSHOP RESPONSES

The parenting for peace and justice support group found other concrete responses coming from the three-day workshop. The Zaleskis, who joined the group as a result of the workshop, were particularly impressed with Jubilee Crafts. They helped organize a simple alternative Christmas bazaar for their local Lutheran congregation. They wrote Jubilee Crafts and got a number of handicrafts on consignment. These items and the *Alternative Celebrations Catalog* (from Alternatives; Box 1707; Forest Park, GA 30050) were displayed in the church hall after worship on the last Sunday in November. The Zaleskis later reported to the support group that this was a relatively "safe" first step in global awareness education for many in their congregation. They felt that participation was high because the project addressed the need of many persons to have an alternative to crowded shopping malls and sometimes meaningless gifts at Christmas time.

Other participants picked up on the suggestion of a "voluntary surcharge." If they were going to continue to buy pineapples and bananas—cash crops imported from the Philippines (and elsewhere) where farm workers got less than two dollars per day for harvesting those crops on land many of them had formerly owned and from which they once had fed themselves—why not set aside 25 percent of the cost of the fruit and send it to a missionary group working with Filipino farm workers? This 25 percent surcharge represents the additional cost of the fruit if the workers had been paid a fairer wage. These participants reasoned that if they benefit from the low Third World wages, they ought to renounce that benefit and put it back into the system as close as possible to workers from whom the benefit was taken. The Maryknoll mission-ary order was suggested as an appropriate recipient by one of the members of the support group who had firsthand knowledge of the work of the order in the Philippines. To involve the children in this activity, it was also suggested that a map of the Philippines, pictures of Filipinos, and a decorated can for the voluntary surcharge be placed in the breakfast/dining room as visual remind-ers of why and how the family was trying to help.

Following the October 1981 workshop, the Zaleskis and another couple joined the support group for their monthly meetings. Those meetings contin-ued to involve only the adults and focused solely on the tasks of planning future educational events and outreach strategies in the Kansas City area.

PROGRAM CHANGES

By the spring of 1982 two couples announced their decision to stop coming to the monthly meetings because of "busy schedules" and their dissatisfaction with "the all-business and primarily adult focus of the group." Peter, as the coordinator of the Kansas City group, attended the March annual meeting of the National Advisory Board of the Parenting for Peace and Justice Network. As a result of this opportunity to see how other groups/teams had organized themselves, Peter made several suggestions for changes in the Kansas City group. First, thirty minutes of socializing could be added to the beginning of the monthly meeting, plus thirty to forty-five minutes during the meeting for enrichment. This segment could include features such as audiovisual presenta-tions on topics like sex-role stereotyping, discussions of suggestions for ways the group could respond to issues in Central America, and discussions on methods of conflict resolution and discipline. The group adopted these changes and made a commitment to plan more family events.

The first family event was a May picnic. Then in June seven of the eight support group families joined three thousand other persons in a local march for peace and disarmament on the occasion of the beginning of the United Nations Second Special Session on Disarmament. The children were en-couraged to make signs or banners reflecting their own concern about peace and the arms race. One seven-year-old's sign read: "Money for Schools not Bombs." Group members reflected after the march how important it was for their children to see so many other children involved in social action. Their children weren't the only kids who had "crazy" parents! In addition the parents shared that the experience of knowing that so many people were working to prevent nuclear war was critical for nurturing their own hope that the world might survive the escalating nuclear arms race and not destroy itself.

FAMILY CAMP

In August 1982 four of the eight families, along with three new families, organized a family camp for three days of learning, playing, swimming, shared meal preparation, celebration, and prayer. Anne and Peter agreed that this was a key event in nurturing the global awareness and communal nature of the group.

Many of the activities of those three days focused on global awareness. Using a new intergenerational program developed by the people at Jubilee Crafts, each of the four support group families took responsibility for one of the sessions. Puppets were an integral part of the activities. In one session "Greedy and Wily Wizard" (a U.S.-based multinational corporation) persuaded the unsuspecting "Usa" (USA) to eat sugar which Greedy and Wily was producing on land it occupied in a neighboring area (the Dominican Republic). Once Usa became addicted to sugar, he was able to be enlisted in Greedy and Wily's effort to squelch the resistance of the neighbors whose lands were used (U.S. military intervention in the Dominican Republic in 1965).

Biblical stories were also an integral part of the two-hour morning sessions. The analogy of the Body of Christ—many different members contributing to the functioning of the whole Body according to the unique gifts and functions of each—was imaged in a mythical animal called a "galliwompus." Building on this image, the differences among the various members of the Body of Christ— different races, nations, religious traditions—were portrayed as beautiful and enriching rather than threatening and something to be suppressed. The attempt to ignore or cover over the differences among races, nations, and traditions was seen as a negative result of the usually well-intentioned effort to overemphasize commonalities within the global family.

The concern for developing a balanced appreciation for both the differences and commonalities within the global family was reflected in the slide presentations following each evening's songfest and campfire. Anne and Peter Sawyer and their twelve-year-old son, Tad, had just returned from a three-week trip to Nicaragua. Their slides provided a view of the Nicaraguan people and revolution quite different from the accounts reported by the U.S. news media. Tad's own slides of Nicaraguan children, schools, sports, and places that touched him (an active volcano, the country's only McDonald's restaurant, a river crossed during a jeep ride) drew enthusiastic comments from the children. The adults, once the younger children went to bed, raised numerous questions about Nicaragua and U.S. foreign policy.

The adults were later to agree that an important aspect of effective family programs was taking time for the adults to pursue an issue further following presentations geared to children. Three of the couples shared that part of the powerful impact on both themselves and their children had been created by stories of several Nicaraguan people. The concreteness of their lives—as dedicated rebuilders of their neighborhoods and country as well as victims of Somoza's repressive dictatorship before July 19, 1979, and then as victims of U.S. policy—broke through, at least partially, their "anti-communist" mindset. In Mark Roberts's words, "The lives and witness of real people have a way of touching our hearts and moving us from awareness to action."

Anne and Peter remembered that this same progression was experienced by other participants during the family camp Sunday morning worship service. Worship had focused on the theme of the oneness of the human family as the Body of Christ. The story of a peasant community in Peru struggling for its land and justice focused attention on a specific group of people to whom the support group could tangibly respond. Following worship the children drew pictures expressing hope, concern, and solidarity on a giant piece of newsprint rolled out on a dining room table. At the same time the adults wrote letters to the Peruvian community's leaders. The story of the community of Jicamarca, Peru, was taken from a book and slides produced by the Institute for Peace and Justice and entitled *Solidarity with the People of Nicaragua and Peru*. Again, many of the couples explained later that from this experience they had learned that specific action-responses to the presentation of a situation of injustice are an essential component of effective global awareness education.

In acknowledgment of the importance of the fun/play dimension of the family camp—from nature walks to cooperative games and swimming—an occasional evening of volleyball was added to the repertoire of regular activities of the support group.

FOCUS ON LATIN AMERICA

In October 1982 the family support group held a workshop in which the "global family" component focused in part on a Nicaraguan group described in *Solidarity with the People of Nicaragua and Peru*, a book that discusses the pairing of North American families, churches, or groups with Latin American partners. In a discussion of creative ways of linking families or family groups, the Zaleskis suggested making and sending family albums to individual Nicaraguan families. Other suggestions included individual families or the whole support group having a "Nicaragua Night," celebrating a partnership day, perhaps when the first package was sent, and establishing specific opportunities for the children to collect and share items identified by their Nicaraguan partners as helpful to their needs. However, it was agreed that sending money or materials should not be the primary purpose of the partnership.

Because most of the adults in the support group participated in this session and because of the exposure and interest generated by the evening slide presentation at the family camp, the group decided at its November 1982 meeting to "pair" with the community of Ciudad Sandino, a large barrio on the outskirts of Managua, Nicaragua. A Sunday evening in January 1983 was selected as the "Nicaragua Night" celebration suggested at the October workshop. Several adults volunteered to plan the celebration. Each family was asked to read the story of Ciudad Sandino and to come to the celebration with pictures and other family mementos which would be put on pages to form a combined "family album" to send to the Nicaraguan community.

The planners enlisted the help of a Nicaraguan woman living in Kansas City. Alicia Montez agreed to prepare a special Nicaraguan dish to supplement the tacos, refried beans, and other Latin American items being brought by group members. She also agreed to teach everyone some Nicaraguan dances during the evening of celebration. The slide show of Ciudad Sandino, which the group had ordered with the book, opened the celebration. Maps of Nicaragua and pictures, including prints from the slides of Ciudad Sandino, were distributed to each family to post in a prominent place in its home. Several families were to choose their breakfast rooms, placing the pictures either on a wall or at an "extra" place at the table. After the Nicaraguan meal, the children began making the family album pages while adults wrote letters to their Congressional representatives protesting U.S. "covert" efforts to "destabilize" or overthrow the Nicaraguan government. At the suggestion of the Robertses, copies of these letters were made the next day so they could be included in the album "as real symbols of solidarity and encouragement to the people of Ciudad Sandino."

The album was mailed the next day to Martha, a Maryknoll sister in Ciudad Sandino who had agreed to be the liaison for the pairing. A few weeks later she wrote to the support group that she had shared the album with ten families in the barrio. Each Nicaraguan family was asked to select one of the ten Kansas City families to be its "partner." By March four of the U.S. families had received a letter from their partner and one had received pictures as well. One of the letters, written by a volunteer health leader in Ciudad Sandino, specified a number of items needed in the clinic where she worked. This information was brought to the April 1983 meeting of the group for a response. The list of medical supplies included baby scales, plastic raincoats, simple medical bags for the barrio midwives, crayons and felt tip markers for clinic posters, staplers, and staples. Several of the adults reasoned that these items offered a number of ways in which the children could participate. The group "allotted" each family one set of crayons and one stapler and encouraged each family to see if it could secure donated items from medical contacts. In addition, group members were encouraged to consider creative ways of raising money to finance any purchases. The Sawyers brought this challenge to their next family meeting. Ten-year-old David suggested that the money gained from their monthly "returnable bottles" (three to five dollars) be set aside for the Ciudad clinic. The $24.14 still in the family "Operation Rice Bowl" box—money generated by Lenten snack-skipping, meal-simplifying, and liquor-skipping— was also designated for this project.

Most of the families in the support group decided on ways of raising money and communicated this to Kathy Andrews, the project coordinator. They raised $150, and with that money Kathy purchased a significant number of medical bags and plastic raincoats. At the group's May picnic all the items were brought and put into three large boxes to be shipped to Managua. At an earlier meeting, Kathy had reasoned that this process would enable the children to see their solidarity in concrete terms. It would also enable the adults as well as the children to flesh out the prayers they would share at the "Peace Pentecost" celebration that followed the picnic. The group had agreed in advance to link its picnic with the Kansas City observance of that May 29 event.

STATIONS IN THE CITY

The twin concerns that continued to occupy the awareness/action dimension of the group—Central America and peace—found other stimuli during the spring of 1983. At the March meeting Peter Sawyer had invited group members to consider joining in a national effort that was to take place during Holy Week and that was to include fasting and prayer for peace in Central America and pleading with God "to intervene somehow and touch the lives of both policy-makers and victims of their policies." The Sawyers found that Holy Week provided them and several others in the support group another experience of the integration of faith and social concerns. In later sharing this experience with the group, Peter affirmed that "People of faith need to experience the call to peace and justice as a call from Jesus and to experience social action in the context of prayer and the liturgical year." As Anne and Peter described their "Stations in the City" experience to the April meeting, they discussed four aspects of it: identifying places and people through whose suffering Jesus "relives his passion" today; identifying ways in which the families involved could respond to that passion; performing those responses; and celebrating the experience together. The places and people selected by the participating families included abused women and children living at a Catholic Worker house of hospitality, an elderly shut-in in the parish, a prisoner with whom the Sawyer family had corresponded for four years, and hungry people in Kansas City and Central America. During the three hours of observance on Good Friday, the family dyed Easter eggs for the Catholic Worker residents, made an Easter basket for the shut-in, colored a collage of pictures of Easter hope for the prisoner, and wrote letters to Congressional representatives on behalf of the hungry. Bread for the World's newsletter provided helpful directions for this last activity.

On the following day, Holy Saturday, the Sawyer family joined two other families to deliver the Easter responses. At the Catholic Worker house the group found an Easter party in progress and were invited to join in. Anne and Peter realized that this had made the event much more of a mutual experience, with children in both groups giving and receiving. Peter reported to their support group that the combination of Easter eggs and political letter writing provided an experience of two other important principles of global awareness education. "First, both the works of mercy—direct service—and the works of justice—changing social structures—need to be part of one's social concerns, awareness and action. Second, one criterion for choosing what issues to address should be that they have both a local and a global dimension. Our family found that the concreteness and immediacy of the local focus offered the opportunity for direct contact. The global dimension stretched us in both our vision and action, making the reality of the oneness of the global family a little more tangible."

FOCUS ON SANCTUARY

Other members attending the April support group meeting suggested additional opportunities for developing awareness about action on peace and Central America. At the end of the meeting the group prayed for the Catholic bishops meeting the following week to vote on the pastoral letter on peace and war, and agreed to join many others at the cathedral in Kansas City on the evening of May 2 to pray together for the bishops. Two other decisions were made. First, the group decided to allot ten minutes at the beginning of its May meeting for political letter writing on an issue proposed by one of the members of the group. Then during the remainder of the meeting individuals could choose to sign or not sign each of the various letters being passed around the room. Second, Peter proposed that the enrichment-time of the meeting focus on the situation of Central American refugees and the possibility of the group providing or supporting "sanctuary" for some of those refugees. There was general assent to this suggestion, with numerous comments that this was a "good idea."

Several members of the group were part of other area groups that had already been considering offering sanctuary to people the U.S. government considered "illegal aliens" or "economic refugees." These were people leaving El Salvador and Guatemala who had been categorized by the U.S. government as motivated by the desire for economic betterment, rather than as "political refugees" who were fleeing because of fear of repression or death. U.S. authorities had already returned some thirty-five thousand persons to El Salvador over the previous four years. Many of those persons were later reported as having been found dead.

At the May meeting the group watched a slide presentation (*In Pursuit of Refuge*) on the plight of Salvadoran and Guatemalan refugees and discussed briefly a "Sanctuary Support Form" that identified nine ways in which individuals or a group could assist in the sanctuary process. In the discussion it became clear that not everyone agreed. There were moments of strained silence as well as some anxiety in the voices of several members. As Peter and Anne later discussed on the way home, the "sticking point" seemed to be the issue of civil disobedience.

CIVIL DISOBEDIENCE

Civil disobedience was not a completely new issue for every group member. The possibility of nonpayment of taxes had been presented in mailings to most of them by the Institute for Peace and Justice in 1982 and early 1983. Although five new group members had come on board since the October 1982 leadership workshop, Anne and Peter had felt that these were people who would be open to the possibility of civil disobedience. The question of civil disobedience was the first one raised after the slide presentation. Peter Sawyer and Mark Roberts both affirmed that while any support (food, clothing, or even a letter of support for another group willing to provide sanctuary) technically made the contributor liable to a charge of conspiracy to violate federal law, the likelihood of prosecution was extremely small. Peter continued, "At the present time the INS and Department of Justice have chosen not to enter the more than seventy-five U.S. churches providing sanctuary. They are neither prosecuting those churches nor the thousands of other individuals supporting those churches." (See the note in the Introduction to the Teaching Note, p. 56, below.)

Because it was clear that several members of the group needed more time to think about the issue, Peter suggested that people read the May 1983 issue of *Sojourners* magazine, which focused on civil disobedience, as well as one or more of the articles on sanctuary in the February 1983 issue of the magazine entitled *The Other Side.* In addition members of the group agreed to read the Bible, particularly the Old Testament prophets, to pray for one another, and to ask the Holy Spirit to guide the group in this matter. Later that evening Peter and Anne discussed the uneasy tone of the meeting. Anne reasoned that many communities go through this kind of dilemma on issues of peace and justice when one or a few members of the group are not ready or able to embrace a particular action or issue. The question became: Should those who are ready and want to act postpone or perhaps even drop the action for the sake of the unity of the group? Peter responded by saying that as the urgency of the action or issue increases, so does the desire to act. He went on:

In this case it is obvious that at least one third of our group, including myself, feels strongly the desire and need to respond to the desperate situation of the Central American refugees entering the United States. Another third is in favor of our action, and the last third seems unsure or has some reservations. We've already written letters to the INS, the Department of Justice, and the Department of State, as well as to our Congressional representatives urging that these refugees be granted "extended voluntary departure" status. This would mean that these so-called economic refugees could legally remain in the United States until the civil wars in their countries are settled. Several in our group have discussed offering sanctuary as a symbol of resistance to what we feel is an unjust law, as a concrete way of performing works of mercy—feeding the hungry and sheltering the homeless—and as a unique opportunity to do effective global awareness. This is a concrete opportunity to educate others, including our children, by giving voice to the story and witness of the refugees and thereby touching the hearts as well as the heads of the members of our group and many others.

Peter had shared with the group several specific ways in which they could respond: provide one or two nights' lodging for refugees en route elsewhere;

pick up and deliver refugees from one stop to another; provide services such as food, clothing, bail bonds, or medical care; support individual families who would do any of these things.

Any of the above activities carried the same penalties as providing sanctuary itself—a felony bearing penalties of five years in jail and a two-thousand-dollar fine. Peter acknowledged his awareness that in light of the legal implications some in the group were feeling defensive because their jobs or family situations were different from those of others. The husband of one woman who was a part of the group did not participate in any way in the group's activities; she had shared that her active involvement in the offering of sanctuary would put a definite strain on their marriage. Some of the members worked for social service organizations or congregations which would be supportive; others, however, expressed concern about "unsympathetic employers."

A lot of things seemed to be happening all at once: invitations to tax resistance, fasting, public demonstrations and prayer vigils for peace, political letter writing, the clinic supplies for Nicaragua. On top of all that, two families had serious job problems, one had a serious health problem, and one woman in the group was only a month away from her wedding. In recalling the evolution of the support group, Anne and Peter agreed that each member had joined for support as well as challenge. The cohesiveness of the group over its two-and-a-half-year history had been tested before. The first time was when the two families had dropped out of the business meetings. Then there were several times when the group expanded and diversified itself by inviting in new members and explicitly affirmed the need to be sensitive to the desires of each new member.

The June meeting was to be at the home of the Sawyers, and they were responsible for its coordination. Peter asked Anne: "As facilitator, how forceful can I be about my own position on sanctuary? And how fast can people be pushed on this or should they be pushed at all?" He and Anne had a lot to discuss before June 10. They decided they would need to discuss plans for the meeting with a number of the members of the group as well.

Teaching Note

TOPICS AND QUESTIONS FOR DISCUSSION

This case not only poses a specific dilemma for Anne and Peter Sawyer as leaders of the parenting group—it also traces the development of the group from its inception and describes a variety of program components. (Note: Since the writing of this case, the legal status of individuals and churches providing sanctuary has changed, and the INS and Department of Justice are prosecuting some North American citizens who are members of the Sanctuary Movement.)

1. The case author, Jim McGinnis, suggests that readers and discussion participants refer to the questions posed by Suzanne Toton in her commentary, below, as a way to look critically at the Parenting for Peace and Justice model. Those questions focus on the training workshops, the role of children in the group, links between various issues and actions taken by the group, the role of face-to-face encounters, and the development of group consciousness for civil disobedience.

2. Another approach would be to trace the chronological development of this particular group. List the various programs and stages which occurred (the retreats, the various levels of relations with the national network, the focus on Latin America, etc.). Which components appear to have been most effective in raising the consciousness and commitment level of the group? Why?

3. In one of the quotes that introduce the case, a participant states, "I didn't join this group primarily for social action. It seems to me we are changing our original focus." What was the "original focus" of the parenting group? Were there changes in the focus? How do you interpret Peter's remark to Anne that "offering sanctuary . . . [is] a logical and responsible step for [our] group to take"? What is the role of establishing goals and periodic goal-review in a group?

4. Consider a role-play of the upcoming June meeting at the home of the Sawyers. However, with the exception of a "group leader" selected to guide the discussion, each participant should "play" himself or herself. That is, the scene is the June meeting, but each member of your group should speak his or her mind on the vital issues that face the parenting group. The role-play could take two stages: first, designing a meeting that would provide for an open discussion of the issues and, second, conducting a meeting which comes to some creative, concrete decisions about future directions of the parenting group.

5. In a period of "de-roling," discuss how you did as a group. How

successful was your design for the meeting? What were the barriers to resolution? What were the most effective steps? Whatever the group decides to do, what resources can the members call on to continue to be an effective group?

6. What did you learn from this case discussion about forming groups to address peace and justice issues?

ADDITIONAL RESOURCES

Carmichael, Carrie. *Non-Sexist Childraising*. Boston: Beacon Press, 1977.

"Children, Race, and Racism: How Race Awareness Develops," *Bulletin* 11, nos. 3 and 4 (1980). Published by the Council on Interracial Books for Children.

Christian Parenting for Peace and Justice, 1981. Published by the Board of Discipleship of the United Methodist Church.

Haessly, Jacqueline. *Peacemaking: Family Activities for Justice and Peace*. New York: Paulist Press, 1980.

Longacre, Doris Janzen. *Living More with Less*. Scottdale, Pa.: Herald Press, 1980.

McGinnis, James. *Those Who Hunger*. New York: Paulist Press, 1979.

McGinnis, James, and Kathleen McGinnis, *Parenting for Peace and Justice*. Maryknoll, N.Y.: Orbis Books, 1981.

Prutzman, Priscilla, et al. *The Friendly Classroom for a Small Planet: A Handbook on Creative Approaches to Living and Problem Solving for Children*. Wayne, N.J.: Avery Publishing Group, 1978.

ALLEN J. MOORE

Commentary on
Parenting for Peace and Justice

The issues involved in parenting for peace and justice are both complex and elusive. Who among us, on the surface at least, would not believe in the centrality of the family and affirm the responsibility of parents to raise children who believe in and practice "peace and justice"? Few of us would deny that the family is a significant influence in the formation of good persons for a better world. The family is central to our way of life, and we revere the parenting role which procreation calls us to fulfill.

We probably would not readily agree that the emphasis and value which middle-class society places upon family life might be in themselves negative forces when viewed from a global perspective. Without critical reflection on the institution of family life itself, all the gestures of solidarity might be relatively unimpressive when seen from the point of view of oppression and the gross injustices of our world community.

Among us there would be even greater disagreement as to the effectiveness of parents educating their children so that they can address the complex political and social structures of the global reality. What is required of families to insure that children will grow up to be morally responsible agents in the struggle for global justice and peace among nations? Is such insurance possible?

OUR CHILDREN AND OTHER CHILDREN

Parenting is the process of nurturing (bringing into being and caring for) the persons we have helped to create as we participate in God's ongoing creative process. When one reflects upon the complexity of the reproductive processes and grasps the uniqueness of each new birth, one has to conclude that every child is truly a gift of God. The problem is that it is easier for us to grasp the value of our own child than to have a social awareness of the worth of each and every child regardless of parental background and location in the social structure. We have not fully grasped the significance of Erikson's concept of "generativity," which broadens parenting from taking care of one's own to a social responsibility for nurturing or "generating" a whole generation of children. Although programs of family enrichment, including those programs in which enrichment has to do with world awareness, do have their merit, we must be concerned if they tend to separate the "good" families from all the others and do *not* call parents and others to the larger responsibility for the community of children.

My Tongan friends remind me that there are no unwanted children in their community, and the welfare of all of the children is central to the parenting concern for one's own children. Even with sparse food, a parent would not think to feed her or his own child while neglecting the cries of hunger coming from a neighbor's child.

Implicit in much of our concern for a better world is the fear that our own child may not survive to grow up. Seldom are we fully aware that in much of the world parents have little hope of their children surviving to adulthood as they daily fall victim to guerrilla warfare, poverty, disease, and exploitation. As Henri Nouwen discovered in personal encounters, the United States is willingly and unwillingly participating in the killing of the *sons* and *daughters* of many Nicaraguans. Our guns—guns which are paid for by our tax dollars—are being used by the counterrevolutionaries to murder children who are valued and loved by Nicaraguan mothers and fathers.

Possibly we can never escape our self-interest in the nurturing of our own children, but deeply ingrained in our assumptions about family life in our society is the belief that our own children have rights above and beyond the rights of other children. As long as our children perceive of their own self-importance at the expense of other children—both near and far—the gestures that we make toward solidarity will carry signs of phoniness. This is why liberationists caution North Americans not to take over the agendas of liberation from the South Americans while we neglect the oppression and injustices so rampant within our own institutional structures.

We desire a good world for our *own* children, and we find that our economic structures generally define that world in terms of our own values and beliefs, our own way of life, and what we believe will be best for the future of our own children. Parenting in middle-class society is largely an egotistical enterprise. Children are consciously and unconsciously viewed as an extension of our own histories, and we desire for them the unrealized goals which we have not achieved. We want them to avoid our errors of judgment and to benefit from our experiences rather than theirs. We enter the experience of parenting with high expectations for ourselves and with great ambition for our children. No wonder our brothers and sisters living in other social contexts often view our gestures toward peace and justice with suspicion—because the assumptions we bring to our family way of life are so incongruent with our gestures.

DEIFICATION OF THE FAMILY

We have come close to deifying the family in the civil religion of middle-class society. The figurative language of the family in our biblical tradition has been literalized, especially among Protestant groups who have always had difficulty in distinguishing between the symbolic and the literal fact. This has led most North Americans to exalt the importance of the family in relation to the larger community of humankind (and of livingkind as well) and to define the worth of persons in relation to their marital and family status. We assume that all persons are to be married and that the end of marriage is procreation and parenting. This very attitude has led us to be exclusive in our religious life and in the kinds of programs we offer as a church community. These naturalistic definitions of marriage, combined with a divine-like mission to replicate the "household of God," has led us to heap judgment on those who do not share these relationships. Such definitions have been the cause of massive injustices, all in the name of family solidarity and the welfare of children. A case in point is the deep prejudice that exists in the religious community against homosexuality because lesbians and gay men do not choose to express what many in middle-class religious groups understand as the natural capacity to reproduce and continue a family lineage.

Ever since the Enlightenment the family has represented the increasing privatization of human life. What Johannes Metz has suggested about the middle class in general is applicable to the family unit in North American society and many other First World societies. The family is no longer sustained by traditions and a commitment to the larger community. The family owes its significance in North American society to an economic and social system that depends upon consumption, success, achievement, and competition for the rewards of society. These economic assumptions are both implicit and explicit in the social systems that are geared toward enhancing the family. It is especially visible in the schooling structures of society. Undergirding the economic and commercial transactions are private values and the doctrine of individualism.

THE FAMILY AS SOCIALIZING UNIT

Two other factors may have social and theological significance in any reflection on the parenting function. The first is the extent to which the family has become dysfunctional as a socializing unit. There is much evidence that in spite of the popularity of marriage at this time and the apparent rebound of parenting among many in our society, the educative functions of the family have been turned over largely to other institutions. This is not to make a judgment on the current practice to turn the child over rather early to day-care centers, nursery schools, or to other surrogate parental structures. As we move beyond the narrowness of the Freudian view of the family, we have come to find some positive ways to expose the child to a large community of influences. Unfortunately, these influences seem to mirror the restrictive view of reality that is fostered by economic structures based upon materialism and consumption. Any attempt by these public institutions to open the windows to the realities of the global society is met with massive resistance. An example of this resistance is the rise of private schooling that is designed to protect one's child from interacting with children of minority backgrounds and to preserve ethnic and economic stratification. It may be that some church communities remain the most free institutions serving families and may remain the most potent influence in the formation of wider communities of concern and the widest avenue to a new global consciousness.

Another factor is the sociological discovery that the family has limited influence in the formation of children's values. Richard Elacks, Kenneth Keniston, and others found that youths often live out the values of their parents, but always under the conditioning of peer-group influence. Children seldom depart totally from parental attitudes and beliefs, but they do at times embrace with some urgency the value-system of their friends and age-group associates.

AWARENESS AND VISION

What all this says in relation to the parenting for peace and justice case study is: Although programs of awareness and of social action are significant gestures, they are no more than that—gestures. Only as we bring families, including both parents and children, to a critical awareness of their own plight will there be hope for justice for humankind and peace among peoples and nations. As long as our agenda remains the plight of others and we do not perceive the destructive values and assumptions that are our own captivity, we will neither be free ourselves nor will we be very effective liberators of others.

What we need most are new visions and purposes for the family in our society. A new basis for marriage and parenting requires a new sense of God's calling and vocation, a mission that transcends our preoccupation with feelings, relationships, and personal satisfaction, and an expectancy of God's coming Kingdom. As Juan Luis Segundo has suggested, only the middle class has the luxury to indulge in seeking better relationships. The majority of the world's people have another purpose, and that is sheer survival.

SUZANNE C. TOTON

Commentary on
Parenting for Peace and Justice

I greatly appreciate the model of "Parenting for Peace and Justice." It suggests that justice education is not confined to the church or school and that adults can and do take responsibility for raising their own consciousness. Also, the fact that this model is being lived gives me hope—hope that efforts that are being made in the schools to educate for justice may be continued in the home.

In order to analyze this as an educational model, it would be helpful to be able to trace more clearly the development of the group's consciousness, their growing sense of solidarity, and their deepening involvement in action for justice. In this light I pose several questions for the model architects to consider.

1. The Training Workshop

a. *Rationale for the Workshop.* Why did the support group decide to offer a workshop in October 1981? Did the need for a workshop emerge out of a feeling among the group members that it was important to share as soon as possible new information and insight? Did it emerge out of a sense of urgency to respond to the problems that plague our world? Or was the group approached by individuals, a church, or another group that asked it to give the workshop?

b. *Role of the Support Group.* My reason for asking the previous questions arises from a concern about the support group itself. Did it feel reasonably comfortable with itself (i.e., Did the members know each other well? Could they rely on one another? Did they know where each member stood on the issues?) and confident that it had enough information and resources to give a workshop? Finally, to what extent was giving a workshop important for the identity and purpose of the support group itself?

c. *Goals of the Workshop.* What were the goals of the workshop? Were they to provide information, raise consciousness, form a network of concerned parents, or add new members to the support group? What indication is there that the workshop accomplished its purpose? Do we see a new purpose emerge? What effort might have been made to keep in touch with the people who participated in the workshop?

d. *Workshop Theme.* What role did the group play in selecting the theme of materialism? In addition to purchasing crafts from Jubilee Crafts, were other alternatives to Christmas buying proposed to the workshop participants? Also, is Jubilee Crafts a viable alternative or is it in itself a form of consumerism (even though proceeds go to a good cause)?

2. The Children

One question that kept popping up for me was: How might the children better fit into the support group? The real question I have is: Did the support group exist for the sake of the parents, the children, or both? If both, then how were the children integrated into the group? Were the information and support that the parents received from one another to "trickle down" to the children? Other than the descriptions of bringing children to a peace demonstration and their collecting money and packing the cartons for Nicaragua, it was hard to get a sense of the relationship between raising the parents' and their children's consciousnesses.

3. Links and Connections

How did the support group decide on the issues and actions with which it would concern itself? Why did it move from materialism to nuclear war to Nicaragua? What efforts might have been made to make the links or connections among the issues? Is there a rationale for groups simply to respond to concerns as they are presented?

4. The Face-to-Face Encounters

One of the strengths of the parenting for peace and justice program is the attempt to pair affluent with poor families. In fact, this model suggests that one of the more successful events was the sharing of Peter Sawyer's slides of Nicaragua at the family camp. What opportunities were explored for the support group to be engaged in face-to-face contact—contact with Salvadoran refugees, relief workers, missionaries, Congresspeople, Senators, etc.? Might some members attend a shareholders' meeting? Another question involves the relation between the Sawyers' visit to Nicaragua and the group's experience. Would there be value in enabling other members of the group to go as well? It appears that the support group relied more heavily on audiovisual and printed material than on face-to-face encounters for its information. Given the concern and makeup of the group, could more emphasis have been placed on face-to-face experiences?

5. Civil Disobedience

Civil disobedience is quite a jump from putting a 25 percent surcharge on bananas. It was difficult to get a sense of a growing or heightening political awareness among members of the support group. In addition to writing periodic letters to Congresspeople, how politically active and sophisticated might such a support group become? How do the members of a group grow together in consciousness and action? The members of the group appear to be very much individuals. One might hope for a new identity to emerge because of the relationships among them. How could this be encouraged?

In summary, I found the case of the Kansas City support group hopeful and inspiring. Such support groups may profit from closer attention to their own inner dynamics and agendas, with special concern for the specific stages of moving toward solidarity and action.

CHAPTER 3

PLANT CLOSURES PROJECT

More than any other case in this book, "Plant Closures Project" raises the issue of the Third World in our midst, and it does so as it deals with local community problems. In the broader context of the global economy, this model focuses especially on the problem of local unemployment resulting from the movement of plants from place to place around the world. The case opens up the class implications of the problem in a California urban area and the challenges posed for the leaders of a particular congregation. It is also effective for evoking reflection about educational processes necessary to any successful attack on the problem. In striving for some helpful resolution of the acute, local, human problems, the model opens up the global dimensions as well.

The case has distinctive value in its dramatic portrayal of the human suffering involved nearby, not overseas, and in its exposure of the relative unreadiness of ministerial leadership organized ecumenically or operating in a local church to tackle such problems with any hope of success. The project presents a model of specific ways to address the issues of plant closures and unemployment. However, the case may raise more questions than it answers, as it contrasts the realities and the ideologies of the unemployed with those of the affluent managers who often dominate church leadership.

Persons and groups seriously concerned about how middle-class churches respond to the challenges and problems in today's world, especially those related to plant closures and unemployment, will find this case a sobering exercise for study and a stimulus toward action.

Program Overview

The Plant Closures Project of Oakland, California, is a coalition of unions, religious organizations, and community groups working together against plant closures that have caused nearly half a million Californians to lose their jobs in four years. Closures have caused a virtual shutdown of basic industry (steel, rubber, lumber, auto manufacture, food processing) in California and have had a devastating effect on individuals, families, and communities. The Plant Closures Project, a central component of the Northern California Interfaith Council on Economic Justice and Work, is committed to community education that enables people to act together for individual and community survival. The project and council believe in education for empowerment of local citizens.

The project and the council see the "personalization" of problems of social justice as a first, necessary step for work for justice. Staff members are convinced that community and church people need to know that the unemployed are real men and women with children, not merely statistics, and that managers and office workers are real people as well. The project and council operate on the assumption that Christians do not turn their back on human suffering; rather, they want to address it. But to do so they need understanding of the causes of injustice and knowledge of specific ways they can address the root causes to bring about change.

The council and Plant Closures Project have found it easy to involve the unemployed in education for action. The unemployed know there is a problem that must be addressed. They need understanding and tools for action and a community with which to act.

It is more difficult, however, to involve members of middle-class churches in social justice issues. They must be shown the problems and have the issues humanized or personalized through meeting and hearing from unemployed workers and union members. They must also be given understanding of the systemic and structural causes of unemployment, be shown that unemployment and economic chaos could easily affect them and their families as well, be given time for biblical and theological reflection, and then be given skills and tools for political, social, and economic change. Finally, they need a community of people with whom they can work for change.

When broken down into segments, this series of steps for educating the non-poor is not complicated. When taken one at a time, these steps can be freeing and empowering. A group which has gone through this series of steps can become an informal community ready to be involved in action for justice. However, the social and ideological barriers to taking the first steps are enormous. For this reason, the following case study focuses not only on the magnitude of problems faced by the unemployed, but also on the deep resistance which the personnel of the project often find in middle-class congregations.

Working with a broad-based constituency, the Plant Closures Project has a series of specific goals and projects for social and economic change. Staff members and volunteers organize support for:

—public awareness of the causes and effects of economic dislocation
—campaigns to stop individual plant closures
—city, state, and national legislation to prevent closures and provide assistance to workers and communities in crisis
—programs of alternative economic development.

Volunteer and project staff members also help workers and communities to:

—recognize early warning signs of plant closures and layoffs
—analyze trends in industry which may put a plant at risk of closure
—draft contract language which will help prevent closures or extend benefits to laid-off workers
—analyze strategies for stopping or delaying closures
—find access to lawyers, counselors, mental health workers, and specialists in worker and community ownership.

Finally, the staff members and volunteers provide:

—speakers for union, religious, and community group meetings
—training sessions for union, church, and community leaders
—a resource library
—a computerized listing of plant closures and layoffs in California with information on unions, industries, and legislative districts affected
—educational materials, including leaflets, brochures, and other organs of analysis.

The Plant Closures Project is developing a network of plant closings coalitions in California as well as a network to be in contact with coalitions, unions, and religious organizations working in other states and countries for similar goals.

The Plant Closures Project depends on financial support from participating organizations and individuals. It has received support from the United Presbyterian Church (Office of Economic Justice), the United Methodist Church (Board of Global Ministries), the Shalen, Vanguard, and Abelard foundations, and from union locals, individual donors, and other community groups.

The Plant Closures Project operates out of the Catholic Charities building in Oakland. The work is carried out by task forces on direct action, legislation, economic development, and national and international connections. An executive and a working committee coordinate the work of the project. Two codirectors/organizers staff the project and coordinate the work of the members/volunteers.

For further information contact: Plant Closures Project; 433 Jefferson Street; Oakland, CA 94607; phone: (415) 834–5656. Or: Northern California Interfaith Council on Economic Justice and Work; 464 19th Street; Oakland, CA 94612.

Case Study
Plant Closures Project

Pastor Ed Harrington unlocked the side door and flipped on the vestibule lights as he entered the new administration wing of the Pacific Presbyterian Church. He checked out the lounge to see if the janitor had arranged the chairs for the session meeting and plugged in the coffee pot. After Ed reviewed the typed agenda for the meeting, he turned to the sheaf of papers he had begun collecting since the Ministerial Alliance breakfast meeting he had attended the prior week. A team of three from the Plant Closures Project had spoken to the gathered pastors asking for their help. In the course of the meeting Ed had been convinced of the need for area churches to support the project. Now he had to convince his fifteen session members who comprised the governing body of the church.

PACIFIC PRESBYTERIAN CHURCH

Harrington had been at Pacific Presbyterian for five years. During his tenure the church had seemed to prosper. The six-hundred-member congregation was largely composed of professionals and managers, with a high percentage of college graduates. As far as Ed knew, a teacher and a nurse were the only union members in the congregation. He knew of several members who had faced brief unemployment, but his people kept their work problems pretty much to themselves. The president of the local Chamber of Commerce was a lay leader; the manager of a local bank and the director of marketing of a large manufacturing firm were active members. Ed also knew that one of the lawyers negotiating the Toyota-General Motors–Fremont plant joint contract was a member of the congregation.

GENERAL MOTORS–FREMONT

Though the suburban community in which Pacific Presbyterian was located was only thirty miles from Fremont, Harrington believed that members of his congregation had not been significantly affected by the General Motors clo-

---

sure over a year earlier. This was not true of surrounding communities. After the plant's doors opened in 1963, General Motors had been the primary employer in southern Alameda County. Twelve hundred workers had been laid off in 1981 when light truck production was shifted to St. Louis. Then in the spring of 1982 GM laid off the last two thousand workers in its one-time workforce of 6,800. For several years Fremont workers had achieved the highest quality-ratings. Base wages at the plant of $9.90 per hour had been negotiated by the United Auto Workers Union (UAW). When the plant doors closed, it was estimated that local communities lost $249 million from wages, benefits, and taxes. The entire area was heavily impacted by the closure.

Immediately following the shutdown, DuPont Paint in South San Francisco announced layoffs, as did Libby Owens Ford's auto glass plant in Lathrop, auto carpet makers in Southern California, Southern Pacific Transfer, and California Canteen. Harrington remembered reading that numerous small machine shops, restaurants, bars, and delis were affected.

GENERAL MOTORS-TOYOTA NEGOTIATIONS

After several months of inactivity, new plans for the plant were publicized. General Motors and Toyota of Japan were negotiating a $300 million venture to turn out two hundred thousand front-wheel drive subcompacts per year, starting in 1984. The Fremont plant would open as a new company under Toyota management, using Japanese production techniques. Plans called for employing three thousand workers.

Harrington glanced through copies of newspaper articles (*San Francisco Examiner and Chronicle,* March 13, 1983, sec. A, pp. 2, 10, 11) which had addressed some of the issues in debate. In the area of labor relations, Toyota was considered Japan's "most conservative carmaker" while it was also considered "the most efficient producer." As evidenced in U.S.-based auto plants managed by Nissan (Smyrna, Tennessee) and Honda (Marysville, Ohio) and in the Toyota plant in Nagoya, Japan, the Japanese production philosophy called for "close, harmonious labor-management relationships." Production workers were known as "technicians" or "associates." Observers analyzing the success of Japanese industry cited its emphasis on "promotion of the workers' sense of participation." The majority of Japanese labor organizations are considered "in-house" unions that "link their fate to their employers' fate." "It's not uncommon for those in 'labor union' leadership positions to move into corporate positions." One of the Nissan directors in the United States was cited as saying that "the Japanese . . . cannot fathom a union that would try to hurt the company." One analyst stated that Toyota managers would "seek loyalty and pride in the product and have little tolerance for militancy." In an interview one Toyota vice-president working on the GM-Toyota venture stated, "Labor management is the key to the success of the venture, and we have no intention of giving priority hiring to former employees of GM."

When asked about the GM-Toyota negotiations and the attitudes of Toyota managers toward the Fremont UAW workers, a sociology professor at the University of Michigan's joint U.S.-Japan Automotive Study responded, "They are scared of them. Most Japanese managers have a view that [U.S. workers] are militant. The Japanese are not used to that. They want flexibility to move people around." An AFL-CIO international representative noted, "Japanese management techniques are every bit as authoritarian as U.S. management practices—if not more so. In fact, present-day Japanese management structure is paternalistic and virtually caste-like in its hierarchy. . . ." Other critics of Japanese management cited Japan's "rigid two-tier system" in which temporary workers, "often wearing different colored hard hats to denote their lesser status," are employed with no permanent job rights.

Another analyst noted that the three Japanese auto makers with plants in the United States had been "extraordinarily selective—both in choosing locations and in hiring employees." Japanese managers had been cited repeatedly as saying that "with proper selection, an American workforce can turn out vehicles as well-made as those in Japan." The University of Michigan sociologist noted that "there is an obvious pattern of Japanese firms in the U.S. to avoid locating in areas of large concentrations of black workers. They are very racist, in my opinion, in the treatment of blacks." A Nissan human relations director responded, "That's not racist; it's where the most productive people happen to be. We use the same criteria that U.S. companies use."

Pastor Harrington had learned from his meeting with the Plant Closures team that members of the Fremont local were adamant in their demand that all rehiring for the GM-Toyota plant be on a seniority basis. One UAW headquarters spokesperson had indicated, however, that the union was open to concessions "to allow the new company flexibility in hiring and work rules."

FREMONT WORKERS SPEAK

Harrington shook his head. He was finding it difficult to focus on the principles of labor management and union negotiations while the primary images flooding his mind were of the Fremont workers whose lives were so drastically affected by those talks. Until the prior week's Ministerial Alliance breakfast, Harrington had been unaware of the impact of the GM plant closure on people's lives. The team from the Plant Closures Project, two unemployed male UAW workers and a woman machinist, had told of marriages breaking up among their old work friends; of soaring alcoholism as well as drug abuse; of family violence; of men in their late forties having heart attacks; of families running out of unemployment benefits and facing foreclosures on homes into which they had put all their savings; and of suicides.

Ed Harrington was most moved by the personal statements made by members of the team and by a research paper he had been given by a graduate student who had interviewed a number of unemployed auto workers. Ed reread portions of the research paper:

THE GATHERING PLACE

The union hall is across from the General Motors plant which fills 441 acres of valley floor, one-time prime agricultural land at Fremont, California. The immensity of the stilled plant, lying silent below California's green, rolling coastal hills, is overwhelming. The air above is clear, the parking lots empty. The following comments were voiced at a meeting of women who were members of the UAW local.

The gathered women were young to middle-aged, black, white, Chicano, newcomers and veterans of the assembly line, many of them single parents. They had turned to auto assembly, it being one of the few fields where women could earn sufficient wages to cover house payments, child care, food, and clothes for growing kids, and that also included a health, pension, and vacation package. Auto assembly had given them the security lacking in traditional female occupations—clerical work, hospital work, fast-food jobs, and the like.

The room was filled with bitterness, anxiety, anger, hostility, and harsh humor. The Women's Group had dwindled from fifty to about sixteen. (At peak employment, one-third of the over 6,000 workers had been female.) In desperation, a number of them had crossed the Bay to jobs in high technology where, people say, "the future lies." This had meant a considerable wage cut for these women.

"So our future lies in high tech? . . ." a blond, blue-eyed thirty-seven-year-old veteran of nine years at assembly commented bitterly. "Let me tell you that's a future I can't afford. Between gas and child care, there's no way I can break even at electronic assembly. Can't keep up on house payments, and that's the only security we have, me and the kids. On the line I got $12 an hour, plus benefits. That came to $16, maybe $17. Electronic assembly pays anything from minimum wage to $6.74. . . . Out of that I'm supposed to pay gas, child care, feed my kids, buy shoes? How the hell am I supposed to survive?

"At GM it was the union that fought and got us the living wage we had. I was part of it. It made me feel good. We had a kind of dignity, a small degree of control over our lives. Now, though, when employers find that I was in the union at Fremont, they're scared of me, think I'll cause trouble. They don't want to hire me. We union members aren't docile the way we're supposed to be . . . the way they hope to keep their present immigrant Vietnamese, Laotian, Hispanic, Chinese, and Filipino workers who the Silicon Valley companies line up to be pitted against each other."

A black woman in her late forties added, "I've gone all over looking for work. They all say they don't want to hire me because they say GM might call us all back, and if they did, we'd go. God, maybe I would. Hard to tell. What are we going to do? Lie? Pretend we never worked at GM, that something that's real important to us never existed?

"Now let me tell you something else. I've been at this plant nine years. You know who qualifies for those supplemental benefits that our local's officers negotiated for? Workers who've worked for GM for ten years or more. So where does that leave us women? Nowhere. None of us have worked here more than nine and a half years. You can guess who worked out that agreement . . . the men who've been here since the start. They looked out for themselves all right, didn't give a shit about us women workers. We need the benefits as much as they. Lots of them have working wives; most of us are the sole support of ourselves and our kids.

"What are we to do? Get electronic assembly jobs by lying about our past, when those jobs are thirty miles away and don't pay a living wage? Move to Silicon Valley when housing there is higher than anywhere in the country? Get training for a new field, when we've no income coming in? How are we to survive?"

Ed Harrington then turned to another page which reported interviews with union men about unemployment.

A male, thirty-seven-year-old, unemployed union service representative spoke: "My job sure wasn't all I lost when the plant closed, not by a long shot. Can't see why people don't realize what happens when plants shut. God, the bottom drops out of your life.

"I lost my friends, my community, my ball team, my drinking buddies, my place to go. We worked together fourteen years here and at the old plant. Take all that away from a man and you wipe him out. It's terrible what I've seen . . . suicides, heart attacks, family violence, marriages breaking up. They were good marriages, too. My friends . . . I just watch them, see all this anxiety and frustration and anger and self-blame build up. Don't really know why guys blame themselves when the plant's laid off 2,000 others, but they do; they feel terrible. There's no one to take it out on, so their wives and kids get it. Guys who were breadwinners last year are alcoholics this year. And I've seen kids right here in California *hungry*. These men were hard-working people, they'd never been on welfare, they were buying homes, cars, putting their kids through school and community college, real self-respecting people.

"The plant closed, and we didn't know what hit us. We knew it wasn't our fault; even so, we felt awful, like we were failures. I always had this feeling that a real man has a job, a real man isn't an unemployed man.

"They tell us, apply for re-education programs through the community college. Now that's something I might do, because I finished high school, and I got some more training in the service. I know one or two others like me. It's fine, if for starters you're English-speaking, and pretty good with words and numbers. But face it, how many guys that are on the assembly line for twelve, fourteen years have a real good aptitude for numbers? Lots of guys took these jobs in the first place because it was a way they could earn a living though their education had been lousy, though their English wasn't much good. A lot of us are black or Hispanic. But let me tell you, even if guys were once good in numbers, they lose it after years on the line. The company kept us as uneducated as they could. They don't want thinking workers: we might take over the plant and run it or something. They're scared to let us use our brains.

"People tell us, get retrained for high tech. A few might, maybe four or five. Now, if we were real good at math, and real good with our hands, could be we could get into the machinist courses. But those are hard, man are they hard. Most assemblers aren't real well-fitted to be machinists. Only a few.

"The training could keep us busy for a while, but we got to have something to live on while we're in school.

"Then you come to a guy who's gotten busy and trained for high tech. He picks up the morning paper and what does he see? Atari, across the Bay, the biggest of them all, is laying off 1,700 workers . . . Hispanics, Asians, blacks. Why? Because $6 an hour is too much. They're going to Hong Kong and Taiwan where the pay is $1.20 an hour. They say they got to be competitive."

A twenty-seven-year-old man spoke up: "Unemployment's terrible on a man. My marriage broke up. I got two kids to support, my ex-wife's working, but she doesn't make that much. We were buying a small house; that's where she and the kids live. By now, I've run out of all my benefits, union supplemental gave out long ago. I got desperate, applied for food stamps. Since I still got my house, they turned me down.

"To get unemployment, you got to be looking for work, you have to take what they offer you. I got this lousy temporary job. They'd call me any hour of day or night for me to fill in on the shift. Supposed to be always available. If I was out somewhere when the company called, they'd report it to the damn department of employment, and they'd cut off my benefits, keeping the rolls neat and tidy, Reagan-like. . . .

"Then a lady tells me a local company is hiring like crazy. I go to apply, the office girl looks at me kind of weird, goes back and whispers to the others, comes back and says, 'No, we're not hiring. You musta got it wrong.' That's what happens in valley towns when they see a Chicano face."

Another unemployed worker joined the conversation. "Let me give you a dilemma we're facing now. We at GM are all on 'temporary layoff.' There's been no clear announcement that the plant's closed forever, though it's sure locked up tighter than hell. So we all hope that if it reopens, we'll be hired back.

"O.K., you got that. Well, look at this for someone who's still getting unemployment. Yesterday they announced they're opening a second shift at another plant, only this one is in Oklahoma. They tell us that the company's offering Fremont workers transfer rights to Oklahoma. If we don't take this offer, the company can say, 'Look, we gave these guys this good opportunity to work, and they didn't take it.' Well, if we don't take it, they have no more responsibility to us, and they can say, sorry, but you're on your own. However, the company offers us no guarantee that the second shift will be there next year, or next month, or next week. So you risk everything, sell your house, move yourself and your family to a far-off place where local workers don't exactly have the welcome mat out for you—all at your own expense. If you find yourself laid off again, where are you? In one hell of a hole, worse off than before. What's a guy to do?

"Take another example. You read in the papers about Toyota and GM making this fancy deal about reopening the plant together. All the union guys and women get all excited. There's going to be jobs after all. But what do we do about retraining, or about Oklahoma?

"Then the next day what do you think? They announce that they're going to reopen after all, but it's going to be 'Japanese style,' no union. Toyota's the most anti-union of the Japanese car makers. Well, all hell breaks loose, lots of protest. Then, the next day GM's president says, 'Oh, excuse me, there was difficulty with the language. The Japanese didn't really mean that,' but then the next day, Toyota's manager says, 'Oh no, no difficulty in language, we mean *no* union.' Trouble again. The union takes it to the NLRB. More silence. Imagine what it's like for us and our families. Then GM and Toyota announce that since this is no longer a GM plant but a brand-new industry, they say Toyota will be manager, GM will just provide the land, the buildings, the equipment . . . and they'll do it Japanese style. The new company will have no obligation to old workers. Hiring by seniority is out the window. More hell raising. Toyota goes on to explain, 'We plan to hire only the *good* workers, the dedicated ones.' (We figure that means no old union troublemakers.) Then Toyota says about those 'good' workers: 'We'll send them to Japan for training to learn to work like the Japanese.' Now, the way I see that, that's not blacks and Hispanics who have good skills but not much education, that's not men over forty or fifty, that's not union leaders. There's lots of us who won't qualify as 'retrainable *good* workers.' Japan's got a lousy record on hiring women. I tell you, people are scared.

"At our union local, men and women talk. They say, 'If they open up nonunion Japanese style with wages cut in half, we won't take the jobs and we'll see to it that no one else does either.'

"But then I worry; if a guy's got hungry kids, he needs *something,* not *nothing.* I'm scared we'll end up bashing up our own buddies. What's a guy to do? Go to Oklahoma, cross a union line, become some kind of scab?"

Ed Harrington then looked for another sheet of paper in his notes. He had been so moved by the last of the three Plant Closures speakers at the Ministerial Alliance meeting that he had taken notes as the unemployed assembly line worker spoke:

So, where's the church in all this? When I was in the service I broke with the church. Didn't see it as involved in the real world. It wasn't taking up any real issues of concern. It left me feeling empty, specially after Vietnam.

I had to be asked back. I went back to Mass, and it stirred up all my beliefs, and I had to re-evaluate everything. I got reinvolved with the church directly through my contact with the unemployed at the union and at the Plant Closures Project, reinvolved in an intense fashion. There's a lot the church needs to do.

You know, Jesus was a political being; His message was always being carried by Him. I figure, instead of theorizing we got to go out and live it. I've tried, and it's brought me to a place where I have an ability to love in ways I couldn't before. It brought out deep feelings not easily explainable.

Without doubt, I see my work now in the total context of taking up the risk we were meant to be taking up—you might say a work designed by Jesus. I don't think I can separate the two anymore. Now this is what we need from you ministers and your churches. . . .

In his notes Ed had then listed the specific requests of the Plant Closures team:

1. Support for laid-off individuals in their local congregations; counseling that would help them understand the causes of their layoffs; counseling that would counter despair and family violence.
2. Legislative work:
   —Support for Assembly Bill 2430 that would call for advance notice of intent to close (one year for large companies; six months for smaller firms), right of transfer to other branches of the firm, continued health and welfare benefits for one year, severance pay (one week for every year worked), extended unemployment benefits, and payment to the community for loss of tax base (at a rate of 85 percent of yearly tax rate).
   —Pastors requested to make personal phone calls to their Assemblyman/ woman in support of the bill.
   —Pastors requested to bring carloads of people from their local parishes to lobby in Sacramento.
   —Pastors asked to speak at rally on the steps of the Capitol in support of the bill.
3. Financial support for work of Plant Closures Project.
4. That pastors be "on call" to meet with members of management when closures are threatened.

The team then asked for the names of any clergy who would be willing to help. Though six of the twenty pastors present indicated they would be willing to do counseling, Ed had been one of only three who had agreed to become more involved and take the issues to their congregations. He had been told by the Plant Closures team that they would come by the church after his next session meeting to find out what sort of support they could expect from him and his congregation.

SESSION MEETING

Harrington's thoughts were interrupted as Frank Barnes, the clerk, and four other session members arrived. Over the next few minutes the other seven men and women came in, offering cheerful greetings. Harrington smiled to himself as the group settled down to business right on schedule. Ed had alerted the group in advance to the importance of the Plant Closures Project proposal and indicated he wanted to have some substantive discussion on the topic. Ed explained the project to his session members, shared his learnings about the personal tragedies of thousands of unemployed workers in their area, and passed out copies of the list of requests.

Dan Richards, a manager and researcher in a Silicon Valley industry, responded immediately: "I don't see the relation of the Fremont workers to me. They got themselves into the situation they're in. They took those union dead-end jobs and milked management for all it was worth. They and their union got high pay for low-skill jobs; they didn't get out and retrain themselves for something better when they could have. They boxed themselves in; they lived high on the hog. All I can say is, they've got no complaint coming. They should have seen the writing on the wall, should have left those union jobs, gone off on their own, gotten training for something else. I really think they were duped by the union."

Ed noted that several of the elders were nodding their heads in agreement. Others looked uncomfortable. Dan continued, "I'm sorry they're having a hard time now, but it's not my fault, and I see no reason why I have to be concerned. They're not my problem, and I don't want my tax money going to them . . . well, maybe a little of it. I guess welfare's O.K. But that's it. Sure, I care about them as human beings, but I say again, they're not my problem."

Clerk Frank Barnes spoke up, addressing Dan directly, "I understand your personal feelings, Dan, but Ed has asked us about our response as a church, and the church is a lot more than individual opinions."

Dan replied quickly, "Sure the church should care, but what's the church to do? I don't think you should confront church people with a problem unless you've got a solution. It's too depressing. I don't see any solution for this."

Frank answered, "Well, that's exactly what Ed's brought us—some specific ways to respond as a congregation. What about a group going up to the State Capitol to push for advance notice on closings?"

Dan responded immediately: "The government should stay out of this. I realize things have to change, but I say, let the economy take care of itself; in the same way, the Toyota-GM negotiations ought to be up to those in management. They pay the salaries—they ought to call the shots. It'll work out, and one day things for those Fremont workers will be good again. Those people will find their place. It'll take a bit of doing, but I'm sure it will be all right. Things have always worked out in the past. Why, I was once unemployed for four weeks. I know what it's like. But it worked out for me. It'll work out for them, I'm sure. Maybe they should go to Dallas or Houston, or somewhere. . . . Those guys—and women too—just got themselves caught in the wrong place at the wrong time. Face it, high cost of labor is the problem, and labor is cheap overseas, so that's where production goes. Basic industry is over in this country, dead, finished. Tough about the people caught in the squeeze, but there it is. We've got to be competitive, and they don't make that happen. They are not our problem. The way I see it, we've all got to simplify our lifestyle, develop backyard gardens, drive less, Retro-fit our houses, go solar. Cut back on expenses. Live simply. Yeah, I realize lots of them live in apartments, don't have backyards or cash for Retro-fitting. But if they did, they could grow their own food, not be dependent on food stamps. They could cut their heating bills, their driving, use public transportation. Yeah, I realize public transportation isn't that available, but it should be an option. Well, anyway, I guess the way I see it, the future lies in high tech. They should learn machine upkeep . . . lots of jobs in that. All they've got to do is apply themselves . . . robot upkeep, that's an idea. They could take night courses, brush up in math and English. Get into data processing, programming."

Emma Clark asked, "What about the women, Dan? How do they retrain with children to care for?"

"The women? Well, the way I see it, there are too many women in the workplace as it is. They should be home with their kids. Kids need moms. The way I see it, if women stayed home where they belong, there'd be more jobs available for the men who really need them. Unemployment could be cut way back."

Dan Richards turned from the group of elders to address Pastor Harrington: "I guess the bottom line here, Ed, is that this Plant Closures Project is no business of ours. I know I've been pretty blunt in expressing my opinion, but I have a good idea that most of the session is where I am on this, and the whole thing could be quite divisive for the congregation."

As Ed Harrington saw a number of heads nodding in agreement with Dan Richards, he was unsure how to respond.

Teaching Note

TOPICS AND QUESTIONS FOR DISCUSSION

1. This case study is intended for use as a tool for social analysis. Ideally the case would do the following: (a) immerse members of a church group or a service organization in the human problems created by the enormous changes taking place in U.S. economic and industrial life; (b) lead discussion participants into an analysis of the barriers to changing dehumanizing attitudes and structures; (c) give participants an opportunity to see how one church and pastor responded to the problems involved and project how they themselves might respond in a similar situation.

2. Participants should be encouraged and enabled to analyze the case from systemic and social perspectives. To encourage that, group leaders should ask participants to discuss the issues unemployed men and women face and must deal with. These might include racism, sexism, lack of adequate education, changing technology (e.g., robotization and computerization), and the lack of social support for working mothers and their children. The participants might also discuss the feelings of the unemployed—the anger, powerlessness, frustration, and despair that they face.

3. To encourage further systemic and social analysis, participants should be asked to examine the professional and managerial response to blue collar unemployment. Participants may identify, for example, the tendency to blame the victim or to give priority to company profits. The group can then explore reasons for these reactions.

4. Participants should reflect biblically and theologically on Christians' call to meet human suffering, minister to those in need, and work to eradicate the causes of injustice. This discussion could be initiated by examining the statement (see p. 76, above) made to the Ministerial Alliance by one of the Plant Closures representatives.

5. Participants can begin to prepare for action together by first examining roadblocks to action such as the paralysis caused by self-blame on the part of the unemployed; the blaming of the victim by those not involved; and a lack of understanding of the causes of layoffs, unemployment, etc. Next there should be a discussion of ways to address the roadblocks and move toward concrete actions. The most creative and effective responses address the specific constituency of those discussing the case. One suggestion that has been helpful for other groups is to arrange a meeting among managers, union members, pastors, laity, community members, and possibly legislators or their representatives in communities threatened by closures. The discussion at that meeting

should focus on: (a) alternatives to closure; (b) possible use of various facilities for retraining if closure is going to take place; and (c) the specifics of the company's closing plans so that pastors and community members can prepare ways to minister to families and to plan for the closure's impact on small business people, schools, hospitals, social service agencies, churches, and so on.

ADDITIONAL RESOURCES

Baum, Gregory. *The Priority of Labor: A Commentary on "Laborem Exercens," Encyclical of Pope John Paul II.* New York: Paulist Press, 1982.

Bluestone, Barry, Bennett Harrison, and Lawrence Baker. *Corporate Flight: The Causes and Consequences of Economic Dislocation.* Washington, D.C.: National Center for Policy Alternatives, 1981.

Canadian Conference of Catholic Bishops. *Ethical Choices and Political Challenges: Ethical Reflections on the Future of Canada's Socioeconomic Order*, 1983.

Raines, John C. "Conscience and the Economic Crisis," *Christian Century* 99, no. 27 (September 1–8, 1982), 883–85.

Stillman, Dan. "The Devastating Impact of Plant Relocations," *Working Papers* 6, no. 4 (July–August 1978), 42–53.

DANIEL L. FORCE

Commentary on
Plant Closures Project

The Plant Closures Project case presents us with a very interesting scenario between pastor and session. The case would be a useful and effective initiator of discussion, but it is difficult to evaluate as a model for *education*.

EDUCATIONAL PROCESS AND METHODOLOGY

It is important to note that Ed Harrington went through a conversion experience at the Ministerial Alliance breakfast: "Ed Harrington was most moved by the personal statements made by members of the team and by a research paper he had been given by a graduate student who had interviewed a number of unemployed auto workers."

It would appear that the testimony of the Plant Closures team became a living experience for Ed Harrington, that he was moved to become involved by entering into that experience, and that he only then began to take notes and collect data to back up what had happened to him. A week or so later he tries to share his experience with the members of his church's session. We would do well as we look at this model of education to remember the absolute necessity of building in some type of experiential component when we try to move people along a continuum. Most educators will agree that a minority of people learn purely from cognitive input and a majority learn from experience. William Bean Kennedy says it well in his article "A Radical Challenge to Inherited Educational Patterns":

> Education for justice happens best when it begins either with involvement with those who are poor or with direct engagement in the struggle against the forces that oppress them. That means active commitment and action, intentional activity, to work alongside those who are already so engaged. Or it means some radical change of context that forces a fresh look at oneself and one's social milieu with its conditioning influences. It means entering some strategic activity at a point of readiness for those getting into it, and, in the process of working actively, growing into a broader critical conscious-

ness of what is involved. It must sooner or later—preferably sooner—require risk, so that the adrenaline flows. Without that sort of immersion in the action there is little chance that the deep current of ideology will be exposed or challenged or changed. "To know" viscerally is essential if learning intellectually is to do more than add another layer to the cocoon of conditioning within which we live [*Religious Education* 74, Sept.-Oct. 1979, pp. 491-3].

Ed Harrington wanted to move the session into involvement and action, hoping that they would eventually lead the congregation onto that same track. Given the approach he chose to use, the odds were against him from the beginning.

There is a school of thought built up around the ideas of such educators as Paulo Freire, Ivan Illich, and Everett Reimer that expounds a totally different concept of education from the traditional approach. Education is seen as a "process" in which what the individual does and experiences is as important as what he or she actually learns; that is, method is as important as content, or even more so. It is a constant two-way process. Such an approach to education is, in itself, ideological in that it demands a total change of current educational structures and organizations. It cuts across any of the distinctions we may like to make between "formal" and "nonformal" education or between "in-school" or "adult" education. In fact, it puts all these concepts into question. Although originating in Latin America, this approach has had profound implications in industrialized countries because of their long tradition of the institutionalized school which makes certificates, degrees, and diplomas not only essential for getting on, but often the only aim of education.

Taking these two approaches into consideration, we can turn to the Plant Closures case study and ask whether Ed Harrington isn't trying to *teach* the session about his conversion experience. We must ask: Does Ed simply want to inform the session about his conversion experience? Or should he rather try to construct an opportunity for the session to enter into a "conversion experience"? The essential problem is how to devise a pedagogical process that will go beyond information and help people to commit themselves to the creation of a more just and humane society. Additional rationale for this approach is summarized in the writings of many; see especially Jørgen Lissner, *The Politics of Altruism,* Geneva, Lutheran World Federation, 1977.

CONTENT ORIENTATIONS

Moving on from some questions about educational methodology and process, we might look briefly at possible content orientations. Within the scenario of the case we find a trinitarian synthesis of service, advocacy, and education. We see questions raised about the relationship of employer to employee. The questions of a just profit and a just wage, the right to organize, the concept of the common good, the theology of service to those in need, and the relationship of charity to justice are important issues that are raised in this piece. The dilemma in the case also presents a good opportunity for community-based global education concerning the role of foreign multinationals, the trend of U.S. corporations taking their operations overseas, the relationship of cheap labor overseas to U.S. foreign policy and U.S. employment practices, the ethnic issues in hiring, and the opportunity to bring together factions of the community that rarely touch—counselors, union leaders, management, and the church.

Within the body of the case, the model—the Plant Closures Project—is never fully described; rather, the problems it is trying to address are described. There seems to be no contact with management. What kind of education is being done with people who are laid off? Have there been any job actions at other GM plants in solidarity with the Fremont workers? Is there any relationship with the International Labor Organization? Are there larger church organizations in the area that are involved in the struggle? Might they not supply some formal organizational support for Ed and the session members who wish to join the struggle? These are questions Pastor Harrington might pursue.

CHALLENGE TO THEOLOGICAL REFLECTION

Richard D. N. Dickinson in his book *Poor Yet Making Many Rich: The Poor as Agents of Creative Justice* (Geneva, World Council of Churches, 1983) points out that experience in educational ventures such as that described in this case study has over recent years influenced theological reflection. He states:

That does not imply a *new* theology but does suggest that diverse contemporary experience has sharpened or helped us to appropriate again, or emphasize, elements in the gospel which were dormant, hidden or not existentially critical [p. 98].

Dickinson gives us a short list of some key points that illustrate this trend:

1. There is a challenge to the nature of theological reflection itself. Is it possible to engage in sound theological reflection without being immersed first in what God is doing in the world—participating in the struggles for justice, liberation, and wholeness? Some argue that without actual engagement in solidarity with the poor, theological reflection is mere intellectual abstraction; authentic Christian theology has to take shape in the soil of struggles for justice.
2. The contextual character of all theology has become more self-evident; the inherent limitations of theological perspectives from any one cultural tradition, including Western or Eastern, are obvious.
3. The role of the poor, not only in social change but also in theological reflection, has become more widely valued.

4. The struggle for global justice has again put the question of the nature of power in the center of theological reflection.
5. Recent recognition of the natural limits of unbridled growth has encouraged a fresh look at the biblical understanding of humanity's relation to nonhuman creation [pp. 98–99].

Finally, I would like to add that this new educational approach has been dynamically related to new concepts of mission. Can one think of the Kingdom and not have it connected with righteousness and justice on earth?

In conclusion, I believe there is a great deal to be learned from the Plant Closures Project case study. It seems to me the challenge presented to the members of the session is either to remain in their class with its privileges or to commit "class suicide"—from a global education point of view, "perspective suicide"—and accept the risk of gaining a new vision of self and worth. A question we need to ask ourselves if we are really going to try to challenge groups to move to a new sense of involvement and struggle is: What kind of educational opportunities do we design and provide for the Ed Harringtons of this world who would seek to challenge their sessions? The assembly of the World Council of Christian Education, meeting in Peru in 1971, put the issue to us in another way:

To educate is not so much to teach as it is to become committed to a reality in and with the people; it is to learn to live, to encourage creativity in ourselves and others; and, under God and His power, to liberate mankind from the bonds that prevent the development of God's image. This will necessarily require radical change in the objectives, contents, and methods of our educational task [see *World Christian Education* (Publication of the World Council of Christian Education, Geneva), 26, 1971, pp. 132–34].

DAVID J. FRENCHAK

Commentary on
Plant Closures Project

The basic question to be addressed by people of God when faced with a social injustice is how to understand God in that context. This makes the reality of plant closings in California primarily a theological issue and secondarily a social issue. To reverse these issues and make the reality first of all a social issue not only lessens the possibility of freeing the non-poor to take action but fails to appreciate the unique character of the church in contrast to community organizations or unions. Theology is a key resource to the awakening of critical consciousness in the non-poor.

Unfortunately, this case study does not illustrate the potential value or role of theology in the pedagogical process dealing with the social reality of plant closings, but instead attempts to deal with the social reality apart from wrestling with understanding God's place in this context. The case is neat and predictable and depicts an all too common occurrence.

There are few agendas more difficult than dealing with labor issues in a church composed of management types. The structure and existence of such a church is sectarian, giving little or no room for objective or subjective dialectic. This case illustrates the dilemma well. If education is done in that church on an objective level it becomes a battle of statistics and facts, and if done on the subjective level, it produces alienation and distance between the oppressed and the non-poor. If the Plant Closures Project is serious about a pedagogical process for the non-poor in churches, it will be necessary for the architects clearly to understand basic assumptions and presuppositions related to that process. The project as illustrated in this case has evidently not done this. There are at least three possibilities for this project that will provide a structure for doing theology with the non-poor; those three processes are the scientific, the professional, and the artistic. It is only the artistic which holds potential for freedom for the non-poor. The first two, however, are more easily adaptable to social issues such as plant closures.

SCIENTIFIC PROCESS

Theology has been deemed the queen of the sciences and many theologians still demand the respect that such a description envisions. The emphasis in this process is on correct thinking that includes an exactness that is primarily objective in nature. Doing theology as a science requires one to establish both a system and a process that can be duplicated so that the same result or answer may be achieved each time the same procedure is followed. The process is structured argumentation that follows along the path of logic and rational thinking. In such a process the steps are clear and the conclusion is equally clear. The purpose of this process is right thinking. There is a right and a wrong way to think about God in relationship to any particular environment or context, and the task is to make sure we have the right way. Doing theology as a science then meets the need of the head, and those who do it well are frequently as qualified to be a lawyer as they are to be a minister. The intended products of doing theology as a science are a clear structure, a provable system, and perhaps a dogmatic statement about God. This process is usually pursued by the learned who work in academic institutions and who write books about these conclusions.

The Plant Closures Project could easily fit into this process, whether intentionally or unintentionally. This process of doing theology suffers from "narrative sickness" and lends itself to sectarianism and may be an obstacle to the emancipation of the non-poor in this situation even while they espouse freedom. Addressing the question of understanding God in a given context from a scientific basis often contributes to the imprisonment of the primary, secondary, and tertiary holders of the issues; they become imprisoned in the "circle of certainty." Already there are overtones of this imprisonment in the project. The issues are already clear and determined in the mind of the organizer. A case is presented rather than a truth being pursued. While there are individual stories of struggle which are told, the big story is not being considered. It is not difficult to imagine that a few people (specialists) have studied the situation and already know its cause and effect and are ready to offer the solution. Subjectivity is used to further the conclusion rather than to function as a contributing factor of reality for those being educated. It is equally easy to imagine that conferences will be held and books will be written all in the well-intentioned category of consciousness-raising or presenting the case. If this pedagogical process is pursued in the Plant Closures Project, it will accomplish little in the education of the non-poor members of the Pacific Presbyterian Church.

PROFESSIONAL PROCESS

The second method of addressing the basic question of understanding God in context is the professional model, in which theology is seen as a tool to get things done. In this process the emphasis is not on right thinking but is on collecting information, acquiring skills, and considering models that will enable one to get the job done. It is assumed that if one simply has the data, the skills, and the tools, then one can accomplish the task. The educational process is one of assimilation, and those who are to be educated are bombarded with information until it is hoped it is assimilated. After the assimilation one is trained to do the same thing to others and is then given the opportunity to apply what has been learned. It is a process familiar to the non-poor and the oppressed alike, but the non-poor usually are more familiar with this process because it is typified in much of their education and training. They like it because it works, and they hate it because it dehumanizes. However, the non-poor have developed excellent defense mechanisms against this process, particularly when it is employed for an objective they have not decided is theirs.

The purpose of employing this educational process is bottom-line thinking, getting things done. If the scientific process is for the head, then the professional process is for the hands. Organizers like to get things done; struggling with the issues often does not seem to contribute to getting the obvious task accomplished. The product of the professional model is to foster greater numbers of convinced people who will become spokespersons for the cause or specialists or even qualified, trained professionals in the field of endeavor.

Much of theological education fits into this pedagogical method. Seminaries are professional training schools. Even in the late sixties and early seventies when there was significant concern about the oppression in U.S. cities, clergy and seminary students went through urban training programs designed to impart information, develop skills, and form a group of religious professionals trained to get the job done.

All social concerns lend themselves to this pedagogical approach, and the Plant Closures Project seems to be susceptible to it. It appears that the project already has its specialists who are capable of addressing the issues as speakers at any place and at any time. They have obtained the information, and it is not hard to imagine the eventual establishment of a training program. Bottom-line thinking seems to dominate this project as it attempts to get things done. While one may have no argument with the goals and objectives of such a process, it is the process itself which may contribute to ineffective education of the non-poor because it so easily becomes an oppressive process.

ARTISTIC PROCESS

While not fully descriptive of the third process of addressing the basic question for the Pacific Presbyterian Church, "artistic" seems to capture the notion of the free expression of God in a given context. The emphasis in this process is on discovery and the identification and description in symbolic form of the presence of God. The process is one of reflection not only on the immediate context but also on history, tradition, including scripture, and personal experience. The purpose of this process is to enable individuals to draw an incomplete picture of God. Variety and pluralism are captured in this process with the emphasis not on one correct picture of God in context but on an art gallery featuring not only different pictures but different art forms, colors, styles, and characters. The product is neither a dogma nor a trained specialist—it is the awakening of critical consciousness and the freeing of the human spirit to express discovery at risk of rejection. An individual who has experienced this awakening has an involvement with the context and environment that is transactional. Communication with the environment that is both objective and subjective results in a dynamic relationship with both things and people. The process does not take place in an institution or a training program but in the immediate context of life. It is done not by authorities or specialists in the field but by people from all walks of life. It is done by the laity, by lovers, by artists, and it is done in community.

The question of what a pedagogy for non-poor persons looks like for the Plant Closures Project is still an open one. There is evidence that tired and worn methods are being employed. It is not a question of the legitimacy of the social injustice, which is a reality, but it is a question of the methodology and process used to invite people to examine their world. It appears that people who have taken up the cause want to do something to or perhaps for people who are not part of the cause. Exploration is secondary to rightness and solution. Such pedagogy works for neither the oppressed nor the non-poor. Authentic education, regardless of the rightness of the agenda, cannot be carried on by "A" for "B" or by "A" or "B" about "C." It must be carried out by "A," "B," and "C" communicating together. The same realization that we now understand to be true about education of the oppressed—that is, that we cannot go to the laborers to give knowledge or to impose on them the model of what a good person does in a particular situation—holds true of education for the non-poor.

There is hope in the fact that the case is not clear, for that means that those involved in the Plant Closures Project may still have the opportunity to shape an effective pedagogical approach to the non-poor. What is clear is that Pastor Harrington has set himself up for a rigorous and volatile debate.

GRANT S. SHOCKLEY

Commentary on
Plant Closures Project

Industrial plant closings have been a major economic and social problem in the United States for almost a decade. Corporate mergers in the 1960s and so-called strategies of renewal designed to vitalize and keep industries "competitive" were followed in the 1970s by the outright closing of scores of factories and plants. This was especially true in three basic industries—rubber, steel, and auto making. Industries such as canning, the airlines, electronics, meatpacking, timber, and cosmetics, as well as department store chains, were also affected.

Underlying these massive dislocations of people and jobs there has been a trend toward a high-technology and service-based economy in contrast to a traditional production-oriented economy. This basic shift has caused drastic changes in the lives, lifestyles, and earning power of hundreds of thousands of people, most of whom have minimum assembly-line skills, but hardly any others.

With the above as a sketchy background, what follows is a commentary on the Plant Closures Project, a model that proposes to educate non-poor church-persons and others to resist plant closings, find viable alternatives to support the victimized, educate those who "feel" unaffected, and articulate a network of support and cooperation that will constructively impact the problem presently and in the future. This commentary will attempt to do several things: (1) articulate biblical and theological issues in the model; (2) delineate the educational issues to be faced by the non-poor; (3) develop the human, social, economic, and political implications of plant closings that are resident in the model; and (4) suggest an integrated model that will deal with the pedagogical issues involved and that will provide some direction for the future.

BIBLICAL AND THEOLOGICAL ISSUES

The Plant Closures Project and the meeting of the Pacific Presbyterian Church session indicate both strengths and weaknesses in approach. The project's goals of organizational support, aid to the dislocated, becoming a public relations and information base, seeking financial contributions, and providing an administrative structure all seem feasible and viable. The design, however, as evidenced by the reactions, questions, and responses at the meeting of the session, is in need of a clearly defined biblical-theological base.

The biblical base could well grow out of the passage in Genesis 1:26 cited in section II:4 of John Paul II's encyclical *Laborem Exercens* (On Human Work): "Then God said, 'Let us make man in our image, after our likeness; and let them have dominion over the fish of the sea, and over the birds of the air, and over the cattle, and over all the earth. . . .' " The exercise of "dominion" implies that persons have the right to work and are expected to work to cultivate the earth for their existence. Work, then, has an ethical base in relation to persons. Further, the dignity of a type of work is not defined by its objective purpose, but rather by its subject, the individual doing the work. The encyclical makes that clear: "The basis for determining the value of human work is not primarily the kind of work being done but the fact that the one who is doing it is a person. . . . Work is 'for man' and not man 'for work' " (*Laborem Exercens* II:6).

Genesis 1:26 puts the human being at the center of any work ethic. Nothing can be countenanced by Christians which challenges or changes that. Likewise, under a Christian ethic persons are not only primary, but they are also responsible for each other (Gen. 4:8–16). "Am I my brother's keeper?" must invariably be answered in the affirmative. Based on this principle, no economic system should deny to human beings their fair share of the bounties of the earth.

In theological terms any pedagogical model that is to be developed must be informed by a basic understanding about the faith of the church and social responsibility. The church is responsible for the personal and corporate life of Christians in the world. Because this is the case, Christians must respond to any act or institution that disregards the sacredness of persons. Such response must be unequivocal and substantial. In *Laborem Exercens* Pope John Paul II speaks to us about this. He makes it very clear that work is a religious issue. It is a religious issue because it is a human issue. As such it is at the heart of the social question of our time and of the faith of our church. Let us, then, reflect upon the words of John Paul II: "We are . . . on the eve of new developments in technological, economic and political conditions which . . . will influence the world of work and production no less than the industrial revolution of the last century" (*Laborem Exercens* I:1). It is unthinkable that the church should not respond to this revolution with integrity and courage.

EDUCATIONAL ISSUES

The non-poor desperately need education in, about, and through plant closures. Three areas of concern come to mind.

First, the non-poor need to be educated about the fact that U.S. corporations are increasingly moving their money and production base from the North and other traditionally industrial areas to new locations in the United States and in the Third World. The object is to obtain labor at a cheaper price. That labor organization is not intensive in those new areas affords an additional attraction. Furthermore, moving plants from traditional locations is a tax issue. Moving to new areas in the United States or out of the country almost always assures a favorable tax situation. Church persons and community persons should be made aware that the human costs and the cost to the community are great and do not square with the ethical and religious standards of the church. The non-poor should also be made aware of the fact that in the new locations the plants and factories often do not pay adequate wages.

Second, much education is needed to communicate to the non-poor the critical fact that high technology together with new forms of automation and even robotization are contributing to the dislocation of thousands of workers. Also, the non-poor need to be updated on the fact that the new "information society" calls for more service personnel and fewer production workers. Further, the service personnel are not necessarily better off, and the communities that house them often provide minimal services.

A third type of education that is needed in this pedagogical model for the non-poor is education about military spending. Economic dislocations invariably result from such expenditures. The reason is fairly obvious. The creation of military goods is not consumer-directed. It is a special market. Such markets cannot, by their very nature, stimulate economic growth. Actually, if cost-overruns are considered, the general economy may be the loser in expanding military spending.

IMPLICATIONS OF PLANT CLOSINGS FOR SOCIETY

Plant closings have major implications for minorities, especially blacks. For minorities the indicators are not good. A fairly typical breakdown of unemployment statistics in the United States reads as follows: "White males 20 and older (3.5%), white females 20 and older (5.3), black males 20 and older (8.5), black females 20 and older (10.9), white teens (13.3), and black teens (36.9)" (*General Council on Ministries Report*, Dayton, The United Methodist Church, 1981, p. 12). Or consider another statistic related to plant closures in California:

> The numbers of minority people laid off exceeded whites laid off—a figure far out of proportion to racial percentages in the general population. Once again minority workers find themselves discarded by a system that had pretended to find them a niche in stable and remunerative employment [Richard W. Gillett, "The Reshaping of Work: A Challenge to the Churches," *Christian Century* 100 (January 5–12, 1983): 12].

TOWARD A MODEL OF RESPONSE

A model of response to plant closings should be multifaceted. With this guiding principle in mind, churches like Pacific Presbyterian can develop a significant program to challenge plant closings and to serve as a model for other action-reflection projects. The following is a list of some steps and strategies to pursue.

Some Steps

1. Study and reflect on the various dimensions of the whole problem of plant closures.
2. Examine the local community to discover illustrations of infringement of ethical labor practices by the non-poor.
3. Envision a future of justice, peace, and liberation as an "upward call" to be achieved in some way in all that is done in the church.
4. Develop an educational plan that teaches people through engagement in praxis and reflection that:
   a. Persons must come first in any program to resolve the plant closures issue.
   b. New strategies need to be developed for the increase (rather than the decrease) of industrial and agricultural production.
   c. A pedagogy should be developed to discover humane uses for technological advances.

Some Strategies

1. Using the skills of the non-poor laity, develop tools for systems-analysis, corporate action plans, and learning-engagement tasks.
2. Develop a sense of solidarity with minorities in the church and community.
3. Recognize that different situations call for different approaches.
4. Through a comprehensive educational program explore the learning potential of symbols, language, myth, and music to reinforce and to challenge.
5. Develop experiences through which the non-poor can realize their oppression within the present systems which they have largely created or contributed to.

CHAPTER 4

BREAD FOR THE WORLD

As with "Parenting for Peace and Justice," this case focuses on a local ecumenical group. It describes the mobilization of persons to do something to alleviate hunger in the world through national political action. The case centers on the organization of a small town group which draws on the resources of the national Bread for the World (BFW) organization and several local persons with previous experience in BFW. The group faces decisions about shifting to a deeper level of commitment with another phase of activity.

This model shows the value of a single issue focus for volunteer education and action. BFW is organized by Congressional district and calls for an ecumenical approach with its advantages and disadvantages. By mobilizing persons concerned about hunger and by using that relatively low-threat entry into global politico-economic issues, the model opens up creative, practical ways of involving people in a local community for transformative study and action.

The commentaries raise provocative questions about the relationship between local and national organizations and about the progression in voluntary associations from a do-it-yourself approach toward raising money to employing professionals to do the work.

Persons and organizations looking for effective ways of moving from simple and often privatistic concern to public political activity will find this a useful case.

Program Overview

Bread for the World is a Christian citizens' movement in the United States, and it is the only national "citizens' lobby" focusing solely on hunger. Our 43,000 members work to promote government policies that give hungry people a chance. We contact our elected leaders and seek bipartisan support for measures that offer dignity and opportunity to those who are desperately poor.

And we get results!

For example, we drafted and mobilized public support for a grain reserve program. It was a long, uphill battle to get the program passed, but we won. Congress and the administration established two reserves—major steps toward world food security. One reserve stores four million tons of wheat that will be used when food shortages develop abroad. Four million tons of wheat can feed twenty million people for a year.

We deal with various foreign and domestic issues that have an impact on hunger. Recent projects include drafting and working for passage of the Hunger and Global Security Bill and legislation that would establish a nutrition monitoring group on a national level.

Bread for the World does not distribute food. Instead we seek action on national policies. We work cooperatively with Christian denominations as well as with Jewish and secular groups that are concerned with hunger.

We work by writing or calling members of Congress or other government officials when decisions are being made that affect hungry people. A monthly newsletter keeps members informed of current legislative efforts and lists persons to contact about the issues.

Bread for the World is organized by state and by Congressional districts. When a specific member of Congress needs to be reached quickly, local membership telephone networks make rapid contact possible.

There are several hundred active local groups, working through churches via a program of worship, study, and action to participate in making government policy. Although Bread for the World is a nonpartisan movement, our standing as a citizens' lobby means that contributions and gifts are not tax-deductible and are not used to distribute food. Contributions support research on the causes of hunger, publications, seminars, staff salaries, and organizing efforts.

Bread for the World is led by a forty-member board of directors. The executive director and founder is Art Simon, author of the book *Bread for the World,* which won the National Religious Book Award in 1976. Forty-three staff members receive salaries based on need rather than position. They analyze issues, publish reports, and work with a network of volunteer state and

Congressional district coordinators and members throughout the United States.

For further information, contact: Bread for the World; 802 Rhode Island Avenue, N.E.; Washington, DC 20018; phone: (202) 269-0200.

Case Study
Bread for the World

Ann Walters, local co-coordinator of the Bread for the World (BFW) group in Hickory, North Carolina, finished arranging the chairs in her living room and looked at her watch. It was 6:45. Everything seemed to be ready for the BFW meeting. David and the children had gone to church for a potluck supper, so the house was quiet. The gentle moaning of the coffee pot in the background reminded her of her own need to relax before people started arriving.

She poured herself a cup of coffee and sat at the front window, reflecting on the history of the group, which had reached a turning point. "This will be an interesting meeting," she thought. She and Paul Timmons worked well together as co-coordinators of the local BFW group. Tonight, however, their normally complementary perspectives might clash. Paul had spoken with the Director of Organizing in the national office of BFW in Washington. The director suggested that the Hickory group might want to sponsor a summer organizing intern from June until September. "All we'd have to do is provide housing, office space, transportation, supervision, and support," Paul had said with his natural enthusiasm. Ann sighed. She looked out the window and thought: "All! Where would our group of fifteen citizens find funds for such a project? And what would we do with a young man or woman from Bread for the World in a community like Hickory? What would an intern do that we can't do ourselves?"

Surely the group could use a boost. Only five to seven of the fifteen came to regular monthly meetings, to pray and study and work together on current legislation and education on hunger issues. It often was the greatest challenge just to stay together. After three years they were still learning how to make decisions together, to divide up and share tasks, and to resolve dilemmas as they occurred. The question of how much commitment they should make to the group still seemed to be an underlying issue for all the individuals. This decision about taking an intern for the summer would challenge them to say what level of commitment they intended. All fifteen members lauded the education and the fellowship and skills they had gained as members. But how far did they have to go? And was an intern a useful addition or a way of handing over responsibility?

This case was prepared by Jane K. Vella and Candace Fair (ed. Robert A. and Alice Frazer Evans) as a basis for discussion rather than to illustrate either effective or ineffective handling of the situation. Copyright © by the Case Study Institute.

The local group had begun three years earlier, after Reverend John Hogan had attended a state-wide seminar of BFW in Charlotte. He had come back to Hickory on fire with the possibilities of organizing a BFW group in their small rural/industrial community of fifteen thousand. Joel Underwood, Director of Church Relations at BFW's national office, had offered to come to Hickory to meet with all those interested to explain the purpose and operation of BFW. John not only publicized the event in church bulletins, but he also got an article about the meeting in the local newspaper inviting all BFW members and all others in the area to attend. The meeting took place just after Ann and her family had moved to Hickory from Chicago, where they had been active members of a BFW group. Their work with the group had convinced them of the importance and potential of BFW in their own education and political effectiveness. She had been very excited to read the announcement of the meeting and to learn that there were also BFW efforts underway in Hickory.

As it turned out, Ann and David had not been able to attend that meeting with Joel Underwood. However, she called and introduced herself to Kathy Thompson, whose number had been listed in the newspaper article as the contact person for BFW in the area. Kathy was delighted to hear from her and told her: "Eight of us, all in John's church, have begun a study group to read Art Simon's book *Bread for the World* and to review the Bread for the World newsletter, which tells us what national legislation affecting the hungry we can work on. However, we want the group to be more ecumenical in its composition and to move into some form of action."

Ann explained that she and David had been active individual members of BFW, but that they had found belonging to a local group was particularly helpful for understanding the complex legislative issues raised in the monthly newsletter, which comes to all BFW members.

"We had about twenty folks at the introductory meeting," Kathy replied. "A lot of them said the same thing. We are meeting next Friday evening at Parkside Presbyterian Church to plan the organization of a Bread for the World group in Hickory. Can you and your husband join us?" Ann agreed that she would be there, perhaps with others from her church.

Ann found the organizational meeting extremely interesting. It began with worship, a beautiful prayer service from the BFW church publication *Leaven*. After introductions, the group of fifteen spent almost two hours developing a plan of action for themselves. Some people had wanted to emphasize studying together, while others wanted to begin to plan outreach events and visits to the members of Congress. Joel had left them materials, including the booklet entitled *Bread for the World: Guidelines for Coordinators,* which helped them establish a framework for future meetings that would combine prayer, study, and action (see Appendix A, below). Paul Timmons, a Hickory businessman, and Ann had been urged by the others to be co-coordinators, for they had the most relevant experience.

Fortunately, their Congressperson, Marie Stevens of District 10, was in her district office the day after the organizational meeting. Ann and Paul made an appointment and went to visit her. During their meeting they discussed the Congresswoman's position on several pieces of current legislation. Congresswoman Stevens had seemed receptive to their lobbying work, promising to give careful consideration to their suggestions. Because she was a member of the House Agriculture Committee, she was frequently involved in legislation that had been drafted and presented by issues analysts on the BFW national staff. For example, at that time she was facing in that committee the BFW initiative on the Emergency Grain Reserve. Ann and Paul realized how important it was for their group to study that issue and to be clear in their letters and telephone calls to Representative Stevens and to their two Senators, one of whom headed the Senate Agriculture Committee. This closeness to Congresspersons was an advantage of being in Hickory. They reported their learnings at the next meeting of the group. During the next few weeks the members began developing profiles of their Congressional representatives using the procedures suggested in the coordinators' guidelines (see Appendix B, below), and they began further study of specific bills coming up in the House and Senate.

As Ann now reflected on the past three years, she realized the Hickory BFW group had won some and lost some, but essentially she was convinced they had been developing well in their own understanding of the issues. Background papers on the grain reserve, on the Targeted Development Aid amendment, which would require more U.S. development aid to be used in projects benefiting the poorest of the poor, and on the Preventing Hunger at Home resolution helped them to grasp some of the complexities of those legislative issues.

The group had set up "Quickline," a telephone tree of members of BFW in the area who could very quickly get word to Representative Stevens and other crucial Congresspersons in subcommittees, committees, or on the floor of the House and Senate when critical votes were about to take place. There were ninety-four BFW members in their Congressional district. Many of these members had agreed to be a part of Quickline. Kathy served as Quickline activator, receiving a message from the Washington office which she could send verbatim along the telephone tree. Their tree had been activated often enough to enable them to feel effective in their lobbying. Not long ago Kathy had received a call from the BFW office with the news that the following day the Targeted Development Aid amendment was coming up for a vote in the House. Kathy activated the hotline, and Representative Stevens's office received thirty-five calls and numerous telegrams from her district urging her to support the bill, all within twelve hours of Kathy receiving the initial call. It had been a great day when the amendment was passed in the House, and Representative Stevens's vote had been critical. Members of the Hickory BFW group were convinced that they had made a difference.

Ann got up from her reverie to turn on the porch light. It was 7:15 and her friends would soon be arriving. She thought again of their experience together, praying, studying, and working on the often lifesaving legislation. Over the past three years they had set up a booth at the town's "Street Scenes" festival, had had an interview and an editorial published in the *Winston-Salem Journal,* had taken brochures and pamphlets about BFW to area churches to display in their vestibules and include in a Sunday morning bulletin, and had helped to promote the CROP walk (a Church World Service fundraising event to which sponsors pledge an amount per mile for individual participants), which had concluded in letter-writing. However, the best memory was of the Hickory Bread for the World Conference held the previous summer, one of twelve national conferences sponsored by the national office that year.

Ann remembered the hardest part as the preconference publicity and preparations. The national office had helped them with a targeted mailing to over eight hundred state BFW members. Posters and announcements were sent to area colleges and universities, to area churches and judicatories, and to other area agencies which shared their concern for world hunger. The focus of the conference was on leadership training. Over one hundred men and women had attended the three-day event at a large church center. Joel Underwood and Candace Fair, from the national BFW office, came, and Representative Marie Stevens gave the opening address. The Hickory group had arranged a full schedule of workshops and seminars on issues such as: Global Hunger: Causes and Effects; Hunger in the United States; Foreign Aid: Help or Hindrance?; and How a Bill Becomes Law. Skills workshops enabled church people to learn how to use the media for hunger education, how to organize BFW groups, and how to work with members of Congress. The BFW conference was organized with help from the staff of the national office; they provided models for the overall conference and for each workshop as well as the expertise and inspiration of Joel and Candace. But the greatest part of the work, and the decisions about the conference, came from the local BFW group. They were proud of this achievement.

During the weeks following the conference, the Hickory group learned of a number of events which they felt had been initiated at the conference. One church group in their district had begun a "hunger watch" in their community, identifying signs of local hunger and developing concrete responses. Student leaders from a local university organized a campus BFW group which focused on the Grain Reserve Bill, developed a World Hunger Day (October 16) program with films, and set up a voter registration campaign.

After the conference, the Hickory group had seemed to gain momentum. Not only were they equipped with new ideas and skills, but they also had gained ten new group members from a diversity of churches. However, in the last few months their energy and efforts had begun to wane. John Hogan had left for a new pastor's assignment in Raleigh, and other members had come and gone, due to work transfers or a loss of interest. It is hard, Ann thought, to keep a community group strong and active. "We are from so many different churches, such diverse backgrounds, with so many other commitments. What can we do to assure continuity and strength?" she asked herself. In fact, it seemed to her that the beginning efforts were withering. Each time she heard her minister speak about the need for Christians to be involved in politics, as he frequently did, she felt more urgently the need to work to strengthen the group.

Now an opportunity presented itself. Could they, this evening, make a decision for a renewed and fuller commitment to the hunger issue through the support of an intern? Ann thought about the people coming to the meeting: Eve Moore, a retired schoolteacher who had spearheaded the planning for the conference; Tom and Sally Engels, BFW members who had come to Hickory from Florida, grateful to find a group in the town; Steve and Kitty O'Brien, whose son had died in Vietnam and who had become politicized in the sixties and were glad to have BFW as a vehicle for their efforts; Tim Shea, a legal services lawyer who helped the group frequently to understand some of the complexities of legislation; Tim's wife, Paulette, who had done all of the printing and secretarial work for the conference; and Paul Timmons, the co-coordinator of the group. They were good, ordinary people whose faith brought them together to do something about global hunger. They needed one another. They needed a BFW group. But did they need a summer organizing intern?

The doorbell rang, interrupting Ann's thoughts. She got up to welcome the first arrival. It was Paul.

"Welcome, Paul."

"Hello, Ann, am I first?" As he took a seat he asked, "Well, have you thought any more about having a summer intern?"

"Paul, I don't know. I've been sitting here for the past hour thinking about our group. On the one hand, we've been doing well just meeting every month for prayer and study and to plan legislative work. On the other hand, I know we need a boost and that we need to grow here in Hickory. It seems to me to be a big decision. Wouldn't it be a big responsibility for a small group like us to take on?"

"Yes, of course it would," Paul replied, "but think where we were a year ago. The conference was a big task, but it strengthened us. . . . " The doorbell rang.

It was the O'Briens and Eve Moore. Soon the Engelses and the Sheas had arrived as well.

"Well," said Ann, "I guess we can begin. Eve, you prepared a prayer for us, didn't you?"

"Here it is," replied Eve, passing out a litany and the songsheet. "This litany is from *Leaven* and the song, 'Be Not Afraid,' is a favorite of mine. The theme, as you can see, is trust and confidence in God in the face of terrible difficulties."

Ann smiled at Paul and said, "This is a great worship theme for us tonight as we shall soon see." Everyone looked at them questioningly as the prayer began.

After the short worship and the review of the current newsletter, which Tim Shea led, Ann opened the discussion of the intern's coming. "Let's hear from Paul what the prospects are," she said.

Paul began, "Well, a few days ago I spoke with the Director of Organizing at the national office in Washington, Kim Bobo. She asked how things are going with our group here in Hickory. Since the regional organizer for the Southeast has resigned to go to graduate school, they do not anticipate sending anyone here for a while. However, there is a summer organizing program through which they recruit young men and women, train them in Washington, and send them to an area for intensive organizing efforts for the months of July and August. The local Bread for the World group provides housing, local transportation, office space, supervision, and support. Usually the summer organizers' travel and personal expenses are covered by their own churches. I told Kim we would consider having one here at Hickory because there is such a need here to expand our operation, and we have gained support in this district from Representative Stevens and from several churches. I am excited about the possibility."

"My goodness!" sighed Paulette. "What a development for us!"

"Does transportation mean the use of a car?" asked Tim.

"Yes, I guess so, especially in an area like this," responded Paul.

"How much money would this entail?" Kitty O'Brien, the practical one, inquired.

"Well, enough to cover work expenses, postage, gas, and the like," Paul answered.

"We could probably find office space, but I wonder about a car and housing for the whole summer. This is a big commitment!" Eve's exclamation drew agreement from the whole group.

"Another big question: What would this person do all summer here in Hickory? How can an outsider do what we here want to be doing?" asked Tim.

"I think it's a risky business, accepting someone we don't know on the word of folks in Washington. I wonder if it's worth the risk," said Kitty.

"Yes" agreed Paul, "it is a risk. And it is a burden that we would take on: both physical and financial. An intern, as I understand it, will work to help us urge local churches to start Bread for the World study and action groups. He or she will enhance our work with the media to highlight the work of Representative Stevens on the House committee and to further encourage her, especially in relation to the Preventing Hunger at Home bill and the Select Committee on Hunger, both of which are urgent issues right now. The Bread for the World intern will help us in giving talks at meetings and at church services, could help us plan an outreach-on-hunger seminar here in the spring of next year, could work in the college to get professors to introduce hunger issues in their courses, and will keep us in touch with Representative Stevens's office in Washington in a new and vital way. Frankly, I am convinced it is worth our effort, although I recognize the problems."

The group fell silent. Ann looked at Paul. In spite of her own reluctance to get involved, his enthusiasm was moving. But the intern could not live on enthusiasm alone.

"It is not unlike deciding to have a baby," said Steve O'Brien.

"Yes, it means choosing to make an even deeper commitment to each other and to our efforts to help bring about a hunger-free world," Eve responded.

"Are we ready for this? Really?" asked Ann. "Is the timing right for us? Can we move better on these urgent pieces of legislation if we have an intern to be concerned about? I'm just not sure. What do you all say?"

Appendix A

NOTE: Appendixes A and B are taken from pages 18 and 19 of the booklet *Bread for the World: Guidelines for Coordinators* (available from Bread for the World; 802 Rhode Island Ave., N.E.; Washington, DC 20018).

MEETINGS

The following are suggestions for a series of three introductory BFW meetings:

First Meeting

1. setting the mood—a "warm-up" period offering the opportunity for those present to introduce themselves and tell why they have come and what their expectations are. Use of the questionnaire from the BFW Education Fund Hunger Course may be helpful
2. scripture reading and prayer
3. *Bread for the World Filmstrip I* (general introduction)
4. update on current legislation and efforts of Bread for the World
5. discussion and questions
6. discussion of possible responses to current legislative agenda by individuals and groups
7. each person tells the group what she or he is willing/able to do

Second Meeting

1. opening prayer
2. to deepen understanding of issue or issues discussed at the first meeting:
   a. *Bread for the World Filmstrip II* (on issues)
   b. a speaker, or
   c. study/discussion of the latest BFW background paper (usually a newsletter insert)
3. exercise on "how to write an effective letter to your member of Congress" on the issue under discussion
4. group decision on an action to be carried out before the next meeting, and assignment of responsibilities
5. discussion of ways to spread the word to others in the local church or in the wider community or district

Third Meeting

1. worship
2. discussion of the BFW Citizen Action Network (e.g., *Bread for the World Filmstrip III* [on network development])
3. planning for a meeting with the Congressional representative; role-playing a question/answer period with him or her (ideas for this are part of the *Election Kit,* available from BFW)
4. decision of participants on how and when to meet for continued self-education/action/worship
5. decision regarding outreach to other individuals/groups in order to multiply effective action

Appendix B

The more you know about those you elect to represent you, the easier it is to communicate effectively. The basic purpose of developing a profile of a member of Congress is to assemble complete and accurate data for distribution to BFW members acquainting them with their Congressperson.

Profile Outline

1. biographical background
2. address and telephone numbers of offices (Washington, D.C., and local)
3. names of assistants or staff aides who deal with hunger issues
4. legislative committee and subcommittee assignments (if representative is ranking minority or chairperson, this should be noted)
5. other pertinent information summarized from news items, articles, speeches, etc. that would give insight into his or her views and possible positions on issues of BFW concern
6. major financial/political supporters of the representative
7. voting record on hunger-related issues

Sources

1. *The Almanac of American Politics* (copublished by E.P. Dutton and the Fund for Constitutional Government)
2. *Congressional Record*—good for reports, speeches, bills, etc. (in your local library)
3. Local and other newspapers
4. Your member of Congress—ask to be added to his or her newsletter mailing list and for copies of speeches and press releases on issues of concern to you
5. Newsletters from public interest groups—the Interreligious Taskforce on Hunger; the League of Women Voters, etc.
6. Local hunger organizations and groups—those that work on food stamp advocacy, welfare reform, social services, etc.
7. *Congressional Quarterly*—on financial disclosures
8. Congressional voting records: available from Bread for the World, the Interreligious Taskforce on Hunger, NETWORK, League of Women Voters, and other groups.

Teaching Note

TOPICS AND QUESTIONS FOR DISCUSSION

1. Based on evidence from the case, who seems to be the primary constituency for the Bread for the World (BFW) organization? Who are the members of the Hickory group? Early in the formation of that group Kathy Thompson raised the goal of ecumenical composition. Ann Walters later voiced concern that the group was "from so many different churches, such diverse backgrounds. . . ." What are the strengths and/or liabilities of an ecumenical group?

2. What underlying vision and specific objectives guide the direction of the Hickory group? What do you see as the primary barriers of reaching those goals?

3. Though there are individual BFW members throughout the United States, this case focuses on the development of a local support group. Trace the development of the Hickory group from John Hogan's state-wide seminar to the time of the group's dilemma over the intern. What role has the national network played in this development? Ann observes that "in the last few months [the group's] energy and effort had begun to wane." What factors contributed to this? How would you respond to her concern for assuring "continuity and strength" in the group? This question could be considered in conjunction with a discussion of the following questions about commitment and the issue of the intern.

4. The case states that the Hickory group members affirm the "education, fellowship, and skills" they had gained over the past three years. What components contributed to the current commitment of the group? Several members agreed that having and supporting an intern would represent a "new level of commitment." What are some possible drawbacks to accepting an intern? What are the advantages? If the group decides to sponsor an intern, what creative steps could be taken to assure that a full-time intern would empower rather than disempower the group of volunteers?

5. What are the accomplishments of the Hickory group over the last three years? Are the members meeting their goals and those of the national organization? Based on your own experience and analysis of the case, are there additional components or steps which would be helpful to this group or the national organization in meeting their goals?

ADDITIONAL RESOURCES

Byron, William. *Causes of World Hunger.* New York: Paulist Press, 1982.
Freudenberger, C. Dean, and Paul M. Minus, Jr. *A Christian Responsibility in a Hungry World.* Nashville: Abingdon Press, 1976.

Grassi, Joseph. *Broken Bread and Broken Bodies: The Eucharist and World Hunger.* Maryknoll, N.Y.: Orbis Books, 1985.

Myrdal, Gunnar. *The Challenge of World Poverty.* New York: Random House, 1971.

Sider, Ronald J. *Rich Christians in an Age of Hunger: A Biblical Study.* New York: Paulist Press, 1977.

Simon, Arthur. *Bread for the World.* Rev. ed. Grand Rapids: Wm. B. Eerdmans Publishing Co., 1984.

JOSEPH C. HOUGH, JR.

Commentary on
Bread for the World

As a social action model, the Bread for the World example has a number of things to commend it. In the first place, it is a model for social action which proposes to focus on a single issue over an extended period of time. One of the great difficulties with models for social action which has surfaced, particularly in the churches, is the diffusion of energy over a number of issues and the rapid shift of issue-emphasis over relatively short segments of time. Programmatic agencies in the churches are not usually geared to single issues, and they usually do not maintain focus on any set of issues for any length of time beyond the normal programmatic cycles of the denomination. Therefore, social action becomes, at best, episodic dissemination of information. It is obvious that the mere dissemination of information, even over a long period of time, does not lead automatically to social action. When, in addition, the effort to dissemi-nate information is episodic, the "program of social action" becomes little more than entertainment. In other words, one is titillated by novelty as the "social-action-in-general" instrumentalities move from issue to issue, but little else really happens. The model before us, with its focus on sustained commit-ment over the long haul, may avoid some of these obvious difficulties.

Second, the model is focused on specific public policies as the avenues for effective social change. When the problem is cast as "world hunger," normally the most immediate reaction is the feeling that the problem is so overwhelming that really nothing can be done. In the absence of concrete possibilities for potentially effective intervention, the outcome is a paralysis of the will mani-fested in social apathy. This model with its focus on specific, achievable objectives concerning specific public policies has a potential for avoiding some of the so-called analysis paralysis which is rooted in the frustration experienced by informed persons who really see nothing they can do which might affect any change in the total problem.

Third, the focus on specific public policy measures provides immediate feedback on action effectiveness. One can discover whether or not a Congress-person votes in a particular way or whether a particular proposed policy is written into law. This presence of some relatively immediate validation mechanism is crucial to the momentum for continuing action. Moreover, the focus on specific objectives or goals (such as passage of particular public policies or influencing votes of policy-makers) provides the basis for constructing an internal accountability mechanism. It becomes possible, at least theoretically, to do serious evaluation, and that evaluation can be made more credible to external observers if the objectives are clear enough to be communicated in ordinary language. When the credibility of the claims for the organization is established in this way, a much stronger case can be made in the attempt to recruit new members in support of the group's goals. The fact that "what-we-have-done" is specific and clear strengthens the claim on potential members who can take seriously the projection of "what-we-can-do."

In this case, each of these strengths of the Bread for the World model is clearly illustrated. The claims for the model are not extravagant, but they are specific and concrete. That something worth doing has been done is felt by the central actors in the case. Furthermore, some few new persons have been recruited by the group, and it has remained focused and often active.

Yet this model also has its problems. There is the perennial problem common to all volunteer groups whose institutional base is not secure: the energy and effectiveness of the group at any given time are almost entirely dependent upon the leadership of particular persons who give the action-objectives of the group top priority in their apportionment of time and energy. The situational analysis of this case itself highlights the problem. Significant leaders have departed. The core workers are tired and reluctant to assume greater responsibilities. In this case, the national organization (perhaps sensing the general problem) proposes a pattern of internships which will be staffed by paid persons. These interns thus offer temporary support to broaden the base of the movement and perhaps to secure a location for Bread for the World in two established community institutions—the churches and the university. On its face it seems to be a move requiring no unreasonable new commitments from the Hickory Bread for the World group. Therefore, the reluctance of the members to accept the rather minor responsibility of the temporary intern bears some comment.

Part of that reluctance may arise from the nature of Bread for the World in Hickory. It is a voluntary organization whose history is dominated by certain key leaders. The cohesiveness of the group rests on the common history of its members and the assent of the group to its leadership, which has been legitimated by its longstanding and enthusiastic participation in the group's social activities. Thus, the offer of the skilled and trained intern is not merely an offer of support. It poses a potential threat to the cohesiveness of the group. A new form of leadership is introduced (rational rather than charismatic) which is not chosen by the group and which is unpredictable. Moreover, even though the group understands its need to expand (and even uses the rhetoric of challenge in the positive sense), the very possibility of expansion is probably experienced as threatening to group cohesiveness as well. To borrow the terms of Ferdinand Tönnies, the intern represents the possibility of diminishing the character of the group as *Gemeinschaft* (community) while strengthening the group as *Gesellschaft* (organization). Expanding membership and securing the institutional base of the group are surely rational moves for an organization seeking to achieve its purposes. However, they are not necessarily moves which will enhance community feeling. In fact, the move from community to organization has often been disruptive and even disabling for some volunteer groups whose energy was derived from a sort of group cohesiveness based on common history, common self-understanding, and charismatic leadership. When that cohesive base is replaced with paid professional leadership or managers, the problem of motivating broad volunteer participation is exacerbated. The perennial problem of volunteer organizational models, then, is how to maintain broad participation and at the same time be effective in the long-term task of achieving the goals of systemic change.

Like most volunteer organizations, Bread for the World has attempted to preserve a healthy balance by developing a national organization which provides resources which enable local communities to be effective on their own while at the same time attempting to promote a sense of common purpose among all the local groups around the country. In this way, the sense of group cohesiveness and also a sense of significant national achievement serve to keep alive the motivation necessary for broad volunteer participation. The temptation on the part of the national organizational leadership is to move beyond these functions toward routinization of all local groups as "branches" of the organization. When this happens, the motivation for active participation of volunteers subsides, and the local groups respond usually by turning over the movement to professionals who "do the movement" for members, who in turn pay them. That sort of history was repeated time and again in the late nineteenth century and early twentieth century among lay volunteer groups. In case after case those volunteer groups were routinized, nationalized, and turned over to professional leadership. The result was that lay people began to lose interest and to diminish their active participation in the groups. Finally, the groups became dominated by professional leaders who developed bureaucracies of their own. Lay participation was finally reduced to fundraising.

In this case, at the suggestion of the national organization, the Hickory Bread for the World group is on the verge of making a move in that direction. The intern will do nothing which members of the group could not do if they worked at it. Furthermore, the subtle shift from participation in group action to fundraising for a professional is obvious. So the decision before them is not merely what to do about the intern. It is rather a broader question. They must ask themselves: If we accept the intern, what will we become?

FRANCES H. KENNEDY

Commentary on
Bread for the World

The Bread for the World (BFW) model has both strengths and weaknesses. There are positive aspects to the single-issue entry point to pedagogy for the non-poor. The model provides an easy and practical way to move from personal to political dimensions of the hunger problem and from theoretical concern to direct action. There are also strengths in the group approach. An individual perspective is broadened through interaction with a group. Groups can be formed of any size and in any location. The model can be used in homes, schools, churches, or community centers. BFW programs can involve individuals or families and are educative for stable or transient citizens of today's mobile society.

There are, however, drawbacks to the single-issue entry point. It can be difficult to move a single-issue group through the complex social construct of today's local/national/global interdependent capitalistic economy, especially as it relates to the Third and First Worlds. Hunger involves food production, grain reserves, transportation, distribution, land use, food as a weapon, and many other justice-related issues. When a local group engages in conflictual politics, it can splinter or take on the challenge. This case tells of successful work with a local member of Congress. These successes are important to the motivation and cohesiveness of the group. If, however, Representative Stevens had not been cooperative, or should she not be cooperative in the future, as the hunger issue expands to aid, jobs, trade, security, and justice issues, the local group could suffer setbacks. There is the additional possibility that national legislative bills will conflict with local community political concerns, which may create tension in the group. To some extent this could be countered by a more comprehensive approach to issues of justice.

A major strength of this model is the strong national office and support network. Contributions, which are not tax-deductible, support the work of some forty national staff persons, according to need. The board of directors consists of diverse individuals, but they do not represent local constituencies. The national staff drafts legislation and encourages local groups through regional seminars. It informs through a monthly newsletter with updates on legislation and contact-data plus background information. A staff director networks with local pastors, who in turn support local group formation.

There are a number of positive factors regarding the role of the network. One is the dissemination of information. Local groups derive strength from knowing there are hundreds of other groups like themselves, from awareness of membership increases, and from reports of successes in influencing Congresspersons. The national staff is also there to encourage expansion and to aid movement of members from group to group. It is ready with guidelines for coordination and models for seminar planning. The national office furnishes background research on issues and current data on legislation.

However, while the national office suggests a variety of programs, local groups assume responsibility for developing their own agendas. Options chosen by the Hickory group include participation in a CROP walk, maintaining a local "hunger watch," showing films, contact with schools and colleges for impact through teaching, aiding college students in action on specific legislative bills, direct pressure on political leaders, and so on. This case therefore models the potential of local groups which can offer social enrichment to members.

Thus the case to some extent highlights the balance between the cohesiveness of the local group and the expanded vision of the national organization. Yet the model also makes it clear that dependency by local groups on a strong national network may be a weakness if it drains creativity from a local group or forces it to respond to national requests before understanding the complexity of the rationale behind a request. This is a drawback to the policy of the national office making decisions on legislation for local groups. In this case study, Ann and Paul have received a suggestion for a summer intern program and are raising with the group the question of whether to accept or reject it. Suggestions from the national office do not necessarily reflect the needs of individual local groups. Finances are a consideration and support for national staffing could be a burden in the future if available funds are expended to support an intern.

BFW as a national "citizens' lobby" provides quick political education on government policy; its bipartisan stance enables it to draw from a varied political constituency, but that stance also means it cannot assume any partisan political support. Its purpose is to affect government policy through legislation, and it seeks to support measures offering dignity and opportunity to the desperately poor. Though the BFW model does not restrict its membership, it seems designed for the middle class, as is revealed by the makeup of the Hickory group. The BFW quick telephone tree assumes access to a telephone, which many poor do not have. A pressure point for the group's success is support or nonsupport of legislators. Many of the poor in the United States are not registered voters, just as they are not part of the network. It is also not clear in what way the poor are present in decision-making or in analysis of their needs in the BFW model. When alleviation of hunger becomes alleviation of poverty and provision of jobs, there must be cross-connecting with other justice networks, which would probably threaten a middle-class-only constituency.

BFW adapts theologically to all churches, communions, and faiths from a biblically-based concern for feeding the hungry. The national office furnishes worship aids, Bible study materials, and book and film resources. Secular groups may use the structure as well. Reading the newspaper on legislation is certainly a helpful corollary to Bible reading! Strength in the BFW independent network must be contrasted with the security of specific church connections which offer sustained obligation and financial support. In this case, support from Pastor Hogan is crucial in the beginning of the group; when he moves away, his loss is felt strongly. The initial hunger concern broadens into deeper analysis because of sophistication of national staff services and that analysis may encourage members to bridge into other network/action models. Hunger need not be a constrictive issue if groups move beyond charity as a way of addressing it. In this case, Ann's group has come together to pray, study, and work on hunger issues over a three-year period. Although only five to seven of the fifteen members are still attending meetings regularly, they have managed to support the Emergency Grain Reserve, Targeted Development Aid, and Preventing Hunger at Home legislation—all involving increased complexity of the food issue. Ann has worked on global hunger and foreign aid workshops, has had contact with a local hunger-observation group, and continues her work with members who were politicized during the sixties. She faces possible further commitment with a summer intern.

The case demonstrates the values of the BFW model—it features a local group that is stimulated by and dependent upon a competent national office staff while at the same time remaining flexible in its educative role in the community. The single-issue limitation may be a handicap for deeper structural analysis, for stronger commitment, or when coalition formation is desirable. But that limitation may be addressed by strong leadership in the group coupled with continued support from the national network of BFW.

CHAPTER 5

WOMEN'S THEOLOGICAL CENTER

The model described in this case, like the Chrysalis Program in the case that follows, deals with professional religious leadership training. However, whereas the Chrysalis model is a program within a traditional theological seminary, the Women's Theological Center is an autonomous institution. The founders were convinced that only in an independent institution could they develop distinctive feminist theological inquiry. The case describes the development of the center and some of the challenges the directors faced during its early stages. The model's significance for this volume lies in its serious attempt to address the major problems of sexism, classism, and racist-ethnic discrimination. The case describes how the leaders from the beginning tried to involve women from a diversity of races, classes, and nations in this theological education experience, and the case depicts the effort it took to deal with the contradictions inherent in that goal. The center also faced the difficulties of combining academic requirements and "standards" with realistic field engagement in various urban situations.

The commentators raise provocative questions about the educational model. They dialogue with the model's architects about the most effective ways of breaking through the powerful institutional structures of higher and professional education and the contextual ideological and structural forces that perpetuate the sexist, racist, and classist patterns of U.S., Canadian, and many other First World societies.

This case will be relevant to those seeking ways to liberate people from sexist, economic, or ethnic oppression, with particular reference to theological education and its discrimination against women.

Program Overview

The Women's Theological Center is an action/reflection program which addresses issues of faith and social justice beginning with the point of view of women's experience. It is an ecumenical program of racial, economic, and national diversity.

The center is organized around two interlocking program components: A Study/Action Program for student participants drawn from across the country and around the world; and a Resource Center, serving primarily the Boston area and open to all people who are interested in explorations of faith and social justice through short-term seminars, workshops, and liturgies which take women's experience as their beginning point. These two aspects of the program are necessarily intertwined in an approach to learning which assumes that authentic learning requires action and reflection and that what one learns depends in large measure on *whom* one learns *with*. The Resource Center serves a broad audience of people involved in a wide variety of community and church-based social action efforts. The Study/Action Program involves a small group of women engaged in social justice work (addressing issues related to homelessness, hunger, access to justice, sexual and domestic violence, Latin American refugees, and urban poverty and disenfranchisement, particularly as these issues affect women) combined with an intensive reflection on feminist theory, feminist theology, feminist spirituality, and institutional analysis and organizational change. The interdependence of the two aspects of the program brings together a diversity of experience that would not be possible in either alone.

The *Study/Action Program* is organized around the personal and communal experience of the participants in action and reflection on work, social transformation, and women's experience. It consists of three components, each of which takes two semesters to complete. The three components are:

1. Field-Based Critical Action—provides a context for women to be engaged in the work of social transformation in the urban area through a minimum of ten hours per week involvement in agencies that address social justice/survival issues. This seminar is structured around issues raised in the field sites, and focuses on developing skills for social analysis and change.

2. Feminist Theology and Feminist Theory—explores the challenge which the women's movement brings to traditional theology and religious practice. Resources for this exploration are women's writings—theory,

theology, poetry, and prose by black, Hispanic, Asian, Native-American, and white women—and the participants' concrete experience of engagement in struggle against cultural and institutional misogyny as it affects their lives and the lives of the women with whom they work in their field sites.

3. Feminist Spirituality and Praxis—focuses on the faith/hope/survival experiences of participants in the personal, political, and religious dimensions of their lives and work. Story, symbol, myth, ritual, and action for justice are resources for this seminar.

Participants in the Study/Action Program come from varied backgrounds, including full-time employment in social justice work, volunteer social justice/political action work, work in schools of theology, and lay participation in church ministries. Those who wish to do so can receive undergraduate or graduate credit through special arrangements with Emmanuel College in Boston or the Episcopal Divinity School in Cambridge, and participants may elect to take one course per semester through either of those schools.

The *Resource Center* serves the larger metropolitan Boston area with respect to questions of women, faith, and social justice. Its task is to address the concerns encountered by a broad spectrum of women engaged in social justice efforts. It draws participants from the many class- and race-defined neighborhoods of Boston, and its programs focus on issues related to the field sites where participants in the Study/Action Program are engaged, thus providing a broader base for reflection among persons of common interest and work. For example, during the 1983–84 term, students worked in shelters for poor and homeless women and in agencies dealing with violence against women, and two Resource Center programs addressed these concerns: "The Unmentionable Sin: Sexual and Domestic Violence" and "The Pathology of Homelessness." In both cases, the women who participated were dealing with these issues in their lives and/or in their work on public policy change and/or in their efforts in community organizing. In addition, the Resource Center provides a setting for communal reflection and celebration through its monthly Womanspirit Celebration liturgies.

For further information, contact: Women's Theological Center; 400 The Fenway; Boston, MA 02115; phone: (617) 277-1330.

Case Study
Women's Theological Center

Sarah Jackson felt both depleted and invigorated as she entered the Women's Theological Center (WTC) office. The "Feminist Spirituality and Praxis" course she was coteaching had once again exceeded her expectations, reflecting the commitment and energy of the twelve women engaged in the year-long program of study. It was a diverse group: there were students from, among other places, Washington, Mississippi, Malaysia, and Haiti; Karen was one year out of college and Meg was in her fifties; there were Roman Catholic, Southern Baptist, United Church of Christ, and unaffiliated women; some were lesbian, some straight, some celibate; there were women preparing for ordination, Catholic sisters, and those seeking no "official" ministry. Not knowing what they would find, they had gathered to shape questions and a community. For nine months they would worship, play, cry, and learn together. They would study feminist theology, feminist theory, and feminist spirituality, and would grapple with integrating the theoretical, spiritual, and practical in their work sites and in the "Field-Based Critical Action" seminar.

Momentarily, Sarah would be meeting with Kate Seymour, fellow codirector of the center. She tried to put in abeyance her reflections on the course and to focus instead on the agenda for their meeting. Once again Kate and Sarah would be exploring how to broaden WTC's constituency. From its inception, WTC had been committed to being a multiracial and economically diverse program. The founders, the faculty, and the board were from various races and represented various class backgrounds; Kate was a white woman and Sarah was black. So far, however, in both WTC's Resource Center programming and the year-long Study/Action component, participants were predominately white and middle-class. Although some Study/Action women were from poor or working-class origins, by the time they reached graduate studies, all were middle-class in terms of options, if not income. How could WTC be shaped into a program shared by black, Hispanic, Asian, and white women alike? The coordinating committee, the organization's working board, would be meeting that night to define the problem and develop strategies for greater inclusivity. Kate and Sarah were responsible for shaping the agenda and offering possible approaches to broadening WTC's participation.

This case was prepared by Adele Smith-Pennington and Nancy D. Richardson (ed. Alice Frazer Evans) as a basis for discussion rather than to illustrate either effective or ineffective handling of the situation. Copyright © by the Case Study Institute.

There was work to be done. Sarah's mind, however, filled with images evoked by the "Feminist Spirituality and Praxis" course. How compelling were the students' vigorous questions and visions! Yet, greater diversification would enrich the Study/Action community by fostering new questions, by challenging all to articulate a faith that crosses class, cultural, and ethnic lines while acknowledging the particular, and by calling together persons from various backgrounds to work to dismantle oppressive structures. WTC held that women's experiences—the personal stories and the collective history—were crucial reference points. Because education grows out of experience, participants shaped what stories were heard, how they were told, and what response was offered.

Among that year's students was Yvonne, who had powerfully outlined her faith pilgrimage in Haiti and the United States, beginning "I was born spiritual." And Lynn, sporting her "Fifty Is Nifty" T-shirt, was three thousand miles from her Dominican community as it underwent a severe test. In an effort to live out a more inclusive understanding, her community had welcomed laywomen to have an active voice in decision-making. The Congregation of Sacred Religious had responded by threatening loss of canonical status. "At times it is difficult being here in Boson," Lynn stated, "separated from the intensity of the decision-making. Since Rome initiated an investigation of the Sisters, I have experienced a heaviness which I cannot discard. Even my initial anger had an underlying grief, which I am searching to understand. It is still hard for me to comprehend the situation. I cannot believe the presumption of those who legislate for a group they do not know, and I challenge the depth of the investigation. A Dominican brother, Edward Schillebeeckx, has said that each person 'has his own responsibility for acting honorably and in accord with conscience, aware of the possible consequences which may follow even for himself in the church.' My concern is that we have the strength to live with such honor."

Lynn had shared with the class how her difficulty in deciding at which field site she would work connected with her struggle to live honorably. She had expressed a feeling of being torn. On the one hand, she wanted to use her skills as effectively as possible. Her previous work as secretary, vice-principal and Director of Apostolic Works had demonstrated her administrative capabilities. On the other hand, she felt an uneasiness because paperwork too often limited her "people contact." Although she was of blue-collar origins and had worked years in low-income communities, Lynn believed this year would be a test. She would have to make a choice, a commitment, on a new level. She could not continue moving between involvement with the poor and her relative security. What side was she on? Lynn strove to make a connection from which there could be no turning back.

Andrea had responded, "I think of field work in the traditional seminary model, and I don't want that. You go out to the parish on Sunday and dress up in your vestments. It's the Lone Ranger. You go out there in your white suit and shoot bullets and you're gone. I am struck, Lynn, by what you said about being so changed by the work that there could be no going back."

J'heh thought aloud what it meant to live honorably—and of the life and death consequences for one's actions. "When I was in the Korean student movement, we went to live and work in the slum. We put on the clothes of the poor. We ate the same food. But I could not become poor. I tried hard, but I am different—in upbringing, in language, in what I see, and in wealth. I have money. I have a comfortable home." J'heh paused. "How can we live, incarnate, our ideals? There is a difference between experiment and experience. Experience comes from being in the midst of life, not from standing aside and watching. I felt that our orientation trips around Boston and to our field sites were an experiment, not an experience. We need something deeper. . . . This year is a luxury—to take a year and be here. There is a sinfulness in privilege. I need confession. Perhaps we all will need confession.

"The more I am aware of injustices, that people are hungry in the midst of extravagance, the more I cannot accept a traditional God. But most Korean Christians believe differently than I. I want to work in community. Incarnation can only occur in community. I do not want to be the person who goes outside of community and criticizes with scorn: 'How can you think that way! You are inferior!' If I deny community, I can't find any place to work for the fullness of life. To avoid schizophrenia, I need to work hard to find a fresh way that I can hold my ideas and yet be in relationship.

"I used to ask what I would die for, but now I ask what I will live for. You see, death is not an abstraction. It is very, very real. Many Koreans have died in working for social justice. I am not free to speak about it in detail. But let me say that the powerful are vulnerable, and when we touch their vulnerability, they strike out. They kill. I need to be here at WTC to make real decisions about life and death, to have my ideas critiqued, to learn how to bring about social justice in my community, to struggle for life. In Korean society, honor is very important, but I no longer worry about my honor. I worry about how to make people alive in the midst of death. And how I can be alive with them."

Searching for some way to bring together her concerns and Lynn's, as well as J'heh's, Andrea had begun, "I think we have a unique community. I hear in our different stories sufficient hope to motivate us to take a year away, to uproot and reflect. I think the power in our coming together is that we shape a collective question. I hear us saying: 'Here I am with a gift of consciousness and a few talents. I am not comfortable with the way I have used my gifts and with what I am leaving behind. I am mindful of the luxury in being here, and yet it is a tremendous responsibility. There is a cost, a discipleship. How not to sin in the field sites, our ministries, our lives? How to bring what we have learned here back to our communities?' "

"Crossing that line so there could be no turning back . . ." "Living honorably in this community and the world . . ." "Incarnating justice . . ." The impossible yet compelling visions filled Sarah's mind. She glanced out the office window and spotted Kate walking her bicycle through the campus. The chin-guard of her Skid-Lid safety helmet flapped in the wind, conveying the image of a jockey leading a horse to the stable.

Kate entered the office carrying her helmet and a stack of letters from the mailroom. There was still no word on the three funding proposals, but there were letters expressing interest in WTC from women in Newton, Massachusetts, Chicago, and Nairobi. Word of WTC was spreading.

Connecting the class to the task at hand, Sarah began, "Today's spirituality class was dynamic. The commitment of the students! The perspectives they bring to the class!" She paused. "Yet I'm convinced that the program would be even stronger if there were more voices from women of color. Here we are again asking how to broaden WTC's constituency so that its programs are shaped and attended by more Hispanics, Asians, Native-Americans, and blacks so that diverse stories are heard, so that together we develop inclusive theologies and strategies for social change."

This challenge had faced WTC from its inception. In 1977 the seeds were planted for the center at a Washington, D.C., gathering of women active in ministry and theological education. Their goal was to have a place that focused on academic study of women's issues. Follow-up consultations led to the formation of a Women's Theological Center and the selection of Boston as the site for the pilot program because of its theological schools and strong women's networks. Kate, who at the time had been on the theological faculty of a Boston seminary, had been approached by the steering committee to be part of the Boston group developing initial planning.

As Kate and Sarah began to discuss plans for the evening meeting, Kate recalled a specific aspect of WTC's history. "Because of my experience with Grailville, Ohio—a program with philosophical, personnel, and financial links with WTC—I didn't want to have an organizational meeting to talk about the possibility of a Boston-based program without women of color being part of it from the onset. If we met with all white women, we would be beginning as a white program asking black women to join. So we began with a biracial planning group. In our meetings, we reshaped what the initial conceivers had outlined. We thought that it would be difficult to justify all the fund-raising for only a year-long program for twenty women, and we feared that the Field-Based Critical Action component would not be enough to offset the classism and racism of the ivory tower. So we designed the Resource Center program for women in the city who either couldn't afford or didn't want to be part of the year-long program. Yet, even with our conscious efforts to cross racial lines, those participating in WTC programming remained predominately white." Complementing the Study/Action Program for academic credit, the Resource Center sponsored activities at sites scattered throughout the city. During the first year, these ranged from monthly liturgies to a conference on homelessness, to a consultation on sexual abuse, to an Alice Walker reading.

"We've had this discussion before," continued Kate. "Probably the first time was five years ago at the Grail Center consultation on 'Women in Theological Education.' We said then, as we believe now, that what we learn is dependent on whom we learn it with. We're building a program based on student and staff definitions of what we need to learn. If the majority of people are white, and they don't think they need to know about racism, for example, they won't define it as a problem. Then dealing with racism becomes an imposition and people will resist it for that reason."

"I can probably guess, but what kind of response did the WTC get during last year's recruitment efforts?" asked Sarah, who had only recently joined the staff.

"The contacts via mail with every local black church—letters asking if we could come talk about WTC and the Resource Center—got zero response, which doesn't surprise me, given my experience with campus ministry."

Sarah concurred. "When I think of black churches—and perhaps it's true of any church—I think of closed societies. Unless you have some personal link, you're bound to meet resistance."

Kate continued, "The Resource Center's program in June, 'Black Women and the Church,' was enthusiastically received by the fifteen or so black women present. There was a lot of energy, and they wanted to know more about WTC activities. So it's not a lack of interest. We're doing things that connect with some black women's interests. Rather, it seems that people aren't aware of our program. And our connections with Hispanic and Asian-American women are even weaker. We have much to learn about different cultures."

"Obviously location is important," interjected Sarah. "I recall that that program was in a black neighborhood, and many of the participants probably knew the facilitators—combining a familiar locale with personal connections. For people not into conference-going, a different neighborhood, no matter how near geographically, can be a deterrent."

"For the year-long program," said Kate, "I believe we had only one black North American woman who was interested, and she opted for beginning a doctoral program at Yale. WTC got buried at the last Black Seminarians' Conference at ITC because the conference was heavily male-dominated in terms of leadership and agenda. Seminaries are also closed societies. But the seeds have been planted. We will be sending a delegate again this year and building upon the personal contacts we have."

"As you speak, Kate, the word 'isolation' keeps coming to my mind, especially pertaining to the year-long program. As a black woman, I'd be wary about participating in the Study/Action Program if I knew little about WTC. I'd fear it would isolate me from whatever meager supports I already had, stranding me in an alien city with strange people with peculiar theories, drowning me in a foreign white sea with the nearest raft—however hole-ridden—miles away."

"I can see that," said Kate. "White people, especially students, generally don't risk as much coming here even if the program proved a washout. They usually have contacts, can take a year out. Most are not supporting kids as a lot of black women are."

"I think there's a serious question: What do we have to offer black women who are going into ministry through traditional black denominations?" pondered Sarah. "I can imagine the tension between those suggesting the WTC experience be included in a denomination's program and the licensure or ordination committees. I suspect that not only would WTC be viewed as a threat to traditional male leadership and thereby critical of the conservative impulses within black society, but after a year of Study/Action, the student would be even more assertive of her rights so that working with traditional structures might no longer be tenable. She would have great difficulty being honest to her role both at WTC and in traditional settings in the black community."

"The black women we know who have been involved in WTC—planning programming, teaching Study/Action courses, attending Resource Center activities—are not from the traditional black denominations. They're Presbyterian, United Church of Christ, and Roman Catholic, not African Methodist Episcopal, National Baptist, or from the Church of God in Christ. And that may speak to a class issue as much as a theological one. In addition to their strong middle-class base, black denominations include poor people, whereas Presbyterians and members of the United Church of Christ *tend* to be more affluent," observed Sarah.

"At the Wellsprings Conference, 'Women's Work/Women's Faith,' I counted five black women in the audience: one was an invited speaker, three were Roman Catholic, and one was Unitarian Universalist. None of that speaks to where most black church women are," added Kate. "That's not necessarily a criticism of WTC but an acknowledgment of the kind of base from which we operate."

"And even for those of us who are outside the traditional black denominations, the question exists as to what WTC has to offer," continued Sarah. "I strongly believe WTC can challenge any woman—black, white, Hispanic, whatever—who is committed to rethinking an inclusive theology of liberation. However, for those sisters who do not know WTC as I do, who have no reason to trust WTC, there could be a legitimate fear of being immersed in what is perceived as a white program. Unless the number of women of color are sufficient, we could be diversifying the program at our expense, draining ourselves in order to be a resource for white women's consciousness-raising rather than devoting our energies to clarifying the questions we need to be articulating. Black women are tired of being teachers and mothers."

Kate picked up, "And there's the issue of whether most members of traditional black churches would be attracted to something labeled 'feminist' no matter what is offered. I don't know the answer. Nevertheless, the contact must be attempted. If we decided, say, to restructure WTC to make it more attractive to women in traditional black denominations, at this point we wouldn't know how to proceed. And we are on even less familiar ground in trying to reach Hispanic, Native-American, and Asian-American women. We won't learn what questions to ask and what changes to make until the contacts are made."

"On the other hand," inserted Sarah, "while we don't want to assume that someone won't be interested before even approaching her, we may want to focus on attracting women of color who are not preparing for traditional ministries."

"I was wondering if the fact we call ourselves 'Christian' and 'feminist' knocks out black women at both ends," Kate went on. "Are people who identify themselves as Christian bothered by the label 'feminist' and people who call themselves feminist excluded by the label 'Christian'? Also, the title 'theological' might convey an unnecessarily heavy academic tone. I really expected black women to show up for Saturday's presentation with Mary Helen Washington and Beverly Smith. Here we had a nationally known, black literary historian and a black freelance writer and media consultant. Although I had no illusions about holding them throughout the entire weekend conference, I did expect to see black feminists on Saturday. I wonder if they read the literature and felt excluded by the word 'Christian'."

"I had thought about the effects the 'feminist' label might have, but not about the word 'Christian'," replied Sarah. "Perhaps we need to make clear in our literature that we are open to diverse perspectives, but I don't think we should eliminate the word 'Christian' because it gives important definition to what we do."

The phone rang. Sarah picked it up and began listening. She felt uplifted by the enthusiastic words she heard. A black woman who attended the previous evening's WTC program on domestic violence had telephoned to say how powerful the event had been. "I feel that WTC is the most exciting thing that's happening, and I mean anywhere in the country. I love it!" the caller said before going on to lament the fact that only two black women she knew were in the audience. She was certain many more of her friends would have been present had they known about WTC. "You're working with too small a circle, mostly the seminaries. And that's not where most black feminists are." She agreed to meet over dinner later that week to share her contacts.

Kate glanced at the clock. "Again I need to be in two places at the same time. There's a meeting at one o'clock over at Casa Myrna." Casa Myrna Vasquez, a shelter for battered women, was a field site placement for some of the Study/Action participants. Field site involvement was the hub of Study/Action. Devoting more time to social concerns than to classroom work, students worked throughout the year at an advocacy/direct-service site, received supervision, and integrated theory and practice in the Field-Based Critical Action seminar which Kate led.

"It's evident from the reports we've had that the students are enthusiastic about the placements. They seem challenged by the work they're doing and are raising significant questions. Perhaps the field sites component is one area in which WTC is making multiracial connections. The sites offer a class perspective which seminars can't. The students are immersed in lower-class communities which challenge middle-class assumptions, incorporate cultural pluralism, and present strategies for survival and change," said Sarah. In addition to Casa Myrna, Centro Presente and the East Boston project worked with significant Spanish-speaking populations. Black women frequented most of the eight field sites which WTC had selected. As with the other components of Study/ Action, the beginning point for the field-based experience was the students themselves. But there was a difference as to the nature of that beginning point: instead of sharing faith stories, which occurred in the initial sessions of the "Feminist Spirituality" class, or articulating the theological questions leading one to WTC, which had focused the "Feminist Theology" course's first meetings, Field-Based Critical Action began with student immersion. In the Boston streets and at the placement agencies, students were confronted with sights, sounds, smells, and ideas that often radically undermined their presuppositions. Kate led them to voice and analyze their experience by asking them to look at which factors in those first days were most surprising, most anxiety-provoking, most hopeful, and most revealing about themselves.

"There are many organizations we could have chosen for field sites," Kate commented. "We were concerned with the type of work being done, that students could be effective with only a nine-month commitment, and that quality supervision could be offered. The racial question comes up because we wanted sites to be accessible to all students regardless of race. Even though we're only a few weeks into the program, most of the student–site matches seem to be successful." Kate paused. "You know, Sarah, I wasn't thinking when I said this would be a good time to meet. I had forgotten about Casa Myrna. Could you tighten the agenda for tonight's meeting and decide how to present the question of diversity?" Kate picked up the papers scattered over her desk and put on her bike helmet. The sunlight through the office windows bounced off the black and white plastic. "Thanks a lot for finishing up. See you tonight." Kate went out.

Sarah turned to her desk. Between the Soelle and Ruether and Walker books for class there were scattered notes about a funding proposal and a brochure rewrite. She found a fresh piece of paper to jot down ideas for the evening's meeting. "Okay. We talked about the need to make connections, to personally contact folks, and to be persistent. But there is also the question of what we have to offer women of color, and the gap is greatest with women of Asian and Latin backgrounds. At the same time we may need to target recruitment, we certainly must build stronger bridges with existing groups." She thought of the Innercity Women's Project, a multiracial program coordinated by the Sisters of Notre Dame and involving lower income people. That fall the project's directors would be adapting some of WTC's conference themes to mesh with their constituency's interests. "One good move. And another issue before us seems to be how we can reshape the programming to reach a broader base. However, we can't do the restructuring until the contacts are made so that even more women of color are involved in the rebuilding. As a black woman I know WTC can have validity for women from diverse backgrounds. The exuberance, the questions, the honesty I sense after so many of the sessions . . ."

Sarah thought back to what had brought different women to WTC and wondered how to widen its base. She remembered Andrea's frankness as she shared her story with the spirituality class. "My family, my parish family, and my seminary family are all rich, white, and economically self-satisfied. And we behave oppressively to anyone who isn't. How can I reach the people God put into my life? Can we change? How? And what about my own classism, racism, and persistent adherence to materialism? How do I reach me?"

Andrea had spoken of the power that the image of El Shaddai held for her. At her seminary in a class entitled "Inclusive Language and Liturgy," she learned that El Shaddai, usually translated as "the God of the mountain," in early texts was "God of the breasts." A very female image of God had been translated out of the text. Andrea went on about her class: "Working with this kind of material, the class became a consciousness-raising experience. And as a group we decided to do something collective as an offering back to the larger seminary community rather than to follow the traditional model of each student going off into separate carrels to write papers. We did a liturgy. But I found that after the service others on campus expected us to be experts on inclusive language, to have a position, to have a cause, something which we had to prove. It struck me that if I were going to have to defend and prove myself at the same time that I was trying to stretch and grow and learn, then I wouldn't stretch and grow and learn along any other path than the path that the questions were coming from. So, for me, moving to WTC for a year will allow me, I hope, to ask questions and not have answers, to find out where I am and not have to defend it at the same time I'm learning. I wish I could say it were as simple as calling God 'she,' but it's not. I wish to have some space in which to experience worship and work with worship in a different way. And then the questions arise: If I have a place where I can worship with more of me, will I be more tolerant with my traditional parish family because I'm being fed else-where, or will I be less tolerant of them because I won't put up with being unfulfilled by them? And these are very serious questions in terms of project-ing my long-term relationship with my parish as a member and a lay reader—as part of the community—and even more acutely as I consider the question of ordination. Will my experience at WTC pull me so far away from the tradi-tional experiences of the church that I can't participate in them at all? And then where do I go with my ministry? Do I wrap it up in a red bandana and hit the road? I don't know."

Women of diverse backgrounds needed to hear Andrea's questions, and Lynn's, and J'heh's, and Yvonne's. And women of diverse backgrounds needed to mold a response. "It is surgery," one woman had said about being at WTC, "and we are both the patient and the doctor." And for what? A vision that could not be established in one's lifetime, if at all? And before a new order could be created, wouldn't the divisions become more acute: a greater impa-tience with church structures, a rejection of former understandings of God, an alienation from one's community? And the gulf between First World and Third, affluent and poor, the powerful and the persecuted—wouldn't it be-come even more undeniable?

In the kaleidoscope abounded the complementary and conflicting images surrounding El Shaddai. Would students be stranded on a mountain cut off from community? Were there ways to use the vision which could come from climbing to the mountaintop without becoming hierarchical? And what of the strength of the imagery—Could it be retained without domination? The breast image—the life flow, the creating—summoned the conversations about community and interrelatedness. The conflicts and problems were abundant: To achieve true mutuality without being sapped, without exploiting individuals in trying to achieve group diversity . . . To create a multiracial community which respected the particular . . . To develop a feminist center which did not translate out—cut off—people from their ethnic community . . . The divided Boston streets . . . The crammed South Korean jails . . .

What was the vision to be seen from the mountaintop? It was a question asked by the students and prospective participants alike, by whites and women of color. And the response, too, needed to be shaped by women representing diverse cultural, racial, and class backgrounds. Sarah picked up her pen and wrote, "How might WTC involve people who embody the richness of women's distinct experiences?" Thinking, she gazed out the window and glimpsed Kate pedaling through the campus gate to join the urban traffic.

Teaching Note

TOPICS AND QUESTIONS FOR DISCUSSION

Suggestions

A dialogical approach to this case is critical as the methodology of the program itself assumes a dialogical mode of learning and teaching. A suggested format is a group of eight to ten people with a facilitator. The facilitator will initiate discussion by suggesting some or all of the questions below and ask participants if they have additional questions that they see as critical to gaining an understanding of the case. If questions are offered, they should be added to the list. The facilitator will suggest a format—including which questions to begin with—and time frame for the discussion, and will then ask for the group's approval.

If the group dealing with the case is larger than ten, it can be divided into two or more groups. In that case, the process outlined above (adding questions, setting format and time frame) would be done in the large, overall group. That group would then be sub-divided and each group would be asked to discuss agreed upon questions for approximately three-fourths of the total time available. When the overall group reconvenes, the facilitator asks each group to shout out responses to the questions (not reports from each group as these get repetitive and boring). All responses are written on newsprint. After this process is completed, the facilitator pulls together learnings and leads a summary discussion/wrap-up.

Questions

1. What are the goals of the Women's Theological Center?
2. What are its strengths? What are its weaknesses?
3. What pedagogical assumptions are made?
4. What are the issues that confront Sarah and Kate in the Women's Theological Center?
5. How are those issues reflected in the pedagogical model?

ADDITIONAL RESOURCES

Cornwall Collective. *Your Daughters Shall Prophesy.* New York: Pilgrim Press, 1980.

Davis, Angela Y. *Women, Race and Class.* New York: Random House, 1981.

Freire, Paulo. *Education for Critical Consciousness.* Translated and edited by Myrna Bergman Ramos. New York: Seabury Press, 1973.

———. *Pedagogy in Process: The Letters to Guinea-Bissau.* Translated by Carman St. J. Hunter. Edited by Martha Keehn. New York: Continuum, 1983.

———. *Pedagogy of the Oppressed.* Translated by Myrna Bergman Ramos. New York: Herder & Herder, 1970.

Giroux, Henry A. *Ideology, Culture, and the Process of Schooling.* Philadelphia: Temple University Press, 1981.

Harrison, Beverly, ed. *Making the Connections: Essays in Feminist Social Ethics.* Boston: Beacon Press, 1985.

Hope, Ann, and Sally Timmel. *Training for Transformation: A Handbook for Community Workers.* 3 vols. Guere, Zimbabwe: Mambo Press, 1984.

Hull, Gloria T., et al., eds. *All the Women Are White, All the Blacks Are Men, But Some of Us Are Brave: Black Women's Studies.* Old Westbury, N.Y.: The Feminist Press, 1982.

Keohane, Nannerl O., et al., eds. *Feminist Theory: A Critique of Ideology.* Chicago: University of Chicago Press, 1982.

Moraga, Cherrie, et al., eds. *This Bridge Called My Back: Writings by Radical Women of Color.* Watertown, Mass.: Persephone Press, 1981.

Mud Flower Collective. *God's Fierce Whimsy: Implications of Christian Feminism for Theological Education.* Edited by Carter Heyward. New York: Pilgrim Press, 1985.

Rich, Adrienne. *On Lies, Secrets, and Silences.* New York: W. W. Norton & Co., 1979.

Ruether, Rosemary Radford, *New Woman/New Earth: Sexist Ideologies and Human Liberation.* New York: Seabury Press, 1975.

F. ROSS KINSLER

Commentary on
Women's Theological Center

The following is a series of concise comments under these headings: "Strengths," "Weaknesses and Obstacles," "Possible Ways Forward," and "Components That May Serve in Other Educational Models." The primary frame of reference for these comments is theological education, a subsystem within the larger framework of church and society.

Strengths

1. WTC ties closely together experience and life concerns with study and reflection; new involvements and skill development with study, reflection, and discussion; personal and spiritual formation with social analysis and practical engagement in issues.

2. The program is based on deeply felt needs and fundamental goals for person, church, and society; it sustains, deepens, and evokes these needs and goals.

3. A participatory style is manifested by the self-understanding of "teachers" and "students" as partners in a common learning pilgrimage, by the self-critical and mutually critical questions they are dealing with, and by their willingness to question the whole enterprise.

4. The struggle with issues of justice and diverse participation is fundamental. The leaders realized that they could not find their way from the outset without the participation and perspectives of representatives of diverse races and cultures; they are unwilling to continue without more adequate representation.

5. The participants are willing to face tensions between various fundamental goals which appear to compete or conflict—for instance, feminism vs. Christian identity. They are not satisfied with the pursuit of one issue at the expense of or in indifference to others.

6. The participants face tensions between conscientization and working within "the system," becoming aware of sin and the dangers of imposing agendas and judgment on others.

Weaknesses and Obstacles

1. The location of WTC and the framework of theological education are elitist; that is, they are bound by the limitations of Anglo, middle-class, intellectual, capitalist cultural patterns and power structures. The formation of another elite cadre within this elite structure provides little leverage in the struggle against elitism, poor access to other races and social groups, and questionable credibility as a program for fundamental social and spiritual change.

2. The individual participants in the Study/Action Program are pursuing their own formation in isolation from their colleagues and social systems; the dominant forces and persons in those systems are evidently not engaged in the process of learning. The participants themselves may be further isolated and lose support through the experience.

3. Representatives of marginalized groups are few or totally absent. Those who enter the program may already be alienated from their poeple; the program may alienate them further.

4. The elitism of the ivory tower cannot easily be offset by the action component of the program or by the Resource Center activities. It is difficult to build genuine partnerships between university women and ghetto women. The latter are apparently not included in the learning community. The social systems and values are alien. Ghetto people can feel used or paternalized (maternalized) in that kind of relationship.

5. In this type of situation, white, feminist women run the risk of appearing to judge or presumptuously to educate people of other social groups and cultural patterns. This can delay the cause of feminism.

Possible Ways Forward

1. Attempts to improve the inclusiveness of WTC's coordinating committee, staff, and participants will probably improve its effectiveness, but the center may need to take more radical steps. The locus, base, and framework may have to change or be broadened or complemented by initiatives taken by women who have other locations, bases, and frameworks which can provide new leverage, greater access to people, and more credibility in their own contexts.

2. The isolation of the center, its programs, and the participants from the power centers of theological education and the churches can be offset by relating to existing networks and caucuses and/or establishing new ones. Extensive preparation and follow-up with the participants in their own contexts will help to strengthen their impact on the local systems where they study and work.

3. The elitism of theological education is being challenged increasingly by innovative, alternative patterns that open the doors of training and certification and ministry to people of very diverse backgrounds and experiences and also open the doors of theology and ministry to the contributions of the wider

people of God. This in turn challenges the presuppositions, criteria, patterns, and style of hierarchical, academic education and professional ministry. WTC could play a significant role in those developments.

4. As more and more women assume leadership roles in church and society, will they be able to reshape the mountaintop in a feminine mode (El Shaddai) so that it will be life-giving rather than domineering? Those who ascend the pyramid will have to work with sisters at other "levels" and in other contexts in order to turn the pyramid on its side, in order not to be coopted themselves by the subtle illusions of leadership.

5. How can the critical questions, tensions, and issues of justice be evaluated in theological education? How can institutions and programs where those questions, issues, and tensions do not arise be challenged? Should these concerns be considered within the criteria for accreditation? The natural tendency is toward self-preservation and opposition to radical change.

Components That May Serve in Other Educational Models

1. The pattern of a study year combining an internship with academic work is suitable to most theological education programs. It is an excellent design and could be an option for every theological institution, cluster, and consortium, not only for the pursuit of feminist concerns but also for urban studies, intercultural studies, focus on local and global justice, and so on. It could be utilized at M.Div., M.A., D.Min., and even Ph.D. levels and for sabbaticals and other educational experiences.

2. The combination of a study/action program and a resource center could be applied to an interdisciplinary focus on issues (as in WTC) or to any of the academic fields. Systematic theologians can and do provide resources and services to the churches as they consider such matters as ecumenical consensus on baptism, Eucharist, and ministry; biblical scholars and graduate students can and should work with congregations and base communities in the development of vital and relevant Bible studies; "practical" theologians need to participate in the shaping of counseling, educational, and other ministries. The learning and benefits of this kind of partnership are mutual.

3. Effective theological education requires an ongoing interplay of identity, issues, study, action, and community. WTC manifests an extraordinary intensity of interplay. Every institution and program should attempt to build in those dynamics from the outset, and review them constantly.

JOAN PETRIK, M.M.

Commentary on
Women's Theological Center

In our eleven basic Christian communities in El Salvador, Maryknoll sisters and *campesinos* used a popular rendition of Freire's method of conscientization. It was hardly thorough, but people did become subjects in their struggle for liberation and creators of their communities. After I returned to the United States I reread *Pedagogy of the Oppressed* and that helped me to sharpen many of the convictions that I gained in my work in the basic communities as well as to give me new insights. While working in the First World I have seen Freire's methods bear fruit in the world awareness workshops that I coordinate for members of traditional Christian churches. It is from this background that I respond to the Women's Theological Center (WTC) model.

The overview of the center explains that WTC developed from a need among women for a center of community and learning. It courageously names traditional religious teachings as misogynous and oppressive, and it names the churches as oppressors. WTC is very innovative in departing from the almost wholly academic program of the traditional seminaries and theological centers. Importantly, it maintains a connection between study and action and between faith and social justice. Although it is not mentioned, I hope the connection between consciousness-raising and structural change is also made.

The excellent Study/Action Program is both experiential and participatory. It is organized around the experience of the participants with both action and reflection on key issues relevant to social change and women's experience. It has three components: (1) a seminar on feminist theology and theory that explores their challenge to traditional theology and religious practice; (2) a field-based critical action program in local social-change agencies that is designed to develop skills in social analysis and critical action/reflection; and (3) a program in feminist spirituality and praxis that uses story, symbol, ritual, and myth to aid participants in understanding and integrating the personal, political, and religious dimensions of their life and work.

Being both experiential and participatory, the content of WTC's programs appears to be shaped in large part by the students and so cannot help but be owned by them. I feel, however, that the program lacks a clear direction toward structural change. The more local situations selected for critical action and reflection need to be understood in the setting of global structures and systems. We need to uncover the root causes of the oppression, causes that exist in unjust structures and systems. Then we can move outward toward structural and systemic change.

In my experience, as the illiterate *campesinos* of El Salvador searched into the root causes of their oppression, they discovered that the structures held their oppressors, although differently, just as enchained as they were. The structures dehumanized both oppressor and oppressed. The *campesinos* then came to understand and be sympathetic to their oppressors. "They are caught, too," they said. Then they understood structural change to be even more necessary. But they also recognized that they, the oppressed, had all the possibilities for the clearer vision and, therefore, the greater responsibility to lead the struggle for change, the struggle that would bring about humanization of all.

As we move into the model, Sarah and Kate are struggling with the problem of broadening the constituency of WTC so that "more diverse stories can be heard." They choose to strategize and reflect around the goal of greater racial inclusivity without clarifying why they chose it over striving for greater diversity of economic class. It would seem that there would be more dissimilarity between the poor and the middle class than between middle-class whites and middle-class people of color. However, the WTC structures make it difficult to include the poor for more in-depth contact.

Already there is a tremendous diversity among the twelve women in the program: there are lesbians, heterosexuals, and celibates; ages range from fifty down to the early twenties; there are women of different religions and nationalities. Sarah is black and there is a woman from Haiti. That and the fact that the center is located in Boston, which has a fairly large black population, probably help to explain why as Sarah and Kate discuss the need for racial diversity, they return several times to specify black women as the target. Confronting white women's racism seems to be a key issue. The question is not only whether black women will want to come to the center to aid the white women in cleansing themselves, but it is also whether that process can take place in the setting of the center. I believe that the oppressors can only reconcile themselves by entering into solidarity with the oppressed, by taking upon themselves the best interests of the oppressed, and that this needs to take place in the territory of the oppressed.

Diversity is important to the women at the center "so that diverse stories will be heard," so that they can "learn to respond to one another" and "to honor and affirm the interrelatedness of all creations," and because "what we learn is dependent upon whom we learn it with." Diversity is vital for them because the experience of the participants "shapes" the content of their learning. But how these experiences are actually used in the learning process is not explained to us. There is much reference to the students' questioning and to formulating some all-inclusive collective questions. But to what does the questioning lead? Is it to the recognition of similarities and differences? To the bonding of women? To the change of structures? We also do not know for whom the question is posed, whether it be for all women, for the churches, or for only the women at the center. Is the question existential? Is it meant to be responded to in the concrete?

I believe that the women's experiences both in the past and in the present at WTC should not only shape the content of their learning experiences but should *be* that content. I believe that there needs to be reflection upon that content and an analysis that is guided by the directors. There needs to be an articulation of clear, concrete questions that lead to better understanding and awareness of our oppression, the internalized oppression of the non-poor. These should be questions that lead to critical action to break free of the oppression, to an understanding of oppression's root causes and structures, and to the creation of alternative structures. That reflection should lead especially to the participants' engagement in the struggle for liberation. Freire says in his first chapter of *Pedagogy of the Oppressed* that that struggle makes and remakes the pedagogy. He says that the struggle is the pedagogy and the pedagogy is the struggle. It is in the struggle that we, like the *campesinos* of El Salvador, discover that both oppressed and oppressors are dehumanized. However, it is the oppressed who "from their stifled humanity" must wage the bulk of the struggle for a fuller humanity for both.

The middle-class women at WTC are oppressed, but they are also oppressors of their economically poor sisters. The oppressors usually rationalize their guilt through paternalistic treatment, keeping their poor sisters and brothers dependent. But the struggle must be waged from the situation of the poor. Solidarity requires our entering into the situation with them. It does not sound to me that the field work in the WTC model allows for that kind of depth. I wonder if the Resource Center could not be restructured to provide the field work. Then, keeping in mind that the struggle is the pedagogy, I would restructure the Study/Action Program and reverse the time frame so that ten hours per week are given to theologizing on the experience of the conscienticizing work among the poor. Andrea could not avoid the challenge of others, and that challenge will probably help her to articulate who and where she is, for the struggle is the pedagogy. Participants may not get full academic credit from other seminaries; changes are not coming that fast. Henri Nouwen says that ministry is entering with our human brokenness into communion with others, and Freire says that the foundations of dialogue are profound love, profound humility, profound faith, profound hope, and critical thinking. There is no better way to practice spirituality. And Jesus gave us his example. We are not going to break into the power structures, but we can create new structures that will eventually "overcome"—structures shaped in solidarity with and from the turf of the stifled humanity of the poor.

CHAPTER 6

THE CHRYSALIS PROGRAM

The Chrysalis model claims attention because it attempts to develop a new approach to education for transformation within the institutional pattern of theological education in North America. The case reports a creative effort to bring three Third World scholars into a seminary and use them in academic courses and clusters of local churches to bring about greater awareness of global issues. The case illustrates the difficulties in the social context within which theological education and church life exist, and provides stimulating insights into how those factors affect formal educational efforts toward peace and justice. The model raises troubling questions about the problems faced by religious institutions in First World societies as those institutions try to develop leaders with critical consciousness about global political and economic problems.

By building on a strategy of bringing into these structures of higher professional education a core of scholars from the Third World, this model reverses the approach of travel seminars (chapter 7), and leads to a comparison of the two methods in regard to cost and effectiveness. The complexities of relating the Chrysalis Program to local churches add another valuable dimension to this case.

All those who look to religious organizations for guidance in working toward peace and justice will find provocative issues discussed in this case. It will be particularly challenging to theological educators in the United States and Canada who are concerned about globalization of theological education.

Program Overview

The Chrysalis Program provides one-semester and two-semester advanced, intercultural study opportunities for selected pastors, church executives, and theological students who wish to strengthen their understanding of North-South justice/development issues by struggling with these questions: What kinds of issues, lifestyles, programs, and institutions are necessary to create a more just international system? What roles can and should North American churches play in achieving those new possibilities?

The Chrysalis Program began in 1981. The basic purpose of the program is to generate in and through the churches a greater capacity to deal with worldwide hunger issues and the more deep-seated and complex economic, political, and intercultural issues of which hunger is symptomatic. The core resource persons for the entire program are three resident scholars in development and theology who come from Africa, Asia, and Latin America. Chrysalis students complete most of their studies under these scholars and may work toward the Master of Sacred Theology (S.T.M.), Master of Arts in Religious Studies (M.A.R.S.), or Doctor of Ministry (D.Min.) degree, depending on their previous academic and church experience. Nondegree study in Chrysalis is also possible.

In addition to academic studies, Chrysalis students give leadership to ecumenical clusters of local congregations in the elaboration of grass-roots study/action programs on hunger-justice issues. Hunger is used as an entry point for understanding the dynamics of North-South problems. By the second year of the program twenty-two local parishes were partners in this aspect of Chrysalis. Chrysalis also sponsors a variety of short-term seminars for clergy, university and seminary faculty, denominational leadership groups, and other interested parties, and conducts two- to three-week study tours to India. A tour to Central America may be added in the near future.

Chrysalis is administered by the Christian Theological Seminary, under the direction of the Chrysalis Steering Committee, an interdenominational group. The director of Chrysalis is Dr. Richard D.N. Dickinson, Christian Theological Seminary dean and vice-president. Mr. Thomas Hunsdorfer is associate director.

Funding for Chrysalis is provided by the following denominations, ecumenical bodies, and foundations: Christian Church (Disciples of Christ), Church World Service, Cummins Engine Foundation, Gemmer Foundation, Maryknoll Fathers and Brothers, Reformed Church of America, United Church of Christ, United Methodist Church, Presbyterian Church (USA), Episcopal Church, Moravian Church, World Council of Churches.

For further information, contact Chrysalis; Christian Theological Seminary; 1000 W. 42nd Street; Indianapolis, IN 46208; phone: (317) 924–1331.

Case Study
The Chrysalis Program

Memo:

TO: Members of the Chrysalis Steering Committee, Christian Theological Seminary
FROM: Richard D.N. Dickinson, Dean and Director of the Chrysalis Program
SUBJECT: Review of Chrysalis Program and Recommendations to the Board

The board of directors has assigned to the Chrysalis Steering Committee the task of reviewing the Chrysalis Program after two years' experience and is expecting a report and recommendations at its next meeting regarding both the coming year of Chrysalis's operation and its long-range prospects.

As we were unable to have a meeting of the steering committee while the key program participants were available, we held a meeting of those key persons and taped the discussion. Attached is my edited transcript of that discussion. I choose to give it to you in this form because it seems to me to raise the basic questions you need to face and also to communicate to you something of the spirit of those taking part in Chrysalis.

Here is the list of participants in the meeting: Father Theo Mathias, a Jesuit college principal from India and one of the visiting scholars; Winnie Petty, lay leader and member of a cluster group, from the First Congregational Church, United Church of Christ, Indianapolis; Pat Cameron, intern student in the program for two years; Tom Hunsdorfer, associate director of the program; and myself.

May I remind you of the meeting of your committee on September 19. In the two hours before the board meeting opens with a luncheon we must arrive at recommendations for the total board.

As I see it, we shall need to address these questions: 1. During this academic year and the next (the final two years of the program in its experimental phase), what changes would we propose and why? 2. What long-range recommendations shall we make about the future of the program, and what implications

---

This case was prepared from a transcript and edited by William Bean Kennedy, Thomas Hunsdorfer, and Richard D.N. Dickinson as a basis for discussion rather than to illustrate either effective or ineffective handling of the situation.

might that recommendation have for the program and the action of the board during the next two years?

I hope that you will reflect carefully on the issues raised in this transcript and come to the meeting prepared for the discussion.

DISCUSSION OF THE CHRYSALIS PROGRAM
BY SOME KEY PARTICIPANTS

RICHARD (DICK): Chrysalis grew out of our assessment of global justice issues and how the United States is involved in either promoting or inhibiting justice in the Third World. Most church efforts in the past have focused on problems as seen in so-called Third World environments. Little attention has been given to how U.S. policies and institutions affect the prospects for global justice. In this program we have tried to say that the problem is not only out there, but is also in how U.S. policies and institutions affect nations. This is often through the World Bank and the International Monetary Fund or through U.S. aid policies. We have said also that our program should focus upon the life of the church, where our seminary can have the most significant influence. We believe that theological education, in order to be effective in preparing people for leadership in the churches, must itself understand mission in its larger context of promoting social justice. On a more practical level, we believe that if we can arouse consciousness in the churches about these issues, the churches themselves and individual Christians working through the churches can influence U.S. public policies and institutions.

We felt that we could help promote social justice by having in residence at the seminary spokespersons from so-called Third World environments to help us understand more deeply how North American churches are implicated in the lack of development and the lack of liberation in the poorer countries of the world. Many scholars in North America know a lot about Third World situations, but they haven't experienced them as fundamentally as have churchpersons who have grown up in those environments. We wanted to have Third World scholars in residence to help us see ourselves as we are actually perceived in other countries. We have put the Third World scholars at the center of our action and vision, and hoped that through them we would be able to train twenty-five to thirty-five younger persons for leadership among the churches in issues of global justice. These students, usually working on S.T.M. degrees in the academic program, have been involved in clusters of five or six churches where they have been able to try out ideas and strategies for impacting local congregations.

Those have been the main components of our program, although we've also had a number of short-term seminars and other events.

In retrospect, we've had relatively few full-time students, only seven to ten officially enrolled in the Chrysalis Program each year, and an equal number of part-time students. We've had very good success in attracting significant Third

World scholars. The programs in the clusters of churches have raised many questions. We've had a number of seminars, most of which have gone well, but there haven't been as many seminars as we had originally envisioned. Those are the programmatic elements. Tom, why have we been unable to attract more full-time students?

TOM: I see at least three reasons: First, the mundane but constant reason is money. For people to come from wherever in the U.S. or from other countries to Indianapolis for ten months is a significant sacrifice. It means students must give up a job and get money to support themselves while they are here. Our inability to offer more scholarship help is certainly one reason. Second, at a deeper level I think that the perception of need for something like Chrysalis here in the U.S. is not that great. Persons who have come are very unusual in their backgrounds and types of ministry. Third, perhaps another reason is the fact that this is an experimental program. Publicity went out in fits and starts, and those who knew about it weren't able to get word about it out into their networks. Perhaps in two or three years there'll be lots of information out about the Chrysalis Program, but it was not as well-known initially as it might have been.

I guess I still don't understand why more persons did not apply. Pat, maybe you can shed some light on this as one who did apply.

PAT: I was finishing my Master of Divinity degree at another seminary and had been pushing all the way through for more of my theological education to be focused on the kinds of concerns that Chrysalis raised. When I heard about the program, it sounded like exactly what I'd been looking for. I'm just surprised that there aren't more students free to pack up and willing to come to the program.

TOM: I repeatedly heard from people from Asia, Africa, and Latin America about how important an idea they thought this was. This was the only seminary program in the U.S. they had heard of that really addressed the needs they face in churches in their own countries. But somehow that was not the case for recent U.S. seminary graduates. They didn't quite know what to do with it. I think that was reflected to a certain extent here at CTS. Many of the M. Div. students here couldn't quite grasp why we were doing this or what persons like Theo were doing here.

DICK: After two years a number of people still think of this Chrysalis effort as directed primarily toward persons from the so-called Third World. They wonder why we don't get more Third World students here. We have been trying all along to say, "This is addressed to North American church leadership," but somehow we haven't been able to get that understood. I guess people are still imprisoned in the analysis that the problems are out there and that we can deal with them by helping the people out there.

Tom: Perhaps the reason it was hard to get large numbers is precisely the reason the program was needed—there is very little perception of our involvement and even complicity in some of the global issues, or awareness that change needs to happen within the U.S.

Winnie: I think we should also address some of the issues facing the clusters of congregations in the program. A minister can have much more influence than an ordinary church member who serves as a representative of the cluster. In the clusters we were frustrated by the inconsistent participation of congregational representatives. We didn't have the same people attending the meetings. Maybe the meetings weren't regular enough. We would also like to have had more contact with the Third World resource persons and with the seminary students. In my church, looking back over the last couple of years, it seems as if we just didn't get anywhere; and yet looking at it again, I feel that we did make a good deal of progress in education. The working together of our Christian education committee and our committee on church and society has made people more aware of conditions in the underdeveloped countries. I didn't think, for example, that we would ever have a Bread for the World contact, but now we have permission to go ahead with that. Considering our church, I think that's a big step. I think that the unique quality of Chrysalis demands that it be continued and developed.

Dick: When we started this program, we thought we would have maybe twenty interns, four or five working in each cluster. As it turned out, there were only two in each cluster, one from the U.S. and one from overseas. In light of our inability to attract students, is it your impression that having a cluster of four to six congregations is simply too big an enterprise? Maybe that many can't work together immediately if they haven't been working together before.

Winnie: It would have been easier if the churches had been used to working together. I don't know whether having more resource persons would make much difference.

Dick: Theo, after the first year, you wanted us to change the pattern and work more with individual churches, because you thought that would have a greater payoff than trying to work with the cluster.

Theo: Yes, I still am of that opinion. One of the purposes for bringing a number of churches together was the very laudable goal of fostering ecumenical action. But that was subsidiary to the major purpose of sensitizing people to First and Third World problems and to justice issues. I thought going through representatives to the churches, hoping that they would then have some influence upon their congregations, was not the best way. My impression was that not much has been done by the representatives, though they are good people, really concerned about these problems, and they wanted to educate and improve themselves.

Whether this is going to have some long-term effect, I don't know. I think that the clusters should have insisted on working through the pastors for contact with the entire congregation.

DICK: In congregations where that contact did take place, like the Fairview Presbyterian Church, there was a very active program. In large part I think it was because the pastor and his wife were integrally involved in the Chrysalis Program right from the beginning.

THEO: Where a representative was sufficiently influential to get one of the scholars or full-time students in touch with the whole congregation, I think more good resulted.

TOM: This situation is a microcosm of some of the global concerns and power structures and of the problem of empowerment. Where certain key individuals were willing to assert themselves in their own churches, saying "We need to get this kind of program going," or "I think we should be a Bread for the World covenant church," things did happen, especially when the pastor was on board. But where people for whatever reasons felt they didn't have permission to do some of those things in their churches, they held back, and if the pastor was lukewarm, nothing happened.

WINNIE: Many of the representatives did educate themselves. I'm thinking particularly of the three-week study tour, led by Theo, which we took to India and which changed my life. And in showing my pictures and talking about the trip, I've made quite a few contacts with other concerned people in our area.

TOM: This raises for me another very important concern, which has to do with where we are in relation to the poor in our own communities. You mentioned, Winnie, that the experience in India was a transforming one for you. It was the same for me. I think the churches in inner-city Indianapolis, which are closer to the problems of poverty here, got going much more rapidly and in some ways with a better understanding of some of the concerns than did churches farther out in the suburbs that may be further removed from local problems of poverty. Is it valid to be looking at global poverty concerns in India or Ghana if we are not involved with the poverty problem and justice issues here in our own city? Pat, you were working in the inner city.

PAT: Yes, I had a very good experience last year and felt good about what our cluster was able to do. All of our churches had been involved in local hunger and justice issues and all the representatives in our cluster came out of that context and with those concerns. The information we were presenting, with speakers coming in, was really keying in to where people were. They could link global justice issues and local issues. We didn't have to fight the battles that we had fought the year before, of trying to convince people that the U.S. did have a responsibility to look at its own policies. This was an assumption built into the group out of their previous experience. So that previous experience with local justice issues helped greatly.

Another factor is that we met with all of the pastors early in the term to plug them in to the program and plan with them how they wanted to see the Chrysalis Program take effect in their congregations. As a result we had four out of the five congregations in our cluster with very ambitious programs. They brought in speakers and had educational awareness programs as well as programs of action within the local congregations.

DICK: From the beginning I wanted to keep the program flexible. I didn't want to put a blueprint program on the clusters. I wanted it to evolve out of their life and concerns and commitments. Perhaps more guidance should have been given to the clusters, so that people who had never worked together before could at least have some clues about how they ought to proceed. I hoped each church would move from hunger to systemic questions, that hunger would be a way of opening the door to the larger questions of systemic injustices. I had a hope that there would be an action/reflection component in all of the programs, that people would not only be learning about the problems of hunger, but would also be doing something practical in the local community so that there would be an interaction between action and reflection. I had hoped that there would be some visible connection between the global issues and the local issues, and people would say, "This is the way that issues of global injustice look on our local scene." But I didn't give sufficient direction to the interns and to the pastors about what kinds of opportunities they might make available to their people.

WINNIE: I suppose that's true. Maybe we didn't know what was expected of us at first. It depends a lot on which persons in the congregation, I guess, are asked to volunteer to be representatives and the concerns of those persons. Maybe we did need more instructions.

THEO: What influence was being exerted here at the seminary? We had only a small number of full-time students attending the Chrysalis Program, and that was very disappointing, because developing the full-time program was our main objective. But there's also the generalized sort of impact that persons living on the premises can have upon the entire seminary community. Furthermore, over the two years that I've been here I think I have dealt on a classroom basis with 120 different people. That may not be a large number, but it is a significant number when you consider that many of them were pastors. The impact of a pastor on his or her congregation as a result of this sensitization I think is incalculable. Those pastors who repeatedly exposed their people to the thinking of the Third World scholars had an enormous impact by bringing these matters to the knowledge of their congregations. In summer courses we had people who wanted in a concentrated dosage the same sort of information.

The importance of these courses should not be downplayed. Most of our students and the pastors wouldn't have come if they had not really been concerned about these problems.

What impact did we have upon the seminary community? I think little. Or at least I should say, not enough. My impression of the regular seminary students who came and took an odd course was that for them it was just another course and they needed three credits so they signed up for it! They saw there would be three somewhat interesting people giving the course instead of the same old professors. But there was not the same motivation. The highly motivated were the full-time Chrysalis students and the older people, the pastors.

Apart from these regular courses, what impact did we have? I think, really, not much. We developed a certain number of friendships, and talked, but this was on a sort of social basis. There were very few invitations from student groups to participate in their meetings. They appreciated our comments at the beginning of the year, but we didn't attract a large number of students. Something here in the family needs to be looked into. Why is it that a seminary consisting of liberal-minded people is not more interested? One would expect them to be open to these problems and issues. Maybe they don't want to get into these problems. They have more energy or inclination for everything else.

Tom: I think you really raise an important point. The Third World scholars helped sensitize me during the first year to both the cultural insularity in general, and specifically as it is manifested at the seminary, and also to the class structure in the churches in this country. Unless you've had a strong sociology background, you're not sufficiently aware of the class barriers between poor churches and middle- or upper-class churches here. Those cultural and class biases are manifested in the student body. But I think the cultural insularity, a general lack of interest, is a real factor.

Pat: How do you convince students and ministers at the seminary that these kinds of concerns are every bit as much a part of the task of ministry as counseling, or preaching, and are not peripheral concerns that you take as an elective?

Dick: If only M. P. Joseph were here! He was a full-time student from India who works a lot with people's movements there and is committed to that. He pretty much came to the conclusion that it is impossible for middle-class, "bourgeois" institutions like CTS and most of the churches to have any effective influence on changing people's attitudes or making any significant contributions to global justice. Whether he did that from ideological grounds or whether he did it on the basis of despair over his experience here, he always confronted us with this question. Is it possible to conscientize the relatively rich, the "non-poor," as the Plowshares people say? Is it possible to conscientize them without engagement with the poor in the context of the poor's own struggle? We haven't been able to address that question adequately in our program.

PAT: We have a parallel situation in our churches with the representatives. It's so difficult to make a dent in members of the congregation, to put these ideas across.

TOM: Winnie, I think your comments about the India study tour and how that changed you are very important. I have often thought that if money were no object, that if you were going to re-create the Chrysalis Program, it might very well include a semester in a seminary in India, Ghana, or Indonesia. This would be an immersion in a different culture, in a different context. Or perhaps there could be a component with the poor in Indianapolis or Chicago. Our distance from the realities is a big obstacle.

DICK: I think this immersion is a very important key in the whole conscientization process. Obviously for lack of money and for lack of a lot of other things, like the capacity of people in poor situations to receive hordes of visitors, it has major problems. But beyond that, I think the immersion ought to take place in communities of people that are going to continue to work together beyond a particular experience. I wanted to have a core group of people, not just individuals in a cluster, but a core group who would have been in the Chrysalis Program for a year, who had common associations, common experiences; who could mutually reinforce one another's ministries in social justice in the years following seminary. With only six or seven full-time people we haven't been able to develop that group of people who can consistently rely upon one another for mutual growth. The immersion experience is good, but how do you get that kind of experience for a sufficiently large group of people who are going to continue to work together, who will reinforce one another's commitments? On our next trip to India we want to have three or four or five seminary professors from here along with us, so that when they come back they'll all have had a common experience and can reinforce and revitalize flagging zeal on these issues.

THEO: The one seminary professor who attended recently told me that the India experience has transformed his outlook.

PAT: The people who went on that tour have spread out to all parts of the U.S. That may be a minus for the seminary, because although they are still interested and are influencing others, they can't give immediate support here.

DICK: The more I work in issues of global justice, the more I'm convinced that we all need continual sustenance and sustaining of the Spirit, and that comes for me primarily through people of similar commitments who try to work out of their understanding of the gospel in certain visible commitments to social justice, to the poor. A lot of people are struggling as individuals and don't feel the support of others who have had similar experiences or who have a similar faith. Theo, you work in the Jesuit community and probably have more of that than most Protestants. I would like to know that each year there would be two or three or four professors who would say this is one of our primary commitments in theological education and ask how can we support each other to achieve or realize those objectives. I recently raised this question in one of my essays; it's entitled "Spirituality for Combat" because it is a constant combat. How do people sense the reinforcing confirmation of other people with similar faith? That's what I'm trying to say about this group of people I had hoped to attract to the Chrysalis Program as interns. It's what I'm saying now about the immersion experience.

THEO: Chrysalis also has a spillover effect beyond its influence upon the seminary community, students of theology, and pastors and parishioners. All the scholars were invited to various colleges, seminaries, church groups. In my two years I have spoken a total of two hundred times. I've been to a dozen universities and to church groups of all kinds, small and large. And all on the same issue, justice. Often I would speak in a spiritual way, of hunger for God and search for justice, about how good churchpeople who want to get close to God cannot do so unless they are also concerned about justice. And justice not only in your community but in the whole world. Recently after I spoke to a group of corporation executives, one of them told me, "We never hear this point of view expressed anywhere in our country. Whatever we read, whatever our pastors say, whatever we discuss among ourselves, we assume that we are in the right, and that everybody else is wrong. It's a good thing that for the first time we have heard someone coming in exposing us to a totally different point of view."

TOM: One of the exciting parts of the Chrysalis concept is the reversal of the historic mission direction of the European and North American churches going out to Asia, Africa, and Latin America. Now we are having leaders and teachers coming from those areas of the world to teach us and help sensitize us. Do you feel that should be a permanent element at the heart of theological education?

THEO: It would be an extremely good thing if seminaries had available to them, at least on a part-time basis, well-educated persons from the Third World. Liberation theology is something to which every student of theology in Europe and North America should be exposed, but this can be done effectively only by someone who believes in it, a person from Latin America, Africa, or Asia.

DICK: Obviously our Chrysalis Program is different from asking a single professor to come and teach a course. We have tried to build a community of persons both at the student level and at the professorial level, a community of persons who could deal together with these issues. But it's been enormously expensive to bring three people from overseas.

THEO: It is a much better program for having three people, because no single person could give a class the different perspectives that come from three continents. Secondly, each one of the three has benefited enormously from the insights of the others. You produced three people who had to develop their experience here and who return home considerably enriched. I can't tell you the extent of my enrichment as a result of these intimate contacts with colleagues from Latin America and Africa, none of whom I had previously met.

DICK: The Latin Americans have told us that they are very much needed now in their own countries, and that it is a large sacrifice for them to be coming here. Isn't there some other way for North Americans to be sensitized? they ask, since they need to be staying home.

THEO: To bring them in for short periods would be less effective, because there would be much less interaction. If you could make provision for these scholars to be busy with other things to a greater degree, other lectures and seminars, it might be more profitable. They could then use their time more effectively and be of benefit to a larger number of people.

DICK: One thing we didn't think of before the program started, but has become increasingly important in my reflection about what we've done, is your involvement, Theo, as a parish priest in Nashville and Indianapolis, and what you've been able to do with those parishes by your monthly presence.

THEO: Three weekends every two months I had Masses for them, preached, and married.

DICK: In a similar way some of the students from overseas have been involved in parishes here on a sustained basis. Their weekly presence and constant participation in the cluster churches gave a reality to what we are all about that maybe didn't come through the formal channels of representatives of the cluster, but which came nevertheless very deeply into the life of that church.

TOM: Chrysalis has been an important part of the experience of all of us and for many other people from our background—all of whom we might be able to characterize as middle- or upper-class individuals. What about results for the poor? In what ways did we get at unjust structures? What tangible or intangible benefits were there for other people? Are there likely to be any?

WINNIE: We had some education about food usage and food dispensers for the poor, and as a result we have a few people who are doing some volunteer work who might not have been doing it otherwise, but I don't know that there are any tangible benefits as a result of our spearheading anything. It has been primarily educational, and consciousness-raising, and maybe there has been some more involvement of a few people in action on issues of justice and hunger.

PAT: The only tangible thing that resulted in our church was the decision to send a sum of money to the Heifer Project in Jamaica, but again that is on a level of charity, sending money over. Although the project is very worthwhile and had an impact on poor people, it won't have a long-term impact.

TOM: One of the first-year students is now working in Florida at a multiracial church, working with refugees, very involved in the justice concerns of the low-income community there.

PAT: We tried a food pantry in a Lutheran church in our cluster.

THEO: Chrysalis was not an action-oriented project. Its first service was not to get these things started and growing. It is an educational program. It was designed to have long-term action effects. To ask to what extent we have produced short-term positive tangible effects might not be fair.

TOM: The key question of the program that some would raise is: What model of education and change was going on? Was it education first, and then action? Or was it our being involved in some action, and then to reflect upon that?

WINNIE: People have to be approached through a direct action project before they can see the results over a longer period of time.

PAT: I think the model that we used was reflection and then action—well, we hoped there would be action. I don't know how we turn that around unless we precisely define what the program is going to do, which is more than we wanted to do. To determine ahead of time what actions the clusters were going to take would in some sense violate the program, but on the other hand if the first step of the clusters was to engage in action, then that would involve them in a context out of which they could reflect on what was happening to them.

DICK: It has to be dialogical, doesn't it? For example, was the raising of money for the Heifer Project used as an educational device, to help people to see both the necessity but also the inadequacy of raising money, to help people come to a greater appreciation of systemic issues of justice?

PAT: In my cluster that connection wasn't made. The education about the complexities of the problem went far beyond the response that came forth in the Heifer Project. Probably the main motivation for that project was that near the end of the year people were frustrated because they hadn't done anything, and this was something they could do and carry to the churches. Some hunger education went on in all the churches as a result, but it was nowhere near the degree of education that the cluster representatives had in reading Jack Nelson's *Hunger for Justice* (Maryknoll, N.Y., Orbis Books, 1980), for example.

DICK: Would it be better, then, to start the whole Chrysalis Program by saying to each cluster church in that component of the program: "This is what we expect you to do," and then use that as a basis for moving on to the broader spectrum of issues?

WINNIE: In our church financial contributions to a public health nursing program grew out of the education first. It was a spontaneous result of education, with action as the result. Partly it was because it was a women's project, and we were particularly interested in women's issues.

PAT: We were talking earlier about exposure experiences in India. Maybe we could set up a weekend-long local experience to help people come in contact firsthand with some of the problems of poverty in Indianapolis and make connections with what's going on in the rest of the world, rather than defining for them what action they are to take. I think a desire and a commitment to action would grow out of that kind of experience.

DICK: Do you think starting with the question of hunger was a good thing? The reason we did it was that people seemed to be willing to grab hold of it, would see it as a problem, and by using hunger we could get into the more systemic questions. I was always afraid to use hunger that way, because first of all I thought we might never get beyond hunger. I was afraid also that the traditional understanding of why there is hunger in the world would preclude people being able to move toward more serious analysis of why there is hunger. Most North Americans perceive it as a problem of production, or of overpopulation, or maybe of distribution. Usually we assume that if there is enough produced, it will get distributed.

WINNIE: I understand why you started that way, but in non-poor churches there's no hunger and no immediate feel for it.

PAT: I think the premise was right. With the larger church population I think the hunger issue has had more receptivity over the years. There is a more natural sympathy for starting there than if we had started with the arms race or U.S. foreign aid. I think it would have limited the audience by starting with another issue.

DICK: Another question: Was it dysfunctional to let people get off the hook easily by giving some money to the Heifer Project? Is it tactically good to let people give money to a project as a part of what we're after in this whole thing? If you do use money, to give to a project, what cautions do you have to build in?

What procedures are needed to keep it from becoming the end-all of what you are aiming at?

PAT: I hadn't thought of that. It might be a good idea for the program in the future to determine that clusters are not to give money.

DICK: But don't you have to let people make whatever expression they can, and then discover ways to move beyond that partial response?

THEO: You confirm the easily accepted thing among well-off Americans—to throw money at a problem!

WINNIE: But in the case of Bread for the World, there will have to be follow-up actions to influence legislation and other responses that will require other things than just giving money. It's another kind of commitment, and we're counting on that for future education.

DICK: I heard recently about a denomination experimenting with how middle- and upper-class women could work with economically lower-class women, to help people with single-parent households, for example. Three or four women from the so-called upper class would work with a poor woman, and could do anything they wanted except give money. They could try to work with the structures of the community, with the agencies that exist; they could give time to that person in counseling and comradeship, but the one thing that they could not do was to give them something of a material sort.

PAT: I think that's the reason that program has been so fruitful, not only for the low-income person, but for the church volunteers, that they are prohibited from getting rid of the problem by throwing money at it. It has forced them to experience the oppression of the system and in turn has raised the consciousness of those people. They have gone beyond just working with that individual. They have gone on to try to change the system.

DICK: Would that work with the Chrysalis Program, to forbid giving any material aid?

TOM: I think perhaps a different version of that kind of a personal relationship would be important, perhaps a parish in Indianapolis and a parish in Ghana or in Thailand would begin a long-term personal relationship that might include an exchange of people and a dialogical way of getting to know each other. Repeatedly we heard of people who were getting too much information, that we had plenty of information about a problem, but that somehow there wasn't the personal touch that could transform. The people who got to know our Third World resource persons approached global justice issues with a more visceral sense because they knew the person.

Dick: Seminaries could exchange some students and professors for at least a semester. We've been trying unsuccessfully here at the seminary to get half of the faculty to take their sabbaticals in the Third World rather than going to the universities of England or Germany. That's a very hard thing to do, because that's the way our typical understanding of sabbatical is, that you go to the great centers of learning. But in my mind a great center of learning is a situation in India, in one of the seminaries there, for example.

Winnie: A woman in our church taught in Africa for a year, twenty-five years ago. That influence has been manifested ever since in our church.

Pat: I understand some universities and seminaries require a trimester or semester in a Third World environment as part of the curriculum. Before you can be a minister, you must have spent at least six months in a Third World setting. Is there a possibility of instituting that here at CTS? The Goshen College undergraduate program has something like that. Several of their students have gone to China. Their ties with the Mennonite Central Committee give them networks all over the world through which they can develop programs like that.

Dick: In any of the clusters were there concerted efforts to try to influence public policy, writing campaigns, other efforts to influence legislation?

Tom: There were several. After hearing from one of our Bread for the World contact people, one congregation generated about seventy letters.

Dick: Were the clusters able to get people to subscribe to *IMPACT* or to other regular information and action newsletters?

Winnie: There may have been some of that, but more likely individuals subscribed, not churches.

Theo: How can the Third World scholars be more fruitfully used? Is it possible for them to hold a seminar for the faculty? We had a very useful seminar for the clergy. Can't we do something with the faculty? Or is it possible for us to hold a seminar for the students? Maybe by groups?

Winnie: That seems elementary, when you think about it.

Theo: We do it for all sorts of other people, but not for our own people here.

Dick: What about shorter courses, for three weeks, two or three times during the year, as our Latin American colleague suggested?

THEO: I don't know that students can take it in such a concentrated course. They need time to reflect upon these things. The personal relationships over a period of time are also an important ingredient.

WINNIE: Perhaps our Latin American colleague should be training people to take their places at home. Ask them what they are doing at home to provide leadership to take their places.

DICK: It could be just as economical to have a person paid on a consultant daily basis, and come more frequently. Or several seminaries could go together and share the costs of travel. That might be more feasible than coming for ten days and rushing back.

TOM: What about the issue of community? Could we build a very closely-knit group of people who are really supporting each other, who are doing Bible study together, who perhaps live together? There are a lot of different ways of approaching that, but it's one of the reasons why I am ambivalent about CTS and Indianapolis as a location for this type of program, because it is hard to establish community here. Many of the students are commuters, who scatter right after class. The Chrysalis people were almost a breed apart. We may need either a different institution or much more planning for how a real community could develop. People from overseas often comment about how apart from each other we are. It's a cultural comment, that families are apart. The Africans always are mentioning that. They just can't believe how separated families are here, how we are all just scattered. We are all so busy doing things that we don't have time to sit and talk with each other. Enrique Dussel, one of our Latin American visiting scholars, told us about his own involvement in a base Christian community, how they studied together intensely for five years, working on readings of Marx and some other things. There was longevity in their covenanting with each other. Dick has talked about what a lonely, draining struggle it can be for those of us who are involved in the global justice struggle; perhaps more than the need for more information about the issues, we need that kind of nurture of each other.

DICK: That surely hasn't happened in our program, in any major way.

PAT: No, it hasn't. There was more of it the first year, I think, but that was sort of accidental. The personalities seemed to mesh together, and there was time, and there were a few people who'd take the initiative to call us together and have a dinner or a party or whatever.

TOM: One of the complaints of our overseas people was that they were speaking to so many old people in our churches, and they asked what were we doing with our youth. One of the campus ministers at the University of Indiana in Bloomington wants Chrysalis more involved with campus ministries.

DICK: The presence of overseas scholars has made our faculty colleagues a lot more aware of bibliographic resources and theology as they are evolving from Third World environments. If you go to the bookstore and look at the syllabi, you see there is increasing attention to non–North American and non–European resources for use in the regular courses.

WINNIE: I think people in the clusters took advantage of the bookstore here, which they would not have done otherwise.

THEO: My two years have been extremely fruitful for me personally, and I think for a huge number of others, to such an extent that I admit a desire to continue on here in the program.

PAT: Two years ago I didn't think about things; I didn't read the newspapers about what was happening or ask how an article or issue might be read from a Latin American or an African perspective. I've begun to do that. I assume that what I'm reading is from a limited perspective. It's hard to explain, but it's a different kind of consciousness I bring to the issues. I'm glad I came because of the community of scholars and students from overseas that had never been a part of my experience before. I hold that up as a more important component of the program than anything we've covered in the way of content.

Teaching Note

TOPICS AND QUESTIONS FOR DISCUSSION

1. The Chrysalis Program did not set a pre-established agenda for program participants. What are the advantages of this approach? The limitations? How could a stronger action component be built into the program without imposing specific goals for participants?

2. The steering committee intentionally focused the program on the issue of hunger, using it as an entry point for understanding and becoming involved in more complex, underlying justice issues. Discuss the committee's rationale. What are the strengths and weaknesses of this approach?

3. What does "solidarity with the poor" mean? What are the various approaches program participants took to develop this kind of solidarity in middle-class churches in the community? Which approaches seemed most effective? Why? Discuss whether or not it is appropriate for churches in First World nations to be involved with justice issues in other parts of the world if they are not also involved with the poor and oppressed within their own communities.

4. Consider the two primary questions which were on the steering committee agenda: (1) "During this academic year and the next (the final two years of the program in its experimental phase), what changes would we propose and why?" and (2) "What long-range recommendation shall we make about the future of the program, and what implications might that recommendation have for the program and the action of the board during the next two years?"

5. In some ways the basic thrust of this program reverses the approach taken by travel seminars in developing awareness of and response to global issues. It may be helpful to study this model in comparison with the "Traveling for Transformation" model which follows. How do they compare in terms of cost? Effectiveness? What parallels do the models contain?

ADDITIONAL RESOURCES

Hessel, Dieter T., ed. *Social Themes of the Christian Year: A Commentary on the Lectionary.* Philadelphia: The Geneva Press, 1983.

Kinghorn, Jon Rye. *Education in a World of Rapid Change* (with *Teacher's Implementation Guide*). 5335 Far Hills Ave., Dayton: The Charles F. Kettering Foundation, 1982.

Marstin, Ronald. *Beyond Our Tribal Gods: The Maturing of Faith.* Maryknoll, N.Y.: Orbis Books, 1979.

Russell, Letty. *Growth and Partnership: An Educational Guide to Church Renewal.* New York: Seabury Press, 1979.

Traitler, Reinhild. *Leaping over the Wall: An Assessment of Ten Years' Development Education.* Geneva: World Council of Churches, 1982.

COLIN GREER

Commentary on
The Chrysalis Program

I

The key question raised in this case is whether educating people to be conscious of the need for social change can be a vehicle for educating those same people actually to contribute to social change.

1. The assumption is that an active concern for social change is produced through personal exposure to the worst sores resulting from existing world systems.

2. Heavy reliance on personal exposure seems to mean very little attention to the diverse class interests of those joining this educational process. Isn't actual social change going to mean some serious confrontation with deep-seated personal expectations, traditions, and investments?

3. If institutional education remains tied to the institutional fabric of a privileged society, can education in such institutions be instrumental in releasing transformative social change?

4. Very little attention is paid to the strengths of people living the problems at issue. While necessarily cautious of trivializing suffering by romanticizing it, the model does not adequately confront the other danger of well-intentioned change-agents simply arriving to solve other people's problems.

5. To be sure, a clear purpose of the program is to encourage participants to work for social change at home—in their schools, communities, and nation. Here the endemic problems discussed in points 2 and 3, above, are most serious. On home turf they have to be.

6. The problems mentioned in points 2 and 3 largely emanate from the higher levels of the process of education and so are seated in the very institutions which at once cement the existing order and provide vehicles for its critique.

7. In the Chrysalis model there is no evidence that the immediate educational context is engaged. The critical question is not asked: Can the educator critique the social order without including the educational institutions, and can change be possible without change in these institutions being the goal of education within them?

8. Certainly the goal of the "missionary" educator has long been to contribute to social change abroad. Purpose, styles, and directions are very different in Chrysalis. However, a clearly postmissionary model is not articulated. The postmissionary model is the Freirian model aimed at learning via social awareness and at social awareness via self-consciousness about conditions in one's home environment; it involves learning to name the oppressor much as Adam named by way of becoming the master/subject. It has to be operative in the education of the educator too. How can that potential be realized?

9. Can the missionary model be superseded if the postmissionary educator does not engage the home-base institutional turf and authority structure of which he or she is victim and beneficiary? Can a non-Freirian education provide fertile soil for the making of Freirian educators?

10. If the Chrysalis Program is to develop a clearly articulated postmissionary pedagogy, then I suggest that as an additional component participants be sent abroad as Freirian educators. Certainly Freirian-style educators can—if they are open to it—be re-educated by their oppressed "students" in foreign lands. Because it is not intended that those educators make permanent places in their host communities, the upshot of their work will have to be engaged back home.

11. Eventually, the decolonized minds of the peoples the educators work with will challenge the global, institutional continuation of colonialism to which newly emergent nations are still subject. The response (responsiveness) of the educators' home country (the imperial center) to such challenge might to a great extent depend on the in-process challenge to home-base institutions.

12. The spiral of social change implicit in this possibility is one which might best be incorporated in the social vision and pedagogic purpose of postmissionary education if it is to be contributed to by educators—like those in the Chrysalis Program—working with the intention of wide-scale social transformation.

II

What signs of postmissionary education are present in the Chrysalis praxis?

1. It is important to recognize that religious-based education is only one form of missionary education. Indeed religious zeal was, in part, long in service to secular power and privilege. U.S. "civic religion" has been the basis for secular missions (the Peace Corps) and military advice and education. Yet, alternative styles, both of individuals and distinct approaches (Freire, Illich), have been influential in the thinking of North American and European progressive educators. Chrysalis aspires to those alternatives but seems trapped by the tradition in which it operates.

2. The framework of Chrysalis is of church-related, higher education activity better developing individuals capable of serving the cause of social change. What is missing is the possible and perhaps necessary parallel involvement of the institution itself and its parent authority system (church) as a

powerful actor in those processes. The difference I refer to is between the institutional politics of reforming educational programs and the role of the institutions of education as political actors.

3. The Freirian-informed framework seems to me to be limited by the college/church structure. The Freirian context involves the identification of condition and authority, with education and development emerging through that process. In this program the students are somehow to engage in that process as workers involved in local congregations and social agencies, but the school settings in which they are trained are apparently assumed as benign authorities. It seems to me that it's critical that the education experience of these students be in isomorphic relation with the social change agenda being advanced. The authorities through whom they receive their education cannot be irrelevant. These wider authority systems are, in Freirian style, the causes to be named as crucial to, and a part of the process of, education and development.

4. Dick, the director of Chrysalis, says: "On a more practical level, we believe that if we can arouse consciousness in the churches about these issues, the churches themselves and individual Christians working through the churches can influence U.S. public policies and institutions." In the discussion that follows Dick's statement there is no refinement of that goal. Neither the how question nor the what question is asked. To be sure, public policy can be influenced by the church—and is. The questions that have to be answered are: Influenced to what end? What process is integral to that end? What education inside the church will provoke the struggle in the church for a role in the how and what questions of public policy and national institutions?

5. I have no doubt the people conversing in this script would have little problem with what I am saying. Indeed, the church is full of struggle. But that struggle is not present in the articulation of the educational process revealed in this model, although it is articulated at the cutting edge of its most conscious actors.

6. Standard educational concerns are very present in the conversation of the Chrysalis committee. An initial concern is recruitment. All colleges and programs need students. How are they to get them? The less mainstream the process and credentials, the less readily viable will a program be in this era. Hence so much "back to basics." There is no back to basics here, but the fundamental of recruitment is central. How could it not be? And yet the discussion is of publicity and money; the questions are of viability and institutional credibility as well as of the pursuit of program goals. But where does the Chrysalis process begin? Why does it not begin in the very character of how recruitment is considered and pursued?

7. Pedagogical invention in Chrysalis is to take the ideal of the pursuit of "justice" as its core. Also, there is a "reversal" of historic mission—the program has leaders and teachers from the developing world come to the United States to teach. Perhaps those teachers will be better than U.S. teachers, and probably a richer perspective will be presented. But the pursuit of better

teachers by those able to employ them is only a little more reliable than changes in fashion. No structural changes, no relational changes are proposed. Better teachers are hired by enlightened program directors and deans, but the structures and relational patterns remain intact. . . .

8. Recall some of the language in the Chrysalis conversation: "There is *very little perception* of our involvement and *even complicity* in some of the global issues." (That is, beyond this band there is little understood. The word "even" suggests much less awareness of global interconnectedness than seemed the case in earlier statements in the discussion.) "The major purpose was *to sensitize people* . . . to justice issues." (What kind of goal is "to sensitize"? How do people get it? Who gives it best? What does it add up to for justice issues?)

The well-meaning social manager motif so comprehensively developed in the Great Society era is apparently strong here. Not much evidence, however, of the counter-thrusts of that period: "maximum feasible participation," "deschooling," "education for critical consciousness," "open education," "popular education."

9. Indeed none of those latter themes seem to have found their way into the planning and intention of Chrysalis as its origins are described in the discussion.

Recall the language again: "How *do you convince* students and ministers . . . that these kinds of concerns are every bit as much a part of the task of ministry as counseling, or preaching?"

10. In the discussion, the *immersion* experience emerges as a key to conscientization. Unfortunately the tone of its use is similar to the above-quoted relational style: people are to be managed, sensitized, conscientized, immersed. The relationship of immersion and conscientization with "continual sustenance and sustaining of the Spirit" is not addressed closely. Concern for this latter process is a route for pedagogical style and imperative which is not evidenced in the text of this worried discussion.

11. Finally, the program views its action-purpose in a fashion which emphasizes management as first priority. The philosophy that education and action are distinct is skipped over as an assumption. The idea that academic learning is a form of action is not considered. That all learning (education) occurs in a context of action of some kind (and is relational) is missed. The standard concern of a college for how best to manage its internship is the overall tone here.

III

Chrysalis's understanding of the need to foster contact with people of diverse cultures is at once hopeful and terribly limited.

1. What opportunity for preparing people to challenge injustice and work on behalf of transformative social change is lost when educational processes miss the chance to expand the conventional understanding about who the knower/

learner is? It is the conventional idea of who the knower is and what is knowable that mitigates any serious challenge to generally held notions about justice questions. In this perspective, there are epistemological roots to oppression and liberation.

2. The struggle to know has proceeded against extant definitions of what particular people can know (and should be allowed to know). Slaves in the United States were long denied access to literacy even after they were slowly included in socialization via baptism. Frederick Douglass, remembering his mistress's (illicit) effort to teach him to read, tells how he learned about the significance of reading only when his angry master forbade Douglass's education. In the space created by oppression Douglass learned about the danger the master experienced when he considered the idea of the slave's education. That danger, and awareness of it, is the trigger to learning predicated on the discovery of and challenge to social and cultural limits.

3. A second view of learning with respect to social justice should also be considered. Not only is access to learning via awareness of the limits to its fullness a transformative force in society, but recognition of the narrow definition of what we regard as learning is also critical. It is this framework of convention which helps solidify class and caste rigidities. Here is where the pool of those who can know is limited by defining what knowing is. When what certain people already know is ignored, then even access to conventional knowing is an empty offer because their progress to this route requires acceptance of their own ignorance, dependence on others for a beginning to learning, and readiness to embrace dimensions of learning conventions. By that route lies an ascriptive framework of social change; that is, a route characterized by winning concessions from the dominant system, not nurturing people's capacity to transform it.

4. Without understanding this distinction between transformative and ascriptive goals, the most well-intentioned processes are frequently reduced to ineffectiveness. At each stage learning about and learning to engage social justice questions must have a values imperative which demands that technical knowledge serve it instead of define it.

5. Poor children and their families, for example, throughout the world have significant strengths, and any public education that is to succeed will have to respond to those strengths. This is not an apologia for obfuscating academic goals, but rather is a vehicle for actually making such goals realistic for populations most victimized. This kind of realism requires that the victimized objects of social processes become the subjects of history. If education is a route in this direction, then it will be through the broadest definition of the knower and knowing.

6. Supposedly new approaches to education in the United States since World War II—approaches which have usually not been focused on broad definitions of knower and knowing—have ended up as deadends and have been easily formularized. Along the same lines, old ideas which provided good results are ignored: (a) because they are believed to be too costly; or (b) because they seem

to challenge the legitimacy of one or another convention. So in public schools, for example, paraprofessionals in the classroom have been virtually forgotten—even though there is some record of promise, and the effort did bring about a practical framework for community-school relations.

7. So too, research on and in schools with progressive social change in view has rapidly become an institutionalized, self-justifying framework. Research has often taken on a "because" (explanatory) quality instead of an "in order to" (action-based) imperative: for example, Coleman's assurance (explanation) in the 1960s that desegregation would not harm the "learning" of white students. Also, the plethora of pedagogic psychology studies (the base of a new post-World War II field), which began by identifying pupil style and learning preferences as the basis of understanding learning and teaching, ended up losing sight of its enabling imperative. Much of this work has merely served to explain why certain students fail.

8. Recognition and nurturance of people's strength represent a deep challenge to what Illich called "schooled" society, at its best a society committed to engineering social improvement for impoverished, deprived people. In the post-World War II world, education has been a crucial instrument in the emergence and then retreat of that agenda. Education was at once the means for training and retraining the professionals and managers of this "schooled" society and the means for including more and more in the rewards of technological advance. The direction and priorities of the society, which for so long grew on the promise that continually greater numbers of the impoverished would have access to the bounty of technological progress, continued to hold those people in reserve even as their condition was to be changed.

Chrysalis, in its values imperative, has been in the vanguard of challenge to the "schooled" society. In its praxis it seems yet to have a way to go. In finding that way it will improve its own work and help us all immeasurably. Finally, the problem with Chrysalis is not of its own making.

KOSUKE KOYAMA

Commentary on
The Chrysalis Program

My experience in teaching the subject of "Theology in Asia" to a North American audience has convinced me that the subject must be presented in its organization and contents as "Theology of Asia in Dialogue with Theology in the United States" if it is not to be perceived by them as unrelated to their life and thought. Subjects related to the Third World must be brought into some kind of concrete dialogue with the world in which the students live and work. This methodology of dialogue—not just an intellectual but a participatory one—is in the spirit of Chrysalis as I understand it.

This participatory dialogue is implemented by Chrysalis mainly in two ways: first, by insuring the active presence of Third World theologians on the campus (even though campus is a "non-poor North American campus"); and, second, by conducting study tours. These two activities of Chrysalis must have the intellectual and spiritual backing of the seminary administration or community. It is important for professors to integrate Chrysalis concerns, such as the issue of world hunger, into their "regular" lectures whenever it is feasible. They must reorganize their lectures and risk experiments in their delivery. Periodically, instructors and professors should get together to plan and discuss possibilities for the integration of these concerns into the curriculum. For theological professors to participate in some offering of the Maryknoll Mission Institute ("Developing Spirituality in a World of Conflict," "Missioners Challenged by Global Economic Inequalities," "Christians Responding in an Urban Consumer Society") would be a good idea.

Union Theological Seminary sponsors a short-term tour for students every January to Puerto Rico and the Dominican Republic similar to the Chrysalis tour of India. The Union group usually consists of about eight persons, and the trip is supervised by a person academically and experientially established in the area. Students are provided with a lecture series and a substantial reading assignment before they take the trip. The cost is relatively small, and the impact upon the students is enduring. There are other such projects already being carried on by seminaries throughout the United States, and we need more information in order to facilitate, in the future, projects which can be done jointly.

Chrysalis is engaged in a vitally important task of conscientization of the non-poor about world hunger. This important task is by no means an easy one. First of all, the people who come to the program come out of a culture which assumes that the United States is the center of the whole world (center complex). It may be true that the United States is the center in terms of wheat, but plentifulness of wheat is not plentifulness of humanization. Christian theology must expose dehumanization, which is idolatry. To allow millions to die from hunger in our world today can only be the result of a kind of social irresponsibility that flourishes in an idolatrous civilization. Lack of feeling and inaction in the face of the fundamental need of starving humanity are the practical results of idolatry. This is the theological focus for the Chrysalis Program.

The phenomenon of apathy that the case speaks about has complex rootages. That apathy does not mean that the people in the affluent United States have no passion for anything. There is a great deal of human suffering and tragedy among the non-poor. How does Chrysalis bring the suffering of the non-poor into dialogue with the suffering of the poor in distant places? In the same manner, How can movements such as those for women's liberation, racial nondiscrimination, and disarmament be shared with people beyond the horizon of affluent North American culture? And in return, How does Chrysalis inspire the non-poor to listen to the problems that are directly affecting the poor? These are admittedly not easy tasks.

I believe that the way in which Chrysalis chooses the Third World theologians must involve a careful process. Beyond their availability there must be questions relating to "qualifications," as in what way and to what extent the theologians would represent the Third World. Should Chrysalis invite the theologians fresh from the Third World country each time, or may it consider Third World theologians who happen to be in the United States? The quality of the Chrysalis Program depends very much on whom it has as campus theologians.

After we are conscientized, what then? There must be a community that can support its members to practice whatever they decide to do in order to eliminate world hunger. Such building up of community is very important. It is in this effort that we may be able to experience the meaning of "eschatology." Christian eschatology is inseparable from the concrete effort to build up conscientized community. It is a community of faith that can inspire and nourish the process of conscientization.

CHAPTER 7

TRAVELING FOR TRANSFORMATION

During recent years educationally-oriented travel seminars have increased in number as organizations seek to provide exposure to other cultures and acquaint their constituencies with overseas projects or partner agencies. This model immerses participants in the culture of a host country through visits with ordinary people as well as with key political and religious leaders representing different approaches to a particular country's situations and problems. The model design also incorporates systematic evaluative research on successive traveling seminars to measure the kind and degree of impact on the participants.

The model claims to provide experiences which lead participants to transform their previous, U.S.-oriented views of the world by taking into account Third World perspectives on global relationships and problems. Participants commit themselves to covenants of preparation, living simply with their hosts, and communicating what they experience and earn when they return home. Thus they become new interpreters of global realities.

The case may be particularly useful to church and community leaders who desire to help pivotal persons in their constituencies become more aware of the global situation. It may also interest communicators who see the limitations of the media in interpreting what is really happening to ordinary people in different parts of the world, and people of political and economic influence whose power can be used to ameliorate some of the conditions that oppress people. It may also attract those who want to learn more directly and personally what is happening in the world today.

Program Overview

Convinced that research can be revealing and that education is a critical step toward global wholeness, an international group of educators established Plowshares Institute as a nonprofit educational corporation in the service of the church. Plowshares takes its name and inspiration from Micah 4:3 and Isaiah 2:4:

They shall beat their swords into plowshares,
and their spears into pruning hooks;
nation shall not lift up sword against nation,
neither shall they learn war anymore.

The vision of Plowshares is that of a world where the conditions for the fullness of life may be possible for all. By God's grace, we seek to move, however slowly, toward the reality of human dignity, solidarity, and transforming love promised in the gospel. Christ's presence with us is one of the few lights in this darkness of suffering, restrictions, and failure in a global village that is still frantically beating plowshares into swords. Our task is to discover ways to abandon the study of war and violence in every form, whether military, economic, or social, and then commit ourselves to concrete strategy and action. The dream for us as one people, as a global community, is to put our hands on the double handles of a plowshare and recognize the earth and every neighbor as gifts of God.

The International Advisory Council and staff of Plowshares Institute are made up of persons whose places of birth span the globe and whose ministry has been shaped by Third World experiences, but who now serve as educators, primarily in the First World. We are convinced that there are three important tasks toward implementing our vision of human transformation based on new understanding: (1) conducting basic research on what factors induce persons and institutions to change their priorities and lifestyles in the light of global needs; (2) being most faithful and effective in facilitating such change; and (3) applying those models to initiate concrete individual and institutional change that reflects global priorities. Acknowledging that the reasons for such changes, apart from God's grace, are not always clear, we have nonetheless identified two factors which seem essential: face-to-face encounters between persons in various parts of the world, and a community of support and accountability that allows meaningful change to begin and be sustained.

The application of models has taken two basic forms. One is to give seminars and programs for church conferences, dioceses, and local congregations on topics such as "Ministry in the 80s in a Global Context," "Thinking Globally and Acting Locally," and "Peacemaking in a Conflictual World: Personal, National, and International." Workshops and consultations on "Living in a Global Village" are offered for educational, business, and government agencies in the United States and overseas. Another model of education which we have found particularly effective is three-week immersion seminars to Africa, Asia, and Latin America. These are made possible by specific invitations from religious, government, and civic leaders in our host countries. Participants are committed to extensive advance reading, to living in Third World homes, and to a year of interpretation of their experiences upon their return.

For further information on published research, seminars, workshops or on the traveling seminars, contact: Plowshares Institute; P.O. Box 243; Simsbury, CT 06070; phone: (203) 651-9675.

Case Study
Traveling for Transformation

"Can travel lead to transformation?" wondered Ronald Kimball, Associate Director of the One World Foundation of Los Angeles. "Or are traveling seminars only a diversion for middle-class folk claiming to be interested in issues of peace and justice?" Ron saw these as crucial questions as he considered recommendations to the foundation selection committee.

The research data were not yet in, but Kimball had to admit that the educational experiences made possible by Plowshares Institute, based in Connecticut, appeared to be transformative as far as participants were concerned. Plowshares had applied to One World for scholarship aid to assist more women and minorities in participating in these traveling, educational experiences. As Ron reviewed his notes, he thought about the long phone conversation he had just finished with Sue Hines, who had been on two traveling seminars to the Third World under the sponsorship of Plowshares. Sue's name had been given to him by Dr. Alan Edwards, Executive Director of Plowshares, as a person who, prior to the seminar, had not been significantly related to Third World issues of peace and justice. She also had kept in close contact with her colleagues in those educational experiences and could draw on the insights and concerns of others with critical perspective.

Ron learned from Sue that, in contrast to other immersion experiences through travel, many of which had a specific focus on political lobbying in U.S. church and government circles, Plowshares had gradually developed a broader format. In comparing the eight seminars conducted by Alan Edwards, Ron noted an evaluation and adjustment process from concentration on single issues—such as hunger or disarmament—for seminary students and faculty to a thematically and geographically wider agenda with a mixed group of clergy and lay leaders. The concern of each of the seminars was on the systemic social, economic, and political problems that are manifest in relations between the First and Third Worlds. Evaluations indicated that participants applied their learnings to different issues in relation to quite diverse constituencies and networks.

Ron found that significantly more preparation and follow-up had been

---

instituted since the first seminars. Other changes involved more thorough screening of candidates who apply; a concentration on regional groups versus individuals; more research before and after to determine the degree and nature of each seminar's impact on individuals and their institutions; regular group debriefings during the seminar; journal keeping; the establishment of covenant partners; and peer accountability and support. Many of these changes seemed to be directed toward a more deliberate process of accountability.

Ron studied his notes on the phone conversation with Sue Hines. She was a United Methodist lay woman from New England who had been on seminars to East Africa and Latin America. She had originally learned of a seminar to East Africa from a seminary professor who was leading a Lenten series in her church. She had told Ron, "He recommended that I apply to participate if I was really concerned about the responsibility of the church in the world. I had never considered such a possibility before. Now I know what a dangerous decision that was! The traveling seminar can change your life, and I was not really prepared to have my life changed. To read about conditions in the Third World is one thing—to experience them was quite another. It was not so much what I learned about Africa or Latin America that caused the change in my life, but rather what I learned about the United States. It puts the priorities of our nation, the church, and myself in a new light."

APPLICATION AND ORIENTATION

To Ron's questions about the application and orientation process, Sue responded, "After submitting my written application, I had a personal interview with Alan Edwards, which is required before acceptance. Each participant is asked to agree to three conditions if accepted. The first condition was to do preparatory study including readings from a variety of perspectives about the religious, political, economic, and cultural conditions of the area to which we had been invited by religious and civic leaders. Second, we agreed to go as 'visitors, not tourists,' and to live ' simply but safely' and as close as possible to the conditions of the people. On both seminars we lived in homes, guest houses, and school or seminary dormitories. Third, we promised to interpret as faithfully as we could our learnings from the experience for no less than one year among our own constituencies, whether church, business, educational, or professional circles. There was no attempt to determine prior to the experience what form our interpretation would take.

"While experiencing enormous anxiety about my health, the three weeks away from my family, and whether I could take the culture shock, I was still pleased to be accepted as a member of the delegation. Our group represented a sort of microcosm of North American Christians—laity and clergy, men and women, black and white, all ages."

In response to Ron's inquiry about goals, Sue replied, "The purposes of the two seminars in which I shared were basically the same, although the content of the experiences was radically different. Each sought to convey the richness and contributions of these Third World nations, leading us to discover what we in the First World have to learn from their culture and especially from the vitality of their church life. The second purpose was to experience directly the consequences of the increasing gap and resulting inequality among peoples of the First and Third Worlds, both between and within nations. The hope is that we might modify individual and institutional priorities that could move us toward a more just, sustainable, and peaceful world community. A premise of Plowshares is that it is the quality of the human encounter that causes transformation. This is especially true when personal encounters reveal issues of injustice and suffering.

EAST AFRICAN SEMINAR

Ron asked about specific seminars. Speaking about the East African seminar, Sue said, "The first three days of our orientation for the seminar took place at a retreat center where we began to build our own community and to assume shared group responsibilities for health, baggage, photography, communication, gifts, etc. Worship, case studies, and discussions were built into the program as we began to integrate our advance readings. It was there that we also began our daily journals of theological reflection and learned some basic Swahili, although most conversations in East Africa would be in English or via a translator. The most important learning from the orientation for me came from a meal and an afternoon discussion with the resident leaders of St. Elizabeth House, a shelter for the poor in Hartford. For the first time I came into direct contact with men and women who had been victimized by our own society, evicted from city apartments, unemployed, and former alcoholics. These were people who now sought to take responsibility for their own lives, who rejected our pity and disdained our guilt. The idea that reoccurred during the entire seminar was that brothers and sisters were not asking for charity but demanding justice form me, and I did not know how to respond.

"What experiences were most formative for me?" Sue repeated Ron's question before laughing and saying, "Not what I anticipated! The most significant encounters were with families in their homes in every country. I remember how terrified I was to spend the first night away from the group in a Kikuyu homestead in rural Kenya. As the van carrying my friends pulled away and I started the long walk with my host up the mud path to the cluster of what I described as huts, I was convinced I had made a mistake. Yet I was soon overwhelmed by the genuineness of my welcome and the exchange of common human concerns about family and work, by the joy in these people's worship— all this in the midst of what I would describe as grinding poverty. I began to wonder who was impoverished and also what were the forces that pushed these new friends to grow coffee and tea as cash crops rather than the corn and millet they so desperately needed. That night, sleeping on a mat in a hut with the animals surrounding us for our warmth and their protection, my eyes filled with tears, and yet I felt more profoundly at home than I had since my childhood. The bonds of humanity are forged in this kind of encounter. It was also imperative for me to be able to share my thoughts, feelings, and prayers with our group when we regathered after each of the home visits.

"As a group we met with numerous government and religious leaders. Our meeting with President Nyerere of Tanzania was the most significant for me personally. Perhaps this was because of his own commitment to a 'more human and equitable society for all.' He pointed out that Tanzania must abandon the illusion of catching up with the United States, which, with 6 percent of the world's population, consumes 40 percent of the world's resources. The USSR and Europe have comparable populations and the same desires. The results for Tanzania and other Third World nations are obvious. Tanzania is seeking to provide basic food, shelter, education, and health for everyone. That is the goal of the government policy of *ujamaa* or familyhood." Sue continued, "That will demand simpler lifestyles and a more just world economic order, which the nations and churches of the First World resist. Rather than submitting to significant changes, we ease our consciences with charity, which only temporarily pacifies the appropriate anger of the poor and marginalized of the world."

LATIN AMERICAN SEMINAR

"My anger as well as my consciousness were really pricked in my second traveling seminar to Brazil and Nicaragua." Sue sped on, with no need for prompting, Ron recalled. "I learned about the poor working conditions at the auto manufacturing plants in São Paulo, Brazil, and the church's support of the workers' strike for better wages and conditions. I also learned that prior to the 1979 revolution the Somoza dictatorship in Nicaragua, supported by the United States for decades, channeled most of the wealth, land, and power into the hands of a few families while the majority of the population suffered high infant mortality, illiteracy, and short life expectancy. Finally, in desperation Christians and Marxists formed a coalition to overthrow the Somoza regime and established a new Sandinista government. This new government, with several priests as cabinet ministers, organized national literacy and health campaigns. This same government abolished the death penalty to stop the cycle of revenge that could have led to the execution of imprisoned Somozan National Guard soldiers who had tortured and killed thousands of peasants during the fighting. As Minister of Culture Father Ernesto Cardenal noted, 'For the first time in Latin America a country set the economic strategy with the needs of the poorest fifty percent of the population in mind.'

"Our group also met with opponents to the Sandinistas in the private sector and the church. It became clear that there was strong feeling, for instance, among the editorial staff of the newspaper *La Prensa*. Most indicated their belief that the revolution against Somoza, which they had supported, had gone astray and was endangering future economic stability through a more radical socialist policy rather than a mixed economy of socialism and capitalism that had been promised. Also, they believed the pressure of U.S. opposition was forcing Nicaragua to rely on Marxist countries such as Cuba. The result was increased infringement on civil liberties in the name of socialist national security.

"However, both the Sandinista regime and their opponents agreed that the U.S. government was actively working to destabilize the present Nicaraguan government through economic and military threats and actions. This, they are convinced, is because the United States believes Nicaragua represents a threat as a communist force in Central America. It is ironic that one of the few countries in which the church overtly identified with the poor in an economic revolution is now being undermined by a nation claiming to intervene on Christian principles. Again, it was conversations with families in Nicaragua attempting to build a new life that were essential to my perspective. Although I know it is a complex and ambiguous situation, I began to see the responsibility of our government in a new way. I discovered Christians in Africa and in Latin America, through their faith, taking concrete, costly actions to seek a more equitable world.

"On both seminars it is clear that the personal contacts were a unique and essential part of the experience. At first I was hesitant about accepting the incredible hospitality offered by our host homes, asking if we weren't exploiting their generosity. However, invitations are reissued by our hosts for future seminars because the benefits are seen as mutual. Access to government leaders by our hosts is sometimes facilitated by our presence, and our hosts repeatedly acknowledge our presence as an affirmation of the support of the worldwide community of Christ. It was also important for us to receive without the North American obsession to 'pay back.' "

CRUCIAL FACTORS

When Ron asked about the crucial factors that made this educational experience so valuable, Sue replied thoughtfully, "The commitment and openness of our hosts and the context of a supportive learning community." She laughed when she said, "But, of course, one must remember that traveling seminars with Alan Edwards are not vacations. The intensity and quality of the experience are probably not possible apart from the personal relationships Alan has developed with our hosts over years of living and visiting in the Third World. They obviously not only respect and trust his commitment to a more just world order, but transfer some of their friendship and affection for him to members of the group. One has to remember that Alan lived through Idi Amin's reign of terror in Uganda as a visiting professor and earned credibility in the field that gets transferred to his companions on a traveling seminar. The leadership of the seminar in quality of instruction, nurture, and demands for accountability is crucial to its transforming potential."

"What are the forms of this transformation for individuals?" Ron asked. Sue thought for a moment and said, "In my case it began with fulfilling my covenant to interpret the experience for no less than a year. I spoke to over thirty groups, reaching over 2,500 people in addition to writing articles and doing local television shows, especially on U.S. involvement in Latin America. Even more important was an increasing restlessness with the trivial concerns of most church meetings. We in the U.S. church spend too much time and effort on our own buildings and fellowship. At the same time the church in the Third World in many cases is fighting to survive while living out the gospel imperative of feeding the hungry, clothing the naked, and freeing the captives. The experience produced a conflict with the comfort and luxury of my middle-class lifestyle in contrast to the desperate needs of those I had met in East Africa and Latin America. Impatient with my lack of direct involvement in issues of peace and justice, I moved from reading theological books on these topics to direct participation in groups such as Amnesty International, Bread for the World, and a peace committee in my town. I also volunteer three days a week as a staff person for an organization focusing on issues of global peace and justice. I still wrestle with the conflicts, but there is no doubt the seminar lived up to the warning that 'it may be hazardous to your lifestyle.'

"Let me give you another example. Father Phil Matthews had some of the same surprises I did," Sue said as she described the impact of the seminar on other participants. "As the black pastor of a predominantly black, middle-class, East Coast congregation, returning to discover his roots in Africa, he was shocked to find that he was seen more as North American than black, while, as he noted, 'Old honky Edwards is greeted like a blood brother.' Phil declared the seminar opened his eyes to the fact that his own congregation was essentially ignoring the needs of black and Hispanic poor in the environs of their own church. A program of 'some considerable distress' for the congregation was initiated to address this upon his return from Africa. It finally led to the unheard-of appointment of a Hispanic associate as well as a new range of programs. The transformation of his congregation was documented later in Phil's D.Min. thesis, for which the traveling seminar had been a credit course.

"Phil shared," Sue indicated, "that he was encouraged by Plowshares's plans for developing a program with several theological seminaries that would involve a similar Third World immersion process in order to take seriously the globalization of theological education. Until the African traveling seminar, other courses on liberation theology or the ethics of peace and justice had been for him just that—another elective course, not the core or even a substantial part of the curriculum.

"Another example is John Turner, a dental surgeon from St. Louis, who told us there were three factors which he believes were central to the changes in his life following the African seminar: the written covenant shared with the whole group, which each person is expected to prepare; the selection of an individual covenant partner to hold each of us accountable; and follow-up by the group. John, like Phil Matthews, really discovered the Third World within his own First World as a result of the African traveling seminar. He is now committed to two nights a month providing dental services with the aid of his staff in an inner-city clinic. In addition, John has sought to organize volunteers in the medical and dental field to give time and services so poor people in his community can have access to health care. Like many of us, John also corresponds regularly with a number of his hosts in East Africa, and during elections sees a candidate's foreign and domestic policies in a new light. John Turner was an unlikely 'lifestyle modification' candidate, as he acknowledges. He now has a goal of moving within five years to serving in self-reliant programs for disenfranchised persons for at least one half of his time as a professional." Ron glanced again at the copy of Turner's covenant (Appendix A, below), one of several that Sue had sent him.

In considering other Plowshares research data, Ron learned that most of the seminar participants had completed a rather extensive research questionnaire; all had had a personal interview prior to participation; and most had filled out a postseminar evaluation using the same research instrument. There was currently a Plowshares design to conduct long-range studies of a random sample of traveling seminar participants versus a control group in an attempt to identify and measure the degree and sustainability of the change and what key factors, if any, were responsible. The Plowshares staff, Sue reported, was convinced this research was critical for developing pedagogical models for social change. It was premature to draw a final assessment, but initial research data revealed there was measurable and extensive attitudinal and behavioral change that was directly attributed to the traveling seminar as a catalytic event. Ron made a mental note to track the results of this research for the foundation, whether or not it made the grant.

The exchange seminar which Sue described also intrigued Ron. "One year after our East African seminar returned, the group made possible an exchange traveling seminar for six colleagues from East Africa. Selecting their own representative delegation of clergy and laity from our three principal host countries and funding an equitable portion of the cost (average 10 percent), the delegation came as guests of the North American groups, which raised the remaining funds from our own resources. The East African group stayed as guests in homes and traveled from Connecticut to rural Pennsylvania to Washington, D.C., and to New York City to meet with church, government, and civic leaders from bishops and lay leaders to state governors and Congresspersons to university and multinational corporation presidents."

Sue recalled the words of the chairman of the investment committee of one of the richest corporations in the United States at the close of a luncheon for the delegation. This followed a morning of "controversial" conversation between the African delegation and his committee. "Our encounter has led me, I confess, to change my mind about several proxy votes of shares we hold in other corporations plus my attitude toward our own investment policies involving Africa. Also, I hope to accept your invitation to pay a visit to the East Africa that extends beyond the Nairobi Hilton!"

Sue continued, "The three-week visit was, I believe, almost as revealing for our African brothers and sisters as our visit to them was for us. I believe the mutual exchange will build enduring bonds of friendship."

CRITIQUE

"In spite of your enthusiasm, you must have some reservations and/or critique of the traveling seminar," Ron said to Sue as their phone conversation drew to a close. "Initially," Sue responded, "I wondered if the group could afford the time in an intense, almost exhausting travel schedule for daily worship, dialogical prayer, and even debriefing sessions plus a daily entry in a theological journal. Although my critique remains that the schedule is so packed that there is not enough reflective space for absorbing the learnings, especially in the midst of culture shock, I am now convinced the disciplines of worship and debriefing are essential to the rhythm of the learning experience. I realized this only upon my return.

"A more foundational question about the traveling seminar relates to its cost. It is obviously a relatively expensive form of education in both time and funds, even though the groups live simply and travel light. Is this cost, even if it is for the best education, justified in a world that we know must modify its own lifestyle? From my perspective, the composition of our learning community is also very important, and many women and minorities don't have the money to participate. However, some scholarships are now available as gifts from former seminar participants, and, it is hoped, from foundations such as yours.

"A third issue for me," concluded Sue, "is whether the impact of the experience can adequately be communicated to others without their actual participation. Initial research indicates that over time substantial changes do occur for seminar participants, who in turn have some impact on their institutions. However, if the implied premise is that transformation requires a dramatic immersion—almost a shock—which challenges one's presuppositions about the world, then duplication or adequately communicating the learning, apart from actually going on a seminar or similar immersion experience, may be futile, or at least inadequate. Also, are the changes systemic and long-lasting, or only partial and temporary? It is too early in the research to answer that objectively or conclusively. Plowshares has committed its existence to what is still a faith assumption.

"Finally, there is a question," Sue confided, "about a relatively open-style educational experience which assumes that intense exposure to alternative view-points and experiences allows a balanced and responsible perspective to emerge. Although members of the Plowshares staff clearly have their own perspectives, they seek to make the seminar open so the participants select and covenant as to the application of their learnings. Plowshares does not concentrate on one area of the world or push specific responses, such as influencing legislation or official church policy. To be sure, that does occur for many, but participant responses are quite diverse and therefore in danger of being diluted.

Yet with my real reservations, I recommend for others and yourself participation and support of these seminars as the best program I know for global awareness."

Ron flipped his notebook closed and contemplated his recommendations to both his foundation and to Plowshares on its educational model. Would his foundation best invest its limited funds in experiential education for basically middle-class people whose lives might be transformed by a traveling seminar to a Third World nation, or would there be more concrete results from direct support for agencies involved in aid to the poor? On his desk was another proposal from an established agency requesting direct support for a literacy program for migrant Hispanics. How was it possible to balance the focus on education for the poor with education for the non-poor?

Appendix

COMMITMENTS FOR THE YEAR COMING OUT OF MY EXPERIENCE IN EAST AFRICA—JOHN TURNER, D.D.S.

1. Correspond with new friends in Africa on a regular basis—some form of communication at least once a month.
2. Be present and supportive of the Kenyan (and other African) students attending school in St. Louis. Be available for holidays when it is appropriate.
3. Have a dinner and slide show for the twenty Kenyan college students at the University of St. Louis by May 15.
4. Acknowledge God each day for my life and its many blessings.
5. Never take anything for granted and limit complaining on any issue to no more than a day.
6. Support local and national conservation programs (e.g., on land and energy resources).
7. Support candidates who are committed to:
   a. less military spending
   b. conservation
   c. support of Third World countries
   d. a global vision—working together
   e. programs that "support" people in becoming self-reliant.
8. Acknowledge people who have made a contribution to my life either directly or indirectly on a day-to-day basis.
9. Appreciate my own contribution to the lives of others.
10. Be active in the Hunger Project committee in St. Louis.
11. Support Plowshares Institute with a financial commitment to be used totally or partially for scholarship purposes or support the Busoga Diocese Project.
12. Be available to assist in hosting a delegation of visitors to the United States from Africa under the auspices of Plowshares Institute.
13. Make a slide presentation of our trip to our "extended family" by May 1.
14. Make a slide presentation to the dental staffs and doctors of Dental Associates by May 15.
15. Write Congresspersons, Senators, and other government officials to support policies and legislation that support the commitments stated in number 7, above.
16. Be available for churches, civic clubs, and study groups to share my experience in East Africa.

17. Read the Bible each day over the next year.
18. With my family look at my personal consumption of the world's goods and make a list of any shifts or changes coming out of my African trip. Do this by March 15.
19. Be active in the inner-city Neighbor for Neighbor Program—donate one evening a month and recruit other volunteers. Meet with the board about opening up the clinic another evening each week. Pledge $100 per month for dental services.
20. Send dental journals to dental colleagues in Kampala.
21. Direct my dental career so that in five years I will be available at least half-time in programs that support the disenfranchised of the world—the rule being "Will it create self-reliance?"

Teaching Note

TOPICS AND QUESTIONS FOR DISCUSSION

1. What are the goals of the Plowshares traveling seminars? What are some of the steps the seminars follow to accomplish those goals? From your experience what factors or events have changed your perception of an issue? What factors have led you to active response to a concern or issue? Are there additional steps you would suggest be included in the traveling seminars? Why or why not?

2. What are the educational assumptions on which the traveling seminars are based?

3. In an effort to have a broad variety of participants, Plowshares has requested funding to include women and minorities who might otherwise be unable to participate. What would be the advantages of a heterogeneous group of participants? How does this goal coincide with the other goals of the traveling seminars? What educational role does the group of participants play for one another?

4. The Plowshares seminars expose participants to a broad variety of First and Third World perspectives, including political opposition groups, and urge individuals to draw their own conclusions and to work with "covenant partners" in terms of tangible responses to new learning. Evaluate this approach in contrast to more focused programs which encourage group commitment to specific political action or community involvement.

5. If you were advising Ron Kimball, what factors would be important in evaluating this educational model?

ADDITIONAL RESOURCES

Birch, Bruce, and Larry Rasmussen. *Predicament of the Prosperous.* Philadelphia: Westminster, 1978.

Brown, Robert McAfee. *Theology in a New Key.* Philadelphia: Westminster, 1978.

De Gruchy, John W. *Cry Justice! Prayers, Meditations and Readings from South Africa.* Maryknoll, N.Y.: Orbis Books, 1986.

Evans, Robert A., and Alice F. Evans. *Human Rights: A Dialogue between the First and Third Worlds.* Maryknoll, N.Y.: Orbis Books, 1983.

Shaull, Richard. *Heralds of a New Reformation.* Maryknoll, N.Y.: Orbis Books, 1984.

Sider, Ronald J. *Rich Christians in an Age of Hunger.* New York: Paulist Press, 1977.

CARMAN ST. J. HUNTER

Commentary on
Traveling for Transformation

The use of the term "transformation" is a strong indication of the comprehensive nature of the goals implicit in the model. What is desired is a complete
reshaping of the participants' view of themselves and of their world. This
radical new orientation is to result in a reordering of values and new ways of
acting out those values in individual behavior and in political and social action
for change. This is a high order for any educational enterprise.

The designers, obviously aware of the inherent blocks to radical change in
most educational models, include elements that constitute the major strengths
of this particular model:

1. The model is experiential. Participants are immersed in another reality
   that challenges their conscious and unconscious assumptions, habits,
   social roles, and relationships;
2. The challenges to all that is familiar are mediated through real people
   whose common humanity cannot be avoided. The daily struggle to
   sustain family life is shared at a deep level. Friendships grow that make
   demands on both sides;
3. The setting is so dramatically different and so geographically removed
   from the habitual world of the participants that, once on the scene, there
   is no escape: sights, sounds, smells, food, schedules, customs are omni-
   present during the duration of the seminar;
4. Religious and political figures, known previously only through press
   reports, become real persons, deeply engaged in action to change their
   worlds;
5. The totality of the experience is designed to create a new vulnerability, an
   openness to questioning impressions previously accepted as "the way
   things are." A willingness to probe one's own prior education and
   cultural conditioning emerges.
6. A supportive structure is created to reinforce the values of the learning:
   a. Participants are not alone; they are part of a community of people all

going through the experience together, able to reinforce each other's new insights and commitments;

b. Preparatory reading, discussions, and a brief encounter with "the Third World at home" set the tone for expecting that life might be different after the experience;

c. From the beginning the seminar was presented as a serious undertaking, demanding disciplined commitment before, during, and after the event itself.

SOME DIRECT RESULTS OF THESE PARTICULAR SEMINARS

Internal evidence in the case study points to some of the results of the Plowshares seminars. Sue speaks of her early awareness that people in poverty are not expecting charity but demanding justice. She confesses that she learned more about her own nation and church and about herself than about Latin America or Africa. She seems to emphasize the fact that through personal encounters she understood better the issues of injustice and suffering. For her the interpersonal encounters with families and leaders in the host countries, with other group members, and with the group leader made the strongest impact. She cites certain changes in her own behavior (more direct involvement as opposed to reading), in that of another member of her group (redirection of priorities in Phil's congregation), and in John's perception of his own professional options and commitments.

The reciprocal visit of a group from East Africa, made possible through the efforts of the North Americans who had gone to Africa, was another concrete result.

From the case study it is evident that individual perceptions and, to some degree, lifestyles were fundamentally changed as a result of the seminar experience. While conclusive results from the research are not yet available, it still seems possible to raise certain questions about the applicability of the model on a broad scale and to look for ways to strengthen the design—even for limited use.

STRENGTHENING AND ADAPTING THE MODEL

A basic strength of the model, according to Sue Hines, is the direct personal encounter between the poor and the non-poor, that is, between the hosts and the visitors. Sue raised some questions, however, about time-commitment and cost. The costs seem high to me also, particularly in relation to the relatively short duration of the exposure. Work-study assignments of several months' duration or extended overseas experience seem more capable of producing lasting change.

Heavy emphasis in this model was placed on the reporting back home required of participants. This obviously had high value for the reporters. Those who hear the reports do not themselves have the benefit of experiential education, and one must question the validity of any claim to the multiplier-effect of the seminars based on what participants can do through speeches. It must be admitted, therefore, that those who can benefit from traveling seminars will always be a small proportion of the population. If we are not to take needed funds from other causes, only the affluent will really be affected. But among the affluent there will always be a high proportion of persons who control key resources and who influence policy and public opinion. For these reasons, the model should be strengthened in order to achieve the greatest impact possible.

Three factors appear to require more attention:

1. While exposure to individuals and families in the host culture remains a key element, would it not be possible to engage in more disciplined systemic analysis *with* representative persons in the host country? It is not enough to see and feel poverty and oppression at a personal level. The non-poor need to hear what the poor understand as the root causes of particular problems and, with them, identify not only personal but systemic and structural changes that must be sought;

2. Would it be possible for seminar sponsors to assist participants in identifying movements, agencies, and institutions back home that are already working with some success to make structural changes and to influence both governmental policy and business practices detrimental to relations between poor and non-poor peoples? It may be that lack of information about appropriate and effective channels for action limits the responses of returnees to personal and lifestyle changes;

3. Would it be possible for seminars to be more selective, that is, to be limited to persons who because of their geographic location, institutional or professional positions, or type of responsibility could develop corporate strategies for their activities when they return to the United States? Networks formed by such persons might be both stronger and more enduring than those formed by individuals casually thrown together— even those who share a common faith commitment.

The positive evaluation of the basic structure of these seminars leads me, also, to ask whether or not we must go so far to hear the voices of the poor. While there may always be a need for international seminars to jolt North Americans from their habitual isolation and complacency, this model offers some guidelines for disciplined encounters between the "two worlds" within our own culture. Admittedly there is always a problem of "using" the poor to provide an education for the non-poor. Such encounters could deteriorate into excursions from the safety of the non-poor world into other people's lives. However, with careful preparation, small groups of poor and non-poor could work together at the analysis and solution of practical community problems. This is a matter demanding careful study and planning, with the poor in charge of the agendas.

EDUCATIONAL AND THEOLOGICAL
IMPLICATIONS OF THE MODEL

The model is based on a firm belief in the efficacy of experiential education. Participants experienced the world of the poor firsthand. But is this experience sufficiently powerful to enable them to embrace the option for the poor? I believe not. People may, indeed, become more aware of reality, may perceive the relationships between their affluence and the poverty of others more realistically in terms of cause and effect, and may, indeed, embark upon a course of action that in some way alleviates the situation, but the real issue is spiritual and theological.

No design can do more than provide the environment that perhaps will enable fundamental change, conversion, to happen. Good will and caring about the fate of others are not enough. We, the non-poor, benefit from things as they are. The cost of beginning to live in a different world can only be overcome by the promise of the gospel experienced in the deepest part of our being.

There are two very important elements of educational design that can assist us in our spiritual pilgrimage. We can learn to objectify our own present imprisonment by identifying the obstacles to our true freedom. And we can be challenged by the stories, both biblical and modern, of those whose option for the poor has been the means of their liberation. The seminars and other educational designs can and do help. They must be constantly evaluated and improved. Transformation is a process to which, as educators, we can contribute. The end is beyond our designing.

G. DOUGLASS LEWIS

Commentary on
Traveling for Transformation

EDUCATION FOR TRANSFORMATION

Ronald Kimball states the issue of the case clearly in the first line: "Can travel lead to transformation?" The aim of the travel seminar is transformation through education. What is transformation? Is it transformation of an individual, of institutions, of a total society, or of all the above? The case implies it is all of the above. The case is not analytic in the sense of providing a theoretical framework for understanding transformation. It focuses primarily on some goals of transformation, such as a peaceful, just, and sustainable world community.

I want to suggest a three-fold framework for understanding human and social transformation. All three elements are implied in the travel seminar methodology, but are not clearly spelled out. They are: (1) a new way of seeing or perceiving; (2) a new way of acting; and (3) a new way of feeling.

A new way of perceiving opens one's eyes to see and understand the world, oneself, relationships, and individual and political actions; in short, it is seeing all of reality through a new set of glasses. For example, the travel seminar's aim is that no participant will ever hear about, read about, or think about the Third World and First World in the same way again.

A new way of acting for individuals flows from a new way of perceiving and a desire to do that which is meaningful and fulfilling. They will act in ways which they perceive will achieve their goals. It is hoped that as a result of the travel seminar the participants will not only think and see in new ways but will act in new ways "back home." Part of covenant-making at the end of a seminar is designed to encourage new goals and commitment to new behaviors.

Total transformation would lead to new feelings: changing from fear to freedom; from anger to joy; from prejudice to acceptance. Many people think that feelings and their cousins, attitudes, are the first things that must be transformed in humankind and society. They are, in fact, usually the last to change. Most of us go to our graves with our deeply-held prejudices, feelings, and attitudes. We cannot wait until they shift to change perceptions and actions. The latter of the two, in fact, can lead the way for the former. Fortunately, the travel seminar concentrates little on changes in persons' feelings and concentrates primarily on perceiving and acting.

COMPONENTS OF THE EDUCATIONAL MODEL

A key premise for the traveling seminar is that transformation in education is dependent on the quality of the human encounter. Much educational theory has assumed this to be true in terms of the relationship between teacher and student. The travel seminar expands this encounter more broadly to include: (1) the indigenous folk with whom the participants meet, live, eat, and talk; (2) the leaders, both political and religious, whom the group encounters; (3) the participants in the traveling seminar themselves; and (4) the leader of the travel seminar.

Human encounter is a central element in the traveling seminar. To proclaim it, however, as *the* cause of transformation overstates the encounters and understates the complex and comprehensive nature of the educational experience. Note the following components which make up the overall educational design:

1. *Drama of the Setting.* The uniqueness of the seminar is its provocative and contrasting educational setting. Taking a group to another culture for an intensive plunge is intended to have shock value, and it does. The methodology assumes that the shock increases the probability of transformation; otherwise, it is cheaper to stay at home.

2. *Human Encounter.* Though human encounter is not the only component in the educational design, it is a key one. Building of community among the participants, living and interacting with local hosts, interacting with authority figures, and confronting the uninitiated back home are all educational encounters.

3. *Preparation.* The seminar requires that each participant read and study documents, books, and sometimes languages of the areas to be visited. The intent is to take a somewhat educated group which can better understand the experience and can participate more intelligently in dialogue with local religious and political leaders.

4. *Follow up.* Follow-up to the travel seminar is urged for all participants, although such activity is obviously voluntary. Some research evidence seems to indicate that through strong encouragement by the seminar leader and some accountability through covenant relationships among members, follow-up in the form of "back home" action does occur among a high percentage of the participants.

LINKAGE, OR SYSTEMATIC POSSIBILITIES OF THE MODEL

The model is adaptable in terms of participants. For example, if one wanted to impact a particular group or organization, such as a seminary, diocese, conference, or local church, the participants in the traveling seminar could be enlisted from that one system and the follow-up design could be focused on influencing other persons within that system. The model also lends itself to linking different groups and subsystems. For example, a seminary could involve a cross-section of its various constituencies—board members, faculty, students, graduates, and supportive friends. A common, intensive experience could do much to foster communication and intergroup commitment to the goals of globalization in that seminary. A diocese or religious conference could use the same model, including members of the conference staff, a leader such as a bishop, and selected clergy and laity from diverse local churches within the area.

STRENGTHS OF THE MODEL

Many positive things can be claimed for the model, but, from my perspective, it has two fundamental strengths. First, it does appear to effect some transformation—in many cases significant transformation—in the participants. The case describes lay persons and pastors alike whose lives and ministries were changed both in their perceptions and actions. In turn they set about changing the social structures—families, churches, and other groups—in which they were involved. The case does not tell us whether the model has been successful or could be successful in transforming a total system, such as a seminary, church, or diocese.

The second fundamental strength of the model is that it focuses on crucial but difficult issues about which society has few answers—the split between the First and Third Worlds and the quest for a peaceful, just, and sustainable world. Confronting these issues constitutes the core content of the travel seminar.

WEAKNESSES OF THE MODEL

As is often the case, weaknesses are the backside of strengths or are the result of inevitable choices that must be made. Ron Kimball in the case asks if the model is replicable. The answer, it appears, is an ambiguous "yes and no." *Yes,* travel seminars are conducted continuously in a variety of groups and in numerous places. *No,* not every model of a travel seminar effects transformation in the lives and ministries of its participants.

The keys are the leadership of the seminar, the local arrangements, the quality of persons to whom the participants are exposed, the dramatic settings in which one is placed, and the commitment to an action follow-up. Not every leader can design and bring off such a complex and intricate educational experience.

Some of its other weaknesses are obvious. The time and financial commitments are heavy and, thus, automatically limit the clientele. One of the most pressing questions is who should go? Finances limit some, but even if scholarships were available, who should the leader of the seminar seek to recruit? If the model does transform or change the participants, they, in turn, influence the society and particularly the organizations of which they are a part. Should not the model then be focused on influential persons who hold significant leadership positions? Should it be an elitist model? Should those like Ron who make funding decisions grant money to an elitist model or to projects that directly benefit the poor?

ADDITIONAL QUESTIONS AND/OR OBSERVATIONS

1. Traveling seminars probably draw on motives in participants which the seminar leaders do not openly acknowledge, or might even put down as wrong if openly admitted. Such things as the romance and intrigue of travel to a foreign country and the pride of "having been" and "showing concern," the great badges of the liberal middle class, surely are instrumental in enticing people into a travel seminar. But the Lord has amazing ways to use the worst of motives and the most problematic of encounters to produce surprising transformations.

2. The case is never very specific about its methodology or amount of research. Are social surveys and questionnaires helpful? What about in-depth interviews? Perhaps one crying need the model points up is for more research and even new methods of research to be developed for measuring the effect of such an educational experience.

3. The travel seminar model may promise too much: a personal and social transformation. These complex changes in personal and social entities take time. Even religious conversions which claim instantaneous change recognize the need to grow in grace. The realization and appropriation of justification do not remove the ultimate goal of sanctification or transformation of total self and society. That reality probably must wait for the coming of the Kingdom to be fully realized, although the travel seminar might be one small step in that direction.

4. The case and the seminar open up the question: What is poverty? What is enough? What is not enough? Sue was astounded by the grinding poverty she experienced. She also made those judgments from the perspective of a middle-class North American. Perhaps there is learning for both sides. For the middle-class North American, lowering of a standard of living may not be a move towards poverty—though it may "feel" that way. For a person in a developing country, as President Nyerere points out, simpler lifestyles shared by a greater percentage of the populace may be a better model.

5. The travel seminar model includes reading and reflection, experience and action. The tendency is to stress the latter two. Sue herself implies that she has moved from reading books about issues to action on them. There is heavy stress within the model itself upon dramatic experiences in new settings and the commitment to action upon returning home. It would be unfair to the model, however, not to recognize its incorporation of reading and reflection as well. There is the preparation ahead of time. There is the encouragement of journal-

keeping and covenant-making. One of John Turner's goals was daily Bible reading and reflection upon return.

CONCLUSION

Those who have been on traveling seminars, as evidenced by the case, tend to return as evangelists for the model. Having been on one of those sojourns, I count myself among those converts. I can only wish for others to have the experience.

CHAPTER 8

GOSPEL AGENDA
IN A GLOBAL CONTEXT

This model relates the work of an international religious order to a specific educational workshop where the order's global involvements with the poor are applied to local education for the non-poor. The model focuses on the problem of land distribution and use. Access to "land" represents the right to health, education, and security, all of which protect human dignity. The Sisters of Notre Dame de Namur, whose members are situated around the world, have developed this study and action project in a systematic way.

Dedicated to a five-year development of the program, the Sisters share their ongoing research into education for transformation by discussing one significant event in the process. The workshop combines narrative reports of situations with theoretical analysis, a study of the Bible and church documents, statistical data, and personal involvement with local people caught in the realities of the problem. It seeks to bring together academic and experiential learning.

All persons concerned about how to use global networks and organizations to relate global and local education for transformation will be stimulated by this case. Mission and development agencies, as well as religious conciliar organizations which work to coordinate action projects and education toward transformation, will profit from probing into this case, as will persons wishing to understand better a sociologically oriented analysis of the connection between global and local cirumstances of injustice and domination.

Program Overview

For several years the Sisters of Notre Dame de Namur have been trying to introduce, in working with the poor, the method of conscientization described by Paulo Freire in his *Pedagogy of the Oppressed*. This is a method of raising to consciousness the political, economic, and social oppressions of one's life and taking action to change that condition. The Sisters have found, as have others, that it is effective. In 1968 the bishops of Latin America affirmed the method when they dedicated their conference at Medellín, Colombia, to its initiator, Paulo Freire. They reaffirmed it in 1979 at their next conference at Puebla, Mexico. The outgrowth of the method, namely, the building of base communities, was also affirmed.

The method of conscientization involves an understanding on the part of exploited peoples that they have a human right to possess the land they need for survival. *The land* here refers not only to territory but also to the health care, education, and security needed to live in simple dignity.

One problem that accompanies conscientization, however, is that in most instances people who hold power are not moved to give up that control except through military force. Military force has no basis in the gospel; neither does the appropriation of land that belongs to the poor. The problem facing educators, then, is to discover a pedagogy for the possessors of wealth and power—that is, ourselves, the non-poor—capable of leading us to yield our grasp on the land the poor need in order to survive.

Education has often taken the form of indoctrination, for the poor and non-poor alike. The Sisters are not naive enough to think they can change the customs of a lifetime; their search for an action-oriented pedagogy is an experiment. They do not presume to have found the tools of a new pedagogy; they are in the process of seeking them.

The Research and Planning Group for this experiment developed a pamphlet which was sent to educators all over the globe. The pamphlet includes a paper that provides a critical social analysis of the current world situation, focusing on the population issue. The paper makes a proposal about our progeny and invites group discussion after the group using it hears five stories, all authentic accounts of a people's dispossession of their land. The accounts are by persons who were there when the dispossession happened.

Educators were invited to discuss the proposal of the paper in view of those and other real-life accounts of dispossession, and were asked to send to the committee the outcome of their extended reflections. The Sisters are in the process of examining those responses and working out steps for new learnings. As a result of those comments, the committee has added two tables, edited the original paper, and made the suggestion that the stories always precede any discussion of the paper. Some groups have added stories using tapes or slide presentations depicting authentic local accounts of dispossession.

This educational approach has been used in a variety of settings from school classrooms to adult groups in parishes to local communities to retreat groups and clubs. The following case describes in detail one particular group engaged in a seminar following the pedagogical principles being explored by the Sisters.

For further information contact: Subcommittee of the Pedagogy Project; Research and Planning Group; Sisters of Notre Dame de Namur; Emmanuel College; 400 The Fenway; Boston, MA 02115 (phone: 617-277-9340).

Case Study
Gospel Agenda in a Global Context

"When the poor reach out to take what is rightfully theirs, what does the gospel mandate the non-poor to do?" The answer was given immediately: "To let go our grasp on the things the poor need in order to survive."

Sister Marie Augusta Neal repeated the question she had asked and the response she had given at the opening session of an institute, entitled "Pedagogy for the Non-Poor," which had been held at Emmanuel College in Boston in 1982. She was in the process of evaluating the pedagogical principles of the institute with a friend whose expertise she valued. When her friend requested some background information, Sister Marie Augusta suggested they had better "begin at the beginning."

FREIRE AND CONSCIENTIZATION

The Emmanuel Institute, Sister Marie Augusta recalled, was only one of over one hundred groups which had wrestled with the above question and response since the summer of 1980. At that time the International Research and Planning Group of the Sisters of Notre Dame de Namur, with which Sister Marie Augusta served, had decided to begin a five-year experiment in teaching the non-poor from the perspective of the poor as part of their ministry for justice.

The Sisters' recognition of the need for a new approach to teaching had emerged from two factors: (1) the realization that many of the people who gather for justice education are in fact not poor; and (2) the need for an effective response to the Sisters' already operative new method of teaching the poor, itself a response to their original congregational mandate to teach the poor in the most neglected places (Notre Dame Rule of 1818).

At their chapter meeting in Rome in 1978 the Sisters had adopted the use of conscientization for working with the poor. At that time they heard from their representative from Brazil about the struggles of those with whom the Sisters ministered and who, through the process of conscientization, had become aware of their rights to the land they needed in order to survive. At the 1980

This case was prepared by Marie Augusta Neal, S.N.D., with Alice Frazer and Robert A. Evans as a basis for discussion rather than to illustrate either effective or ineffective handling of the situation. Copyright © by the Case Study Institute.

research and planning meeting one of those Sisters told how, in using this method, the people had confronted the ALCOA company, which had sought to use their land. Listening was intense at the planning meeting as Sisters from Kenya and from inner-city Cincinnati and Hartford recognized the problem of dispossession that occurred in similar ways with the poor with whom they worked in community organizing efforts. These Sisters felt that conscientization could work as effectively in their locations as it did in the Brazilian missions. They knew it as a method developed by Paulo Freire and described in his book *Pedagogy of the Oppressed* (New York, Herder and Herder, 1970). In Freire's approach oppressed people learn literacy as they simultaneously reflect on Bible passages, raise to consciousness the political, economic, and social oppressions of their lives, and take action to change those conditions. Through the method, used since the late fifties, the poor—at first in Latin America and later in various other parts of the world—rapidly learned as communities to read and write while reflecting biblically on the unjust conditions of their situations.

THE RESISTANCE OF THE NON-POOR

Through Freire's approach in basic Christian communities, people became aware of their human rights and their own capacities to struggle to achieve them. However, the Sisters at the 1980 meeting had reported that when the poor became engaged in struggles for the land, they met resistance from their non-poor neighbors. While the poor were having these wonderful experiences of the gospel come alive, literacy occurring, and new solidarity in a Christian community, they were confronted with the harsh reality of resistance from those who had control of the resources the poor needed in order to survive. Those who were opposing them were of the same faith, rooted in the same Bible, but still did not see the situation with the same eyes. The non-poor were opposing the human rights of the poor in their own community whose resources they not only controlled, but, with real power, resisted sharing.

Sister Marie Augusta recalled how at the 1980 meeting the Sisters who had come from working with those poor called for action. They urged the research and planning group to devise some effective way of educating the non-poor members of the Christian community to the gospel mandate to respond to the just demands of the poor. They saw the mandate based on the understanding that the earth's resources are to be shared with all, and especially with those of greatest need.

Discussion led the Sisters to the conclusion that they were at that time better equipped to help the poor examine the injustices of their lives. The Sisters could assist them to have the courage to develop the solidarity they needed to reach out to take what was rightfully theirs as mandated by the early church Fathers (see Charles Avila, *Ownership: Early Christian Teaching*, Maryknoll, N.Y., Orbis Books, 1983), by St. Thomas Aquinas (see *Summa Theologica* II-II, q. 66 r. 7), and by church documents including *Pacem in Terris* (see no. 44) and

Gaudium et Spes (see no. 69). However, they were less equipped to educate the non-poor to make an effective response to those just demands. The Sisters agreed that to their knowledge no effective pedagogy for such a task existed. They agreed also that whatever they invented to effect such an outcome would need careful testing and reporting. It was necessary to determine if the approach did any more than make people feel they were doing something effective. The Sisters decided at that time to assemble a program for effective education from tested elements that seemed essential, design a five-year plan of action, and begin trying out the method. Sister Marie Augusta recalled that from that discussion came plans to draft the program described in Research Paper #1, entitled *The Gospel Agenda in Global Perspective* (available from the Sociology Department; Emmanuel College; 400 The Fenway; Boston, MA 02115).

The institute assembled at Emmanuel College in the summer of 1982, which Sister Marie Augusta was reviewing, was preceded by several other institutes and workshops in the United States, England, Belgium, Japan, Australia, New Zealand, and Scotland. All had used Research Paper #1, and many had critiqued the method, made suggestions for improvements, and made recommendations for modifications in the original program. The sequence followed at the five-day Emmanuel Institute had since been followed by several other groups. This model seemed to promise some reduction of the non-poor's reluctance to let go of the things the poor need in order to survive. Among some participants there was an enthusiastic move toward participating in an ongoing way in the transformation of unjust structures.

In an attempt to review the model, Sister Marie Augusta traced the specific program followed by the Emmanuel group, a group of 125 North Americans gathered for the five-day workshop. The institute had been advertised nationally, primarily in Catholic publications. Participants, both lay and clergy, came from across the United States.

STORIES OF THE ORGANIZED POOR

On the first morning, just after the question of an appropriate response of the non-poor was posed and answered, the group heard the story of a group of Kenyan farmers who had lost control of their lands when the Delmonico corporation brought in machinery that cut pineapples of only one size. The corporation then bought land through the Kenyan government to assure uniformity of the pineapples. In the process the people whose land it had been for centuries were deprived of a heritage (see Appendix A). Institute participants then heard a second story about a man who could not buy land in Brownsville, Tennessee, because he was black (see Appendix A). They pondered those stories of the poor.

Those stories were followed by three others: one about a family losing its residency in a housing project in Cincinnati; one about multinational control of the cashew nut industry in Brazil (see Appendix A); and the third about the loss of health insurance for coal miners in West Virginia. Through discussion of the stories of the poor, the institute group began discovering that it was not shortage of initiative on the part of the poor that prevented their move to more powerful relationships with the land, but the very initiative itself. The initiative was perceived by the non-poor as dangerous. In fact, it was often categorized as "communist" and hence worthy of abhorrence, even when the initiative was shown to be grounded in biblical reflection. Sister Marie Augusta recalled that this observation elicited some uneasiness among the institute participants, as they shifted in their chairs and looked uncomfortable.

POPULATION DATA

The stories were followed immediately with the beginning of a critical social analysis given in semilecture form with graphs and tables from the Population Reference Bureau, and a news article about the "lifeboat ethic." Sister Marie Augusta, who is professor of sociology at Emmanuel College, presented the analysis and raised the question posed by the population data: Who are our progeny?

She also asked the participants to write their responses to three questions to be discussed in the course of the afternoon: "(1) How many people are there in your community? (2) What is different about the map displayed this morning [it had Africa, rather than the United States, at the center, and all continental land masses were intact] from the one you customarily see in the North American classroom? and (3) What geographical division in the world is fraught with greatest danger: East/West or North/South?"

The critical social analysis focused on the first graph, which demonstrated the doubling of the population of the world from one billion to two billion between 1850 and 1950. As Sister Marie Augusta Neal recalled, those statistics for most people generated anxiety about overpopulation. They learned that it had taken at least nine and a half thousand years (the period of recorded artifacts) for the first billion people to appear on the surface of the earth, while the second billion were produced in a single century. Looking further at the graph, workshop participants discovered that in the following twenty-five years (1950–1975) the population doubled again. The second graph showed that the rates of growth of the peoples of the First World (the predominantly white populations of the industrialized countries of Western Europe and North America) as well as those of the Second World (the Soviet Union and Eastern Europe) were all decreasing because their rate of natural increase was approaching zero. In contrast, the population of the developing nations of Africa, Latin America, and Asia was increasing. The impression given by the data was that the peoples of the Third World would in the not too distant future be almost totally dominant. Furthermore, the population of the developing nations seemed to be increasing at rates beyond the capacity of the resources of the planet. The tables of figures provided a basis for Sister Marie Augusta to define poverty as the condition of peoples with low life expectancy and high infant mortality. The figures also provided evidence that this condition was associated with a low gross national product per capita. In Sister Marie Augusta Neal's opinion, using these data, derived from United Nations research, gave the institute members an understanding which allowed them to begin to speculate on why First World people fear others taking over.

The lecture-discussion led by Sister Marie Augusta Neal then focused on how fear of losing access to resources affects the decisions people make. The group looked at the uses of the "lifeboat ethic thesis," developed by Dr. Garrett Hardin at the University of California in Santa Barbara, which had effectively influenced U.S. government policy to withhold help from poor countries with few resources. His thesis was based on the assumption that it was technically impossible to save both the poor of the Third World nations and ourselves, the non-poor, given the limitations of human resources. Professor Neal speculated that willingness to produce armaments beyond any need of defense is also grounded in this unconscious anxiety about there not being sufficient resources for "them and us" and the high probability that the arms we produce will kill them rather than us. This was a difficult idea for the institute participants to discuss. Sister Marie Augusta Neal had noted that the resistance level was high.

Statistical evidence was then presented that the world population would probably taper off at about 10.5 billion around the year 2110 (see the *World Population Data Sheet, 1980*; annual data sheets are available from Population Reference Bureau, Inc.; 1337 Connecticut Ave., N.W.; Washington, DC 20036). People relaxed somewhat, especially when they saw evidence from the United Nations that world resources can actually supply such a population. However, it was also made clear that starvation results from poor food distribution; this occurs when "people lack the money they need to buy the food that is abundant" (United Nations pamphlet, *Toward a World Economy That Works*, 1980, p. 45).

Then the three questions posed earlier were considered. Sister Marie Augusta was not surprised that very few participants had given a "global" response to the community question; most had not responded that there are 4.5 billion people (the estimated world population in 1982) in their community. Most tended to think of their more immediate surroundings. When the question about the map was discussed, the map with Africa in the middle and all the continental land masses left intact was again displayed. Participants discussed briefly what happens in their thinking when the United States is centered in a world map and the USSR and China are divided. As North Americans, many had the impression of being surrounded by communist countries. Finally, the issue of North/South versus East/West was raised and the conclusion was reached that the more serious division was not East/West but was between the advantaged northern hemisphere and the predominantly deprived southern countries.

At that point a reporter from a conservative Catholic newspaper on the West Coast objected to what he called "the bias that gave the impression of communists as equal partners." He criticized the notion of viewing the First and

Second World nations as a unit, and he observed that a noted Catholic, Michael Novak, had presented evidence denying the North/South distinction. The reporter spoke with strong feeling. Sister Marie Augusta observed that other workshop participants looked at their data, listened to his impassioned plea against brainwashing, and began talking to him earnestly about evidence. They showed him from their own tables the differences between the Third World countries of the southern hemisphere and the First and Second World countries of the northern hemisphere: infant mortality rates, the statistics about food and other resources, the GNPs, the rates of population growth. Some participants agreed that the world had a problem with a technical solution; people only needed the will to solve the problem. One institute member remarked that "we do not have to resort to ideological name-calling."

The reporter acknowledged that the group's responses had helped him to understand the direction of the discussion, but another participant raised the question of whether the non-poor had the will to seek solutions to questions of human deprivation when they were not deprived. There were some who expressed discomfort with considering statistics and graphs as the agenda for religious education. The stories, yes; the data—well, maybe, maybe not. Most agreed, however, that the data were compelling in challenging the assumptions of the lifeboat ethic.

THE WORKSHOPS

The morning sessions were long, two hours and a half with a short coffee break. On Monday and Friday afternoons participants could choose one of five workshops. The offerings were led by a group of people who had previously participated in the pedagogy project and were directly experienced in the content they presented. The workshops included one on "Racism in the City," conducted by two registered nurses with long experience in city hospital work in the Boston area. One was a member of the first black family to live in the Columbia Point Housing Project. They were both black and both property owners in Dorchester. They moved their workshop participants into an examination of the experience of black professionals and community people in Boston.

Kip Tiernan, the leader of a second workshop, was a public relations professional turned street activist years ago. She had founded both Rosie's Place, for poor and homeless women, and the Poor Peoples' United Fund, an agency operated by a board of poor people who organized self-help groups. Streetwise and articulate, in Sister Marie Augusta's judgment, Kip discussed effective organization for state legislative action on behalf of the poor. Her analysis was critical of "do-gooders" who wanted to help the poor but did not hear the poor.

In the third workshop the resource leaders were five Sisters of Notre Dame de Namur; all were teachers who had employed the pedagogy project in classroom settings. These were: a first-grade teacher; one with middle-grade students; two high-school teachers; and a teacher who had spent a great deal of time working with parents of school children. One of the high-school teachers shared how she had taught a high-school workshop in the heart of Boston using the same graphs and tables employed at the Emmanuel Institute. These teachers discussed the problems and promises of the pedagogy project, providing ideas of how to share the material with different age groups. The first-grade teacher had slides of her students examining neighborhood housing as well as tapes of their classroom discussion as they related their own experiences to those in the stories the institute had heard.

In the fourth workshop a black Sister and a white Sister provided an account of what they called "a school with a difference." St. Francis de Sales, a Roxbury experimental school with a genuine black culture, had been operated by several Notre Dame Sisters and Sisters of other congregations for over ten years. They demonstrated how a community which emphasizes black culture can satisfy a mixed population, develop community pride, and create a promising learning environment.

In the fifth workshop two Sisters from the D Street Housing Project in South Boston and three Sisters from the Columbia Point Housing Project recounted the experience of living and working in an urban housing project. The workshop included a discussion of the issues faced by the poor when public housing is converted into private developments.

THE CHURCH'S TEACHING AGENDA

On Tuesday morning, alerted to some engaging issues from the Monday afternoon workshops, the assembled institute examined the church's historic response. Sister Marie Augusta, through lecture and discussion, examined a set of social encyclicals of the Catholic church on the rights of workers and the development of peoples. The presentation began with *Rerum Novarum* (1891), on the conditions of labor and the rights of the worker to a fair share of the profits of industry. Sister Marie Augusta moved through: *Quadragesimo Anno* (1931), which affirms the right to strike and boycott; *Mater et Magistra* (1961), which calls Latin America to account for the vast disparity between the rich and the poor in a Christian continent; *Octogesimo Anno* (1971), which is a call to all Christians to move to effective political action to transform the structures of their societies in line with the standards of social justice; and *Laborem Exercens* (1981), which recognizes the rights of workers to ownership of the means of production. Sister Marie Augusta found that those who were familiar with these themes of human rights in church documents welcomed it as a review. Most, however, stated they were hearing about these encyclical themes for the first time. Several participants commented that they identified the themes as communist rather than as Catholic. Sister Marie Augusta then looked at *Pacem in Terris* (1963), in which Pope John XXIII called peace, poverty, and human rights the central concerns of the committed Catholic. Through an examination of *Populorum Progressio* (1967) and the synodal document *Justice in the World* (1971), the institute participants were shown how the work of the United Nations in the development of the Human Rights Covenants was assisted by the work of the church. Also explored in an ecumenical dimension was the development of church thought as recorded in *Church Alert*, a publication of the World Council of Churches.

GLOBAL AND BIBLICAL PERSPECTIVES

On Tuesday evening a group of women just back from Nicaragua presented the struggle of the people there to complete their revolution. They recounted, through story and song, what was happening and what needed to be done in Central America. They reviewed the deaths of Maura Clark, Dorothy Kazel, Ita Ford, and Jeanne Donovan and showed the slide show *El Salvador: Country in Crisis*. People watched, listened, sang, asked questions, and pondered. At this point some murmured about too much social analysis and not enough gospel. Sister Marie Augusta recalled jotting in her notebook that for many in the group the link was not yet clear.

On Wednesday she began to forge that link by focusing on the gospel agenda from a biblical perspective. She led a group discussion of Leviticus 25, which announces the sabbatical year, in which all are called to renew their commitment to the people, and the jubilee, every fiftieth year, in which the people are to have their ancestral lands restored to them. Also examined was Luke 3, in which repentance is constituted by giving food and clothing to those who have none. Many in the group concluded that depriving people of these, when one has more than one needs, constitutes sin. Considering Mark 10, participants found the rich young man turning sadly away from the mission of Jesus because he has many possessions, and Jesus comments how hard it is for the rich to enter heaven. That is harder, Jesus claims, than for a camel to get through the eye of a needle. The good news to the poor in Luke 4 is that they will possess the land.

Sister Marie Augusta then shared how she saw Jesus calming our anxieties about there not being enough for us if we follow all these mandates. Jesus reminds us of the flowers and birds being clothed, as is recorded in Matthew 6. She felt people's spirits rise again. They seemed to be assured that they did not have to struggle alone. But Sister Marie Augusta continued to question the group: What is the way the gospel gets done today? What does this gospel ask of us now?

DISPLACEMENT OF THE URBAN POOR

On Wednesday afternoon the participants boarded buses to find out who will be living in Boston in 1990. Accompanied by the leaders of the "Racism in the City" workshop, the group went the route of the water's edge. They rode along Commonwealth Avenue, with its old brownstones newly converted into condominiums. Next came downtown Boston's old red-light district, or "combat zone," which is being transformed into elegant Park Plaza, a complex of expensive hotels and stores. The group learned that the adjacent Chinatown community was moving out to Brighton and Allston on the edge of the city. In the North End, next to the new government center and Quincy Market, they saw where burned out buildings produced by five years of "arson for profit" were being refurbished as condominiums and the wharf's warehouses were being transformed into luxury apartments. In some areas local organizations, public monies, and church action were providing housing for the elderly, and some local organizers had redevelopment in process with federal aid. Throughout the tour, from South Boston to Roxbury to Dorchester, the leaders pointed out neighborhoods that had once been dominated by Jewish and Christian European immigrants and that had then become black and Hispanic areas and that were now giving way to elite housing and living. Rents were soaring. The dominant image was of the poor, displaced by the gentrification process, being forced into smaller, more overcrowded, ill-equipped living units. The group saw that ordinary people were soon going to lose their city unless they acted together to claim their land. But how is this to be done? This was the question the leaders raised with the group.

On Thursday and Friday institute participants looked critically at the idea of triage, which Sister Marie Augusta explained as the notion of letting one-third of the population die, both locally and all over the world. She discussed sociobiological theories which discourage altruism and focus on a struggle of self-interest. The participants examined capitalism and socialism as ideologies. Church perspectives were included in the critical examination.

COLUMBIA POINT

Thursday night focused on the documentary film *Down the Project*. Some of the D Street and Columbia Point residents who are in the film were present. From Columbia Point came several very expressive young black men and one gentle, contemplative elderly lady, as well as those who led the Monday workshop on housing projects. These residents were seeing the film for the first time. In Sister Marie Augusta's opinion, their expressive comments on seeing themselves on screen disarmed everyone and generated a tone of solidarity in the auditorium. When they and the women from D Street then recounted some differences they had concerning the message of the film, the institute participants listened intently. The film predicted the closing down of the publicly-funded housing project at Columbia Point, a beautiful, now coveted spot on the harbor right next to the new Kennedy Library and the University of Massachusetts's new Boston campus. The project had been built years before, when the site was considered a wasteland. The project now housed only 350 of the original 1,500 low-income families. The Columbia Point residents and the organizers from D Street were seeking concrete support for their efforts to hold onto their land rather than analytic predictions of loss of the land to the "powers that be" for private development. Institute members shared their responses with the group. They said they were "impressed," "moved," and "sobered." However, Sister Marie Augusta was unsure whether any of the non-poor participants had actually been moved to action.

In retrospect, Sister Marie Augusta discovered the most telling comments in participants' responses were associated with the field trip on "Who Will Be Living in Boston in 1990?" and with the encounter with the residents at Columbia Point and D Street who were in the film. The residents had demonstrated a will to hold onto their land and housing. They challenged the institute members by an expression of faith that those who had come to hear their stories would stay to help in the struggle. Sister Marie Augusta heard some participants suggest that the next steps might include a supportive community of the non-poor who recognize and affirm through specific action the rights of the poor. But Sister Marie Augusta found herself wondering if they would assume the initiative to form those communities.

Institute participants departed with Research Paper #1 in hand. The International Research and Planning Group would soon be sending them and participants of all of the other intensive seminars Research Paper #2, entitled *Faith and Pedagogy* (available from: Sociology Department; Emmanuel College; 400 The Fenway; Boston, MA 02115). In that paper the Brazilian Sisters recount step-by-step how they work directly with the poor. The Research and Planning Group would then be asking each of the almost five hundred people who received these pieces: What have you done? What are you doing? What will you do? What difference has it made that we are now willing to learn from the poor? What impact comes from linking critical social analysis with the gospel mandate for a world community? What impact can that linkage have on a world facing a choice between destruction or life?

Sister Marie Augusta closed her notebook and turned to her friend. They both agreed that members of the Research and Planning Group would be pleased if the responses were significantly concrete and positive. But she also needed to consider recommendations for changes in the pedagogy project if the responses were either inconclusive or if the seminars did not seem to be making a difference in the lives of the non-poor. "How can the project be modified? Do we have yet the elements of an effective pedagogy for the non-poor?" she asked.

Appendix

NOTE: the following are sketches of three of the "stories of the poor" discussed at the Emmanuel Institute. The stories were reported by the Sister or Sisters listed at the end of each piece.

TENNESSEE, USA

In trying to make contacts for the formation of JONAH (Just Organized Area Headquarters), we asked a black woman if her church would make an announcement about our working in the county. She looked at us with tears in her eyes and said, "I am ashamed to tell you that we have only nine families in our church. Of the nine families, only one lives near the church." Then, after a pause, she said, "No, I am not ashamed to tell you that. Let me explain why. In the 60s when all of us blacks were struggling for the right to vote, the big landowners in most areas of the county put the people off the land and burned down their homes so they could not return. All those families fled to the north, leaving our church and community. Today our numbers are few."

What we knew as a common reality in the northeast of Brazil suddenly became a harsh reality here. What happened in our own country in the 60s, and still continues through foreclosures and partition sales of black-owned farmland, makes it evident that unscrupulous acquisition of land by the powerful is a constant in the history of oppressed peoples.

Another incident. One day, one of the leaders of our JONAH group, who wanted to buy a piece of land to raise hogs just as his father had, saw a farm for sale. He went to the land bank to make arrangements for a loan and gave the necessary information about the location and price of the farm. The banker told him to return the next day to sign the papers.

When the young man returned to the bank, the banker informed him that they could not make him a loan and that the farm was being sold to someone else anyway. The young man knew he had enough collateral for the loan and that the land had been available to him the day before. He also realized he would not get a loan to buy land in Brownsville because his skin is black.

Sister Maryann Gillespie and
Sister Jo Anne Depweg, S.N.D.
Brownsville, Tennessee, USA

KENYA

Kariuke is a small farmer who works in Kenya. He and his family have planted pineapples for years, and the market has always been reasonably good.

In more recent years, the market became particularly accessible through Delmonico, a multinational corporation which set up small factories for buying and processing pineapples.

Delmonico at one time suffered severe losses because, while the pineapples were of varying sizes, the corporation only had machinery for a standard-size cut. Because of this difficulty the corporation bargained with the government for land. Concessions were made and advantages offered on both sides, with the result that an incredible amount of traditional family farmland was sold by the state to Delmonico. Most of the farmers continued with the company, by working as unskilled laborers with no rights to the land.

Ann Ronayne, S.N.D.
Kenya

NORTHEAST BRAZIL

Antonio is a poor farmer working on free state land in the interior of the state of Maranhao, Northeast Brazil. His big cash crop, the cashew nut, comes from a small fruit tree grown apart from the regular crops in a reserved area and flowering once a year. He also has his regular crops for family consumption: beans, manioc root, and small portions of squash, melons, and greens.

Antonio has seven children. The four small ones work on the farm, and the three older ones are in the capital studying so as to escape the plight of their parents. In the city, they live on the edge of the water in houses on stilts, gaining their living from day to day as unskilled workers and studying by night. Their studies will conclude with high school at best, and they will continue as unskilled workers. The "system" needs their labor at low cost.

Antonio's wife, María, is a stable organizer of all the children's activities and of the farm, for Antonio also works hard in the organization of the small farmers through the Farmers' Union and Cooperative. Both Antonio and María hope for better days for themselves and their children.

The family is typical of approximately 80 percent of rural Northeast Brazil. What will happen to their crops this year is predictable. The drought in Northeast Brazil has dried up the beans, so production will be much lower than in other years, and they will have less to eat. The drought has also caused the *cajus* (cashew) to flower early, which means less fruit and fewer nuts this year. Antonio will probably make only $200 instead of his expected $500, and that will have to last till the next harvest.

Won't the price of cashews go up if production is down? Yes. But here's what will happen. The bank will refuse to lend money to the cooperative because a specialist in *caju* has not guaranteed the cooperative's crop; the bank will make the loans to the local landowners who are also merchants. The cooperative will be forced to sell to the merchants at lower rates and so the small farmer will gain less. Where will the nuts go? The merchants will transport them to the capital and sell them to large companies which, in their turn, have direct sales contracts with multinationals like Nestlés.

Eventually, the same thing will happen to the land. Real estate firms already are sending out intermediaries who through any means buy and resell state land to the big farmers already contracted to sell directly to exporting companies.

To put it in a nutshell, the First World controls the food of the starving Third World through elite control of land, crops, transportation, processing, and marketing. All the landowners are Catholic. When the members of the Farmers' Union and Cooperative demand respect and appeal to the Christian principles of justice and equality with regard to their land and lives, they are repressed and labeled as subversive.

Barbara Ann English, S.N.D.
Brazil

Teaching Note

TOPICS AND QUESTIONS FOR DISCUSSION

1. One helpful way to get an overall view of this seminar is to develop an outline of the week-long program. This can also be helpful for discussing the relationship and order of the various components.

2. Reread the three stories in Appendix A. What pedagogical role is played by the stories of the poor which began the workshop? How could those stories be utilized most effectively? What is their relationship to the "story" of the Columbia Point Housing Project?

3. A distinctive component of this model is the sessions on critical social analysis. What role does that component play in the seminar? How would you respond to those participants who questioned the appropriateness of "statistics and graphs" for religious education?

4. Apparently the field trip and the encounters with the Boston residents had the greatest impact on the participants. Why was that so?

5. Discuss how this model seeks to respond to the question of one of the seminar participants: "Do the non-poor have the will to seek solutions to questions of human deprivation when they are not deprived?" What assumptions do the model architects make about motivating forces which lead to transformation of the non-poor? What barriers to change are implied by the design?

6. Discuss Sister Marie Augusta Neal's final questions: "How can the project be modified? Do we have yet the elements of an effective pedagogy for the non-poor?"

ADDITIONAL RESOURCES

Avila, Charles. *Ownership: Early Christian Teaching.* Maryknoll, N.Y.: Orbis Books, 1983.

Cardenal, Ernesto. *The Gospel of Solentiname.* 4 vols. Maryknoll, N.Y.: Orbis Books, 1976.

Dorr, Donal. *Option for the Poor: A Hundred Years of Vatican Social Teaching.* Maryknoll, N.Y.: Orbis Books, 1983.

Freire, Paulo. *Pedagogy of the Oppressed.* New York: Seabury Press, 1971.

Gutiérrez, Gustavo. *The Power of the Poor in History.* Maryknoll, N.Y.: Orbis Books, 1983.

Holland, Joe, and Peter Henriot. *Social Analysis: Linking Faith and Justice.* Maryknoll, N.Y.: Orbis Books, 1983.

Míguez Bonino, José. *Doing Theology in a Revolutionary Situation*. Philadelphia: Fortress Press, 1975.

Neal, Marie Augusta. *A Sociotheology of Letting Go: The Role of a First World Church Facing Third World Peoples*. New York: Paulist Press, 1977.

O'Brien, David J., and Thomas Shannon. *Renewing the Earth: Catholic Documents on Peace, Justice, and Liberation*. Garden City, N.Y.: Image Books, 1977.

Population Reference Bureau. *World Population Sheet* (published annually). Available from: Population Reference Bureau, Inc.; 1337 Connecticut Ave., N.W.; Washington, DC 20036.

Sisters of Notre Dame de Namur Pedagogy Project. *The Gospel Agenda in Global Perspective*. Research Paper #1. Available from: Sociology Department; Emmanuel College; 400 The Fenway; Boston, MA 02115.

Sisters of Notre Dame de Namur Pedagogy Project. *Faith and Pedagogy: A Journey*. Research Paper #2. Available from: Sociology Department; Emmanuel College; 400 The Fenway; Boston, MA 02115.

Tamez, Elsa. *Bible of the Oppressed*. Maryknoll, N.Y.: Orbis Books, 1982.

United Nations. *International Bill of Human Rights*. New York: United Nations, 1978. Pamphlet no. 36494–OPI/598–June, 1978–35M.

United Nations. *Toward a World Economy That Works*. New York: United Nations, Department of Public Information, Division of Economic and Social Information, 1980.

DOUGLAS JOHN HALL

Commentary on
Gospel Agenda in a Global Context

This description of the attempt on the part of Christian educators to communicate the message of love and justice to non-poor Christians is both impressive and instructive. It is also somewhat inconclusive and frustrating, and leaves me (with Sister Marie Augusta) "wondering."

The first part of my commentary will be a critique of the constructive and integrative elements I have found in the pedagogy of the model—elements from which we may glean lessons for future use. Second, I shall offer what I hope is a positive critique of the procedure adopted in the model. Third, I shall attempt to suggest some ways in which the approach could be enhanced. Fourth, I shall urge use of the model within the context of Christian congregations.

CRITIQUE OF THE CONSTRUCTIVE AND INTEGRATIVE ELEMENTS

Both the variety of experiences and the ordering of them are impressive. The educators have used almost every available resource for getting at the issues they address. Beginning with explicit instances ("stories") of oppression puts the whole discussion into the worldly arena in a way that a theoretical statement of the problem would not do. It is also provocative that these stories were carefully selected to demonstrate what the members of the institute needed to find out quite soon in their exercise—that it is the very *initiative* of the poor that the non-poor perceive as "dangerous." This introduces an existential note into the discussion from the outset: the members of the institute are turned from an objectivizing stance with respect to the oppressed to one which makes them conscious, as the "threatened" group, of their own subjectivity.

Shifting the discussion then to population data reintroduces a sort of interim objectivity, thus preventing the group from rushing into an emotional response lacking sufficient intellectual rigor to sustain itself. There is much yet for them to *learn*! Then, the population discussion gradually moves them from the imbibing of "data" to the recognition if the immediate significance of the data:

they (or at least the whites among them) are an endangered species. I was first a little surprised at the hint of "fear-tactics" in this part of the program, but upon reflection it seemed legitimate. It is part of the truth that the "haves" must assimilate, as Barbara Ward and many others have been attempting to tell us for years.

When Sister Marie Augusta Neal moved from that to the suggestion that arms production may be related to the fear of whites, she was verging on the overly dramatic, I think. A necessary *perspective* might have been introduced if at this point some "hard data" about the arms race had been offered, thus turning to a better use (namely, a constructive *political* critique) some of the personal guilt which seems to have been experienced by the group. It is no doubt pedagogically effective to make people realize that they are personally capable of violence; but a more lasting effect can be gained from the shock of such recognition if it is combined with social analysis.

I was at a loss to understand why, at that juncture, the apparently comforting information was introduced that world population would taper off at 10.5 billion around the year 2110. "People relaxed a little." Perhaps they needed to. But they might not have relaxed so much if they had realized (which surely we must) that this quantitative escalation and "tapering off" could never occur *in reality* without drastic qualitative changes in the lifestyles of the "haves" of the world. *Perhaps* the earth can bear 10.5 billion human beings, but it certainly cannot do that without the "non-poor" being introduced to what many of us in the First World would probably consider sheer want!

It was clever, though, to help the group discover that even after all that, they had not grasped the point that "their community" consists of the whole human population of the globe. The myopia and provincialism of the average North American are truly astonishing.

I do not know whether someone planted that "conservative Catholic newspaper" reporter, but he played his part beautifully. What could have been better pedagogy at this point than to have the position against which the group is struggling represented so simplistically that the group itself would become staunch defenders of the position it has gradually been developing? And then to have the brash reporter admit publicly that he had learned something!

All of this "classroom" activity needed to be combined with practical experience, certainly; and the workshops, the tours of the downtown area, the meeting with representatives of oppressed peoples in other parts of the world, and other activities obviously provided such experience. I found it particularly insightful of the planners of the study to choose young, outspoken black men and an elderly "contemplative" woman to represent the displacement of the poor at Columbia Point. Those experiences also combined provocatively, it would seem, with the study of carefully selected biblical passages and the review of Roman Catholic tradition as expressed in papal encyclicals. Having wrung from the group (or some of the group) the confession that they had regarded as "communist" ideas which turned out to be thoroughly biblical and impeccably Catholic must surely have been one of the high points in the whole experiment.

In terms of teaching, then, I must conclude that the educators in this model have gone about as far as they can go. However, I doubt that it is far enough. The model contains many constructive and integrative elements, but I suspect that at the end of the five-year period Sister Marie Augusta will still be uncertain about the overall effectiveness of the model.

CRITIQUE OF THE PROCEDURE

This does not of course imply that I think the experiment should be stopped. It could well be that, partly as a result of this approach, some persons will experience the kind of *metanoia* that is needed. However, the "repentance" that is required here cannot, in my opinion, be produced by pedagogy.

I wonder if the Christian educators in this model do not have a too idealistic preconception of what they can achieve *as educators*. Specifically, the question has to be raised whether methods applicable to the pedagogy of the poor are applicable in the case of the non-poor.

For one thing, the problematic facing the Christian educator of the non-poor is quite different from that which confronts the educator of the poor. Educators of the poor encounter in those they seek to influence a situation combining ignorance and lack of initiative. They must seek to move the poor from the condition of illiteracy and insufficient awareness of their total circumstances to one of informed awareness, and from the condition of passivity and fatalism respecting their destiny to one of active hope, struggle for social change, and so on. In order to achieve that, the Christian educator engages in a program of literacy which at the same time opens the community of the poor to a new self-image as human beings whose potentiality for fullness of life remains to be developed.

With the non-poor the problematic confronting the educator is different— qualitatively so! While certain things may and can be taught the non-poor, ignorance is not their fundamental barrier to life. Neither is their problem the lack of courage or assertiveness, though many middle-class persons feel "locked into" the rituals and expectations of their social stratum. The predicament of the non-poor at its most rudimentary theological level of expression is their lack of *caritas*—not "charity," but "suffering love" (agape).

The Christian educator must seek to move the non-poor from the state of anxious *self*-concern to that of concern for "the other." This is a tall order. It is one thing to approach persons with the message that the Christ wills to free them from their oppression and despair and give them freedom and hope; it is something else to approach with a gospel that aims to free them from their possessions and give them love. All "rewards" of faith are rather obvious in the first instance—even from a secular point of view. They are not at all obvious in the second—even from a *Christian* point of view. History is not overflowing with masses of Christian believers who walked the *Via Dolorosa* gladly.

SUGGESTIONS

I would conclude, therefore, that the educators of the non-poor need to acquire a very realistic assessment of what, qua educators, they can do for and with the non-poor (including themselves?). Through contact with the poor of the Third and Fourth Worlds; through contextually-conscious biblical study and a new exposure to the silent parts of our Christian tradition, such as that *most* silent tradition Luther named *theologia crucis*; through sociological, demographic, environmental, and other types of studies which can expose them to the actual truth about planet Earth; through psychological study of the function of "property" and "possessions" (something that the present study did not touch upon); and, of course, through the use of models such as this one, it is possible to put the non-poor *in the way of the metanoia* that is needed to alter their (our!) condition from one of anxious self-seeking to suffering love for the neighbor. But I think that we are naive in the extreme if we imagine that we can develop *techniques* for effecting that *metanoia*. Some will be changed, and some will acknowledge the contribution of the educators in bringing about that change—and that will be entirely sufficient as proof of the importance of Christian education. But at bottom what is required in the case of the non-poor is *a fundamental and ongoing conversion of the spirit*, namely a "continuing baptism"—the "drowning" of that within all of us which grasps after ultimate *securitas*, and the birth of that "new being" which reaches out to "the other."

At one point in the model I sensed an expression of this more realistic assessment of the goal of pedagogy for the non-poor. This was in the statement: "This model seemed to promise *some reduction of the non-poor's reluctance to let go* of the things the poor need in order to survive" (emphasis added). This, it seems to me, is what can be reasonably and legitimately aimed at by pedagogy as such: clearing away some of the debris, so to speak, so that the light of the gospel may get in. But if such a goal is what we envisage, then we should not proceed on the assumption that a "conscientization" program for the poor can be applied *mutatis mutandis* to the non-poor. It *is* hard for the rich to enter the Kingdom! Our pedagogy should not assume that it is anything else than hard, terribly hard. Fortunately, there are "possibilities" that transcend *our* pedagogy.

THE MODEL AND CHRISTIAN CONGREGATIONS

A final question I have about the model has to do with the actual make-up of the Emmanuel College Institute. Nowhere are we informed who these people were—racially, sexually, economically, educationally, or in terms of their relatedness to one another. It would seem to me to make a great deal of difference, for instance, whether one attempted such a program as this with persons chosen at random from a wide population base or with persons who were in some other way "in community" with one another—for instance, members of the same Christian congregation.

To my mind, it would make much more sense—in the light of the final sentence in the preceding section—were such a model to be used *within Christian congregations.* Because in that case, besides the influences coming to such a group from the program described in the model itself, there could be many other concomitant contributions to their overall nurture in the faith: the preaching of the gospel, the prayer and spiritual life of the congregation, a wider and longer-range study of the Christian tradition, and so on. These "ordinary" Christian activities, especially if they were sufficiently coordinated with the special pedagogical content of the model, could help to provide opportunities for the non- or trans-pedagogical "possibilities" which, to my mind, are necessary if the "leap of faith" (*metanoia*) to which I have referred is ever to occur. And, of course, it has to occur over and over again—so an ongoing *koinonia* is the *conditio sine qua non* for the deployment of this model.

MARY ELIZABETH MOORE

Commentary on
Gospel Agenda in a Global Context

The Sisters of Notre Dame de Namur know the connections between those who are poor and those who are not, and they want others to know. Furthermore, they know the connections between Boston and Brazil, Tennessee and Kenya. Their knowledge is not the empty "banking" of information which Paulo Freire bemoans (*Pedagogy of the Oppressed*, New York, Herder and Herder, 1970), but the knowledge which penetrates and motivates.

The Sisters seek a pedagogy for the non-poor that will correspond in impact to Freire's method of conscientization with the poor. As they state in the Program Overview (above), they particularly appreciate that in Freire's method the exploited people come to understand "that they have a human right to possess the land they need for survival." The corresponding pedagogy needs to help the non-poor understand that they, who possess the land, must let go of it so that these others can survive.

This is not an entirely unique endeavor. Churches have given considerable attention in recent years to social and ecological education for the non-poor. To date, however, this educational work has been directed largely to questions of personal lifestyle, and the audience has been primarily middle-class (including neither the very wealthy nor the very poor). The effort of the Sisters of Notre Dame to create concrete linkages between the poor and the non-poor and their particular emphasis on possessing and letting go of the land are their unique and penetrating challenge.

The center of power in the Sisters' pedagogy is their own conviction that the way the non-poor see the world *must* change so that their actions *will* change so that the poor *can* change their situation. This power of conviction is like gravity pulling non-poor persons toward the earth for a new look. The gravity defies the forces of fear, comfort, or blindness which propel people up and away from reality. It attempts to ground people so that they will deal with what is on the ground with them.

The elements of the pedagogy itself are legion. The teachers include the people serving in the impoverished areas, the poor themselves, and, to a lesser extent, the gathered members of the institute. The methods include situation analysis (global and local case stories, statistical data, interviews, and field trips with persons directly involved in oppressed situations); analysis of Christian tradition (particularly drawing upon the church's encyclicals on social mission and biblical texts on land ownership, wealth, and giving); and action strategizing (offering information about modes of action with the poor). To name these multiple elements is to call attention to the Sisters' apparent assumption that encountering the multiple aspects of poverty leads to fuller understanding and more motivation to respond. They further seem to assume that crossing over into the world of the poor is a vital link for understanding and response. Their ability to communicate these multiple aspects and to create bridges for crossing over should not be underestimated. The elements are easier to identify in theory than to duplicate in practice.

EDUCATIONAL ISSUES

Certain educational issues are raised by the pedagogical method the Sisters have developed, and within each issue is a possible block to the effectiveness of the model.

First, to what extent is the effectiveness of any educational methodology influenced by the attitudes that persons bring into the situation? In the case described, no clear openings were created to invite people to explore and share their own ideologies and attitudes toward the poor or toward the questions of wealth, power, and land possession. Some of this apparently emerged, as in the observations of several participants that the encyclical themes sounded more communist than Catholic.

Secondly, to what extent is indoctrination (see the Program Overview) avoided when the leaders are trying to convey their own ideas of the basic problems and solutions? Does action-oriented pedagogy necessarily avoid indoctrination? The Sisters seem to assume this, and this assumption could lead to lack of criticalness about their own point of view and a lack of openness to reforming it.

Related to this is a third issue. To what extent do we need to look at radically different points of view in a situation of oppression and hear counter-arguments? Certainly, the Sisters created an opportunity for the voiceless to speak, but in not offering a dialogue with persons of power whose views are different, they have not provided an opportunity for institute participants to hear those persons and to evaluate their counter-arguments. More than one well-intended conference-goer has returned to a local parish or congregation with new insight about the poor or multinationals, only to be blasted by persons whose perspectives are different, whose vested interests are great, and to whom they are not at all prepared to respond.

Fourth, to what extent does an educational methodology need to include a component that summarizes and ends the discussion of the issues and leads to a decision for action? The Sisters seem to assume that knowledge about the oppressive situation and possible steps for action will, in fact, lead to action.

This is a questionable assumption, for new information may be only one component in social change. Certainly, they are offering the possibility for changed perspectives, and in the final components of the institute and the follow-up mailing they are encouraging active response. They are not, however, offering the opportunity for participants actually to name the issues and come to a decision about response.

On this last point James Botkin, Mahdi Elmandjra, and Mircea Malitza have challenged the educational community to develop innovative learning to respond to the rapidly changing world (see especially their book *No Limits to Learning*, Oxford, Pergamon Press, 1979, pp. 17–44). They describe innovative learning as both anticipatory and participatory. The Sisters have given quite a lot of attention to anticipatory learning, for example, anticipation of global population statistics and of shifting population and ownership patterns in Boston. They have given less attention to participatory learning. The possibilities in their model might be multiplied if the institute were based in parishes, where people could examine and reform their own actions in relation to the problems raised and in relation to an ongoing community of support and accountability. Further, active work *with* the poor might further enhance the learning and response.

This leads to the fifth issue. To what extent does a pedagogy require a communal base and communal action? The Sisters' case reveals a great deal of group interaction throughout the five-day institute, but the building of a communal base of support is not evident. How might learning have been enhanced by the building of a communal identity, by working at communal decisions, and by developing networks which would function during the follow-through period?

THEOLOGICAL ISSUES

The title of this project, "Gospel Agenda in a Global Context," suggests that there are tasks to be done in the particular context of today's world. This agenda is made very clear in the Program Overview. But where is the transcendent dimension? The case is very clear in stating that the poor have need and that the gospel mandates the non-poor to respond. What is less clear is what God is doing in the midst of these problems and what difference that makes. The failure to ask these questions may actually limit our vision of the gospel agenda.

The hiddenness of transcendence in the project is carried into the biblical interpretation. The texts seem to be approached as instructions for particular situations and mandates for action. The question of what God is doing or promising to do in the texts is not asked. Certainly mandates *are* spoken in those texts, but how much might those mandates be undergirded and radicalized if we precede our moralizing with theologizing? (This distinction is made by James Sanders, who understands the biblical witness—and, hence, hermeneutics—to be concerned first with God's grace and faithfulness. See particularly his "Hermeneutics," in *The Interpreter's Dictionary of the Bible, Supplementary Volume*, Nashville, Abingdon, 1976, pp. 406-7.)

Similar to these issues is one other. What is the role of the church's tradition in educating persons to respond to the poor? In the case presentation the church's relation to the poor is stated with a selectivity that supports the agenda being put forth, but it does not call attention to the church's mixed teaching and action regarding the poor. Neither does it call attention to other doctrinal issues which bear on the questions of poverty and response to the poor. For example, the doctrine of salvation, when interpreted in individualistic and other-worldly terms, undermines the view of the gospel agenda being put forth in this case study. People need to deal with those teachings which have supported oppression as well as with those which have rejected it if reformation is to take place. With full awareness that no project can, or should, deal with all church perspectives and doctrine, I raise the question whether the church's tradition might have been engaged more fully and more fruitfully.

POWER IN PEDAGOGY

The power in this pedagogical method offered by the Sisters of Notre Dame is in its compelling appeal to see and hear the world and to respond. The power lies in stories, in direct communication between the poor and non-poor, in the guidance of tradition, and in concrete guides for action. The most fundamental power lies in the people who have lived these stories, shared them, worked together to define and address the issues, and participated in the institute in hopes that they might make a difference.

PHILIP J. SCHARPER

Commentary on
Gospel Agenda in a Global Context

Sister Marie Augusta Neal states clearly the basic problem of education in the Gospel Agenda model: "to discover a pedagogy for the . . . non-poor capable of leading us to yield our grasp on the land the poor need in order to survive." It is important to recall her definition of land as "not only . . . territory but also . . . the health care, education, and security needed to live in simple human dignity."

The non-poor must let go of the things the poor need. But close to the core of the problem—if, indeed, not the very core itself—is the fact that so many of the non-poor do not consider themselves to be in that category. In their eyes they are members of the great North American middle class, struggling just to get by, "to survive," in the phrase used by Sister Neal precisely in reference to the poor. For this reason, an effective pedagogy for the non-poor arouses fear and defensiveness, even as an effective pedagogy for the poor arouses hope and positive action.

Basic to the pedagogical task, then, is to devise methods to convince the non-poor that by any standard they possess land in abundance compared to the truly poor in North America and throughout the world. However, if and as that realization of privileged position at the earth's table develops within the non-poor, another dragon often appears to bar the path of an effective pedagogy. The human person is an unfeathered biped that cooks its food, is capable of almost infinite self-deception, and creates myths and stereotypes about what it fears or hates. So the non-poor, when forced to recognize the existence of the poor (who comprise more than half of the planet's population), fall back upon such comforting observations as those they learned at home, at school, or even at church or synagogue: "The poor are poor because they are lazy and lack motivation," "The poor are really happy with their lot," "The poor are ungrateful, despite the foreign aid we lavish upon them and the welfare billions we squander here at home." Far too often education of the non-poor on global issues of peace and justice is bread cast upon the waters which often returns as simply wet bread.

INSULARITY OF THE NON-POOR

One of my concerns is whether "Gospel Agenda in a Global Context" fully confronts the basic educational problems of shaping liberating pedagogy. The problems to be addressed include:

1. To the non-poor the poor are all but invisible. President Reagan was rather typical of the non-poor when he expressed surprise that so many millions went hungry in the United States. It was also a typical action to appoint a commission to study the problem. "I was hungry, and you . . ."
2. The non-poor are not accustomed to thinking globally. A telling example was given in the case. When asked "How many people are in your community?" very few thought in terms of the planetary community, the entire human family.
3. The non-poor seem unaware of the systemic causes of poverty. When confronting poverty (which the non-poor seldom do), it is secondhand through stories of poverty in Appalachia, Kenya, or Brazil.

Unfortunately, this insularity of the non-poor threatens to deepen. A foreign language is no longer demanded in many colleges either as an entrance or a course requirement. Also, most of us get our daily injection of world news from television; the text on prime time half-hour news shows would not fill a single page of the average North American newspaper. Minimal educational requirements, superficial media coverage, and lack of direct contact maintain our isolation.

THE CHURCH'S OPTION FOR THE POOR

The fact that this case study is presented by a community of Catholic nuns is significant far beyond itself. It reflects a profound change which has been taking place within the Christian churches, which now, with varying emphases but with impressive clarity, are proclaiming their option for the poor. However, if church leadership, including educators, continues both to voice and act upon this option, they may find themselves shepherds without sheep or deeply embroiled in controversy, as is often the case with the National Council of Churches. Yet this option for the poor is thick-rooted in the Scriptures and glows throughout the Christian tradition. Part of the churches' pedagogical task, then, is so to teach the Scriptures that the roots are laid bare for the Christians' option for the poor.

EDUCATION AS "RIGHT QUESTIONS"

One definition of education is that it is a process which teaches the taught the right questions. The list of such "right questions" is extensive in terms of a gospel agenda in a global context. To cite but two which should be asked in our seminaries and church schools:

1. If, as we believe, the human person is a living temple, then why, as we look around the world, do we see that most of the temples seem jerry-built, falling into decay, or even desecrated?
2. If, as the Scriptures proclaim, all of humankind is made in God's image and likeness, how do we, as Christians, relate to a society which seems to put possessions and profits ahead of people?

To ask these questions is to suggest that Christianity, or at least a strategic sector of it, become a counterculture, as was the Christianity described in Luke, Acts, and the writings of Pliny.

It would seem, then, that a pedagogy for the non-poor, the setting of a gospel agenda in a global context, should have at least two goals: one negative, one positive.

The negative goal is to end the privatization of religion. "I know no Gospel but a social Gospel," wrote John Wesley, "no spirituality but a social spirituality."

The positive goal is to attempt, through our channels of Christian education, to make sure that, by the grace of God, those who occupy both pew and pulpit are creative malcontents, prophets who speak with lips cleansed by burning coals from the altar, and are willing to accept the fate which usually befalls the prophet. Oscar Romero and Benigno Aquino in death—and Paulo and Elza Freire in exile—remind us, if we needed a reminder, of what that fate may be. They serve to remind us also that what concerns prophets principally is not sinful individuals, but sinful structures, sinful institutions, the sinful society. To the degree that we have privatized religion, we have also privatized sin. "Although my sins be scarlet, yet shall I be made white as snow."

We must learn—and teach—the reality of social sin and sinfulness. Among the "right questions" to be asked are questions such as these: Is my country sinful? If so, why? If so, to what degree? Is my church sinful? If so, why? If so, to what degree? Is my seminary or Christian university sinful? If so, why? If so, to what degree?

THE VIRTUE OF HOPE

Every educational theory from Plato to James Fowler hopes to lead those educated to some *virtus*, some quality which will in turn be a goad to action. One might suggest that a major virtue to emerge from a pedagogy of the non-poor might be the virtue of hope. This is not hope in the syrupy sense so often memorialized in our hymns, but hope as the "wretched of the earth" have come to understand it; hope as St. Augustine understood it.

"Hope," wrote Augustine, "has two daughters—anger and courage." Anger that what should be is not, and what should not be, is. Anger, and courage.

Courage so to act that, so far as in me lies, that which should be shall be, and what should not be, will not be. This is the hope which sustains our brothers and sisters in Central America, the Philippines, and Eastern Europe. It is the hope which brings us into dialogue, not just on this model but on the global application of the Gospel Agenda.

PART TWO

REFLECTIONS ON TRANSFORMATIVE EDUCATION

CHAPTER 9

CONVERSATIONS WITH PAULO FREIRE ON PEDAGOGIES FOR THE NON-POOR

These conversations were edited by William Bean Kennedy from tape transcriptions from the Consultation on "Pedagogies for the Non-Poor," Claremont School of Theology, November 17–18, 1983, and from workshops for the Association of Professors and Researchers in Religious Education and the Religious Education Association, November 19–21, 1983. Questions and comments in the text were from participants in the consultation. They appear in italics, as do the editor's comments. Paulo Freire's statements are in roman type.

EDITOR: *The group asked Paulo Freire to comment on the theme itself: "Pedagogies for the Non-Poor."*

It is a question of the liberty or the freedom of the rich and the lack of freedom of the poor. This obviously has to do with the education of those that you here call the non-poor as well as the education for liberation of the poor. For me it's not possible to talk about the freedom or liberty of the rich as a thing by itself. Then, it's disconnected from the liberty or lack of liberty of the poor. The liberty or freedom of the rich is always in relation to the lack of liberty or freedom of the poor. If you look for these two things in connection with each other, you see that the liberty or freedom of the rich resides in the nonliberty or the lack of freedom of the poor.

The freedom of the poor is in their process of liberation. Every attempt at liberation of the poor appears to the rich as a threat, and every attempt at liberation of the poor is seen by the rich as a restriction of their own freedom. The understanding of this dynamic relationship throws some light on how the process and the pedagogy for liberation of the poor differ from the process and pedagogy for the non-poor or the rich. When somebody asks who educates the rich, I say "the rich," but the irony is that the rich educate themselves to continue rich and they educate the poor to continue poor. And the rich educate the poor to accept their own poverty as a normal and natural thing.

EDITOR: *After further discussion of the non-poor, the group began to explore the term "education for transformation" and how it related to the various models, especially the case "Traveling for Transformation."*

That creates a series of problems for educators. I'll touch on one only, but it seems to have a relationship to all the models we have talked about here. That's the question of transformation. I have no doubt that all of the pedagogies discussed here that are implicit in the different models are capable of realizing a change of attitude, a change in the way of seeing, the way of knowing, in the people who are engaged in them. The real question for me is how to transform the new comprehension of the concrete, of what is, into action to transform that concrete reality. For me that is the question. The question is not to describe clearly the world but to transform it. How can we transform the process of transformation?—a play of words. How can we transform the process of transforming the comprehension of the world into a process of transforming the world?

One of the risks and temptations people have, especially Christians, is to get stuck at the level of the spirit, the soul, the subjectivity. It's whether they're thinking of transformation or liberation—do I free myself when I have a better judgment of people and of the world? This is what I call the transformation of the person at the level of the purely subjective.

Liberation is a social thing with an individual dimension. It's not the individual dimension that explains what is liberation. Salvation is also a social question with an individual dimension. For this reason I think that salvation comes after liberation and not before. In the same way justice comes first and peace later, or simultaneously, and justice first and charity later.

This temptation, this risk of being caught on the individualistic, subjective way of seeing—it is especially true for us as educators. We end the day being so elated by having a new kind of intellectual grasp of subjects.

Some of the questions that have to be related to this whole process of transformation are: Why transformation? Transformation for what end? Transformation of what? Of whom? Transformation against what? Against whom? In favor of whom? In the very beginning we have to be asking all these questions about the basic concept. I think these same fundamental questions have to be related also to methodological questions. For example, transform how? How to be transformed? Transformation with whom? It's obvious that transformation is historical, social, political, economic, and it's radical transformation of the system.

In relation to the particular case ["Traveling for Transformation"], I felt again how difficult is this task, the education of the so-called non-poor. This task involves options, alternatives. They are political options and not pedagogical options. It involves dreams, and they are political dreams, not pedagogical dreams. And the options have to do either with the preservation of what is or the transformation of what is. And the so-called non-poor don't necessarily have the dream of changing, of being transformed. These people do not necessarily want to change, but there are some who do. I myself have for some time been trying to do this, but I am one of the non-poor, according to the definition that we gave. But what I want to emphasize is that people among the non-poor do not customarily want to be transformed or to give up the privileges which they have enjoyed, and they're not ready to accept or engage in the kind of education which involves the giving up of those privileges.

At its base, you can't talk about education, or think about education, without certain qualifications. Education involves power; that's one basic thing. And there is the question of ideology, the ideology of power which seeks to reproduce and emphasize the interests of the dominant class, as well as ideology understood as a possible confrontation with the dominant interests.

EDITOR: *The discussion led further into the question of ideology.*

We have to be aware of this question of ideology when we are discussing and making education. When we are thinking of the so-called education of the non-poor, ideological aspects come up, constituting traps for the educatees and the educators in the same level of position of class. For example, one of the traps is that we need to give some help to the poor. Of course the non-poor speak about the poor, no? And the poor, finally, need to be helped. Sometimes "They are poor because they don't work well." Sometimes "because they are lazy." Then one of my tasks is precisely to tell them, "Stop being lazy." (If they stop being lazy, necessarily they will overcome the state of being poor.) Sometimes the non-poor think the poor are poor because they made their choice: "They prefer to be poor." Sometimes because "the poor are ignorant"—and then it's necessary to make the poor to know. And the knowledge is the knowledge of the non-poor, never the knowledge of the poor. Sometimes it's a question of whether the poor are poor because they live in tropical areas; or a question of a mixture of race, or because they are blacks, or *Capucus,* or *Morenos.* All these things are ideological traps which we have to confront. And there are others, other ideological ways of thinking among us, the non-poor, ways of defending our interests, privilege, and to preserve, to immortalize, our history.

Sometimes we say these things in a different way, with a different discourse or speech. We say "Oh, yes, the poor. There is poverty, misery, but it is natural. This is not a question of lack of justice. It is like this, and no need for changing because we always have the poor, because the poor are necessary in order to call poverty to our attention and for us to be engaged in charity. If we didn't have the poor, how would we show our charity? It's necessary." It implies, of course, a certain fatalism. Then we have to accept it. Because of that, we have nothing to do but to make some changes that will preserve, not really in order to change. No, it is mere reform.

I am not saying that all those who are non-poor think like this. What I am saying is that it is normal that the non-poor think like this. This is the ideological aspect of our experience. I think the experience was talked about in this way here, with this model ["Traveling for Transformation"]. Sometimes, even independently of the wish of those who plan and go on a travel seminar, it can provoke a different reaction, a negative reaction. But on the other hand, such a trip can help people learn that the reasons for the misery are not the climate, or, secondly, that it is not the wish of God.

If we accept to work with the non-poor, it's not a question of telling them they are reactionaries, that they are bad. No. We have to understand the power of ideology. Of course we don't have to accept their explanations about poverty, about justice. I think that we have to discuss with them. Because it is so difficult to work with the non-poor in this kind of experience, I prefer to work with the people of the *favelas* and the slums. They have much more knowledge for understanding all this.

Another question should be this: What are the possibilities for continuation of the experiences for those who themselves experience this kind of education? How can they come together, mobilize themselves, organize themselves in some kind of political organization in order to change? Because this is the question. It is not some kind of intellectual game. Education cannot be understood as a kind of game, an intellectual game. No. Education is a question of really making love, and not masturbation. Perhaps I am a little strong in my metaphor at this moment, but I hope you understand me in my metaphor. This is a question for me. We have to try to become really committed. And not just talking, discussing every Tuesday in some meetings, repeating the same analysis.

EDITOR: *The discussion then moved on to explore further obstacles.*
Another difficulty we have in this kind of education is that we cannot separate the non-poor as educatees from their circumstance, from their reality. It would be impossible. And the question, not exclusively in the United States but fundamentally here in a society like this, is that the reality of the non-poor is so complex, so difficult to be understood, so hard for us to perceive the ways to touch reality. This is why societies like this create undoubtedly a very, very strong feeling of impotence. In societies like yours we have a strong fatalism, with much more difficulty to be overcome than the fatalism of Latin America or Africa, for example. Yes, because the peasant says, "It is God's will," and that is easier, with a good theological approach, to overcome. But here the question is not a God, it is the establishment, it is the technology, it is all these things you know better than I, which prevent us from perceiving even a minimal possibility of change.

Then, it is tremendous, because the twin of fatalism is despair. And a consequence of despair a lot of times is cynicism, and immobilization. And we become cynical. We don't commit suicide, personally, of course. But at the same time we don't perceive even a road, a street to walk in order to change. In some moment, we say, "No, let us stop thinking about that, and let us begin to get the dollar. It's absolutely necessary to get the dollar, okay?" No, I am not saying I do not need to get my salary, but that's not the question. The cynical approach is another thing, which is very next to fatalism, immobilization, all these things. And the more we are prevented from seeing and from understanding, from changing, the more the things which should be changed will continue not to be changed. A lot of the problem in this kind of education is to think that in this situation we have nothing to do.

No, no. I think we have many things to do. The question is to discover how to do it, what to do, and when to do it. We have also ingredients in societies like these which also distract us, that lead us astray. Like, for example, the emphasis on techniques, on psychological, behavioral explanations, instead of trying or acting, of doing something, of understanding the situation globally, of thinking dialectically, dynamically.

The act of knowing, which education implies, must be understood in connection with organization for changing, for transforming. The transformation, for example, about which we talk, constantly, has to go beyond the understanding we have sometimes of transformation as something which happens inside of us. We have the tendency to stop the understanding of transformation at the level of some change in our way of thinking, in our way of speaking, for example, and it is not enough. The individual dimension of transformation has to be completed by the objective transformation, or the transformation of the objectivity, of reality, and it is a question again of politics.

EDITOR: *The question then became: How can these obstacles be overcome?*
The question is to take the blocks or obstacles and find their interrelationships, to pose them to those who are learning as things that can be turned into objects to be known. The question is also how to put on the table ideology as something which must be understood. We are immersed in ideology but we don't know that we are. We need to understand the ideology in its different ways of being theoretically understood.

One of these ways is to understand ideology as false consciousness, as distortion or inversion of the real reality or the real concreteness. It's something which puts a kind of veil over reality and over the world. It's something which says that A is B, and not A is A. There are interests, social interests, which make it possible for ideology to operate and work. But in certain moments what is true for ideology becomes concrete for those who are ideologized according to that ideology. It is the truth. This is one of the reasons why I confess to you I am afraid concerning the end of the world, because the power of this is big. Some of you talked about your reactions last night after the film,* and it is one more reason to be afraid.

The Day After was first aired on ABC-TV on November 20, 1983. The drama depicts the devastating human and material effects of a nuclear strike on Kansas City and the surrounding area—ED.

Take, for example, again, how easy it is for us to think that people are poor because they are lazy. "They are not serious, so they do not work well." "They don't have punctuality. We say ten o'clock, and they arrive at two." "They are lazy . . . they are dark . . . they are dirty . . . they don't speak well . . . they are incapable." It's not a scientific approach, such statements. It is an ideological approach. I don't want to say that with science we also don't find ideology, but if I am mistaken concerning a measuring instrument, if my misunderstanding is just because of some lack of scientific knowledge, it is easier for me to overcome if you say "Look, Paulo, it's not like this because scientifically it is . . ." But if my misunderstanding is based on some ideological assumption, it is very difficult to adjust. Then my tendency is to consider you one who comes to teach me, maybe as a communist. Because of that, I think that one of the first steps you have to take should be to discuss not theoretically or with abstruse speech, but through analysis of the practice they [the non-poor] are engaged in every day.

A fantastic philosopher from Czechoslovakia, Karel Kosick, describes in his book *Dialectic of the Concrete* his analysis of the alienation of daily life experience. Generally we never take into our hands our daily life alienation experience in order to understand it. We never ask ourselves about ourselves, and about our own experience of being alienated. We never discover the raison d'être for our distortions, precisely because many times we need not to discover well. In the depths of ourselves, it's necessary sometimes for us to follow the distorted, the ideological distortion about reality, because for us it is funda- mental. It has to do with our privilege.

And then how to reject our privilege? If I change the way of understanding you, instead of making charity I have to make justice. And it is too expensive to make justice, no? Then ideologically I continue to deny and I don't want to learn. This is for me the main obstacle we have with this kind of people, among whom we are. We are, no? But if it was possible for us to overcome that, it's possible for them, also. Individually, but not as class. As social class, no. But as individuals, yes. But the question is to re-invent, and we don't have prescrip- tions for that. We have to invent ways to challenge the participants, with a "problematizing" way of educating. In the last analysis you are challenging, and maybe we can say that challenging is educating. In some aspects it is almost a type of cultural, political, social, and economic psychoanalysis.

My experience in Africa gave me very concretely the *politicity of education*. This word does not exist in English? Politicity—it is a beautiful word, because it means the quality of being political. Because of my experience I really became much more consciously a politician as an educator. I continued to be an educator, because there is also in the political phenomenon something which I could name the educability of the political as well as the politicity of education. It's impossible to be a politician without being an educator and vice versa. The question is to know what kind of politics the politician does, or the educator does, because both are politicians.

The non-poor, generally speaking, suffer on the one hand the fear of losing what they have, and on the other hand, the hope of having more. This is very serious, because it has to do with ideology. Because of that, generally, the non-poor are, first, the maximum liberal people. Secondly, they generally are progressives just when historically their social segment is moving up. But every time in history when the non-poor see the possibility for the poor to move up, they become reactionary. We must be clear concerning the difference between the individual and the class, or we become naive.

One of the things that I have observed here is a relationship between practice and theory. When I first came to the United States people would say they needed to get at the facts. I used to say, "Yes, indeed, I also respect and want the facts, but the facts don't have a life of their own, unrelated to other things." Over the last few years, there seems to be a greater ability here in this country to accept and work on the philosophical, theological questions without repugnance.

QUESTION FROM PARTICIPANT: *Is there any possibility that when the poor become rich that does not make the rich feel threatened? Is there any other reality? I am looking for some kind of crack in the status quo wall that I can put my screwdriver in. There is a wasting of life among the rich, among the poor, among the middle-class. Of course we recognize that the enslavement of the rich is different from the slavery of the poor, but enslavement is enslavement. Is there a clue or a crack in diagnosing the human situation?*

Sure, there is an enslavement of the rich and an enslavement of the poor which are interrelated, but the enslavement of the rich is so enjoyable, so comforting, that it doesn't even seem like enslavement. For example, it does not make sense to go to the *favelas* in Brazil, the slum people, and say to them, "Look, finally no problem because of course you suffer, you don't eat, you don't get money to dress, you don't have health. But because of that you are less enslaved than the rich. And because of that maybe you are much more next to heaven. And then, it's good, it's good to be like you." But before making this speech, maybe we ate a very good Mexican meal. That does not make sense for the miserable, the poor. The question is to create heaven here. And for us, as Christians, not to create heaven in the heavens, but to start creating it here, in the world. And it is easier if you recreate the heaven here; it's easier to be in the heaven than to fly to it.

QUESTION FROM PARTICIPANT: *If the only situation is that the rich have to keep the poor poor, in order to stay rich, is there any way to look at the reality in such a way that having the poor be rich is to the advantage of us all? The reason for the question is, I'm not sure what education can possibly do if there's no way to think about that, because then your only choice is obviously revolution in which the poor take power by force. That's not what I want to argue against, but that's not an educational task that we are facing. Is there a way to work with the rich in which we can say it's in all of our self-interests that we change, and is there a way to talk about that?*

Look, the question is one of the fundamental ones we have as educators: the relationship between education and power or lack of power. It is impossible to think of education without thinking of power. Every time we think of education without thinking of power, first of all we are not understanding just what we are doing. It's absolutely impossible. Secondly, it is impossible to think of transformation without thinking of getting power to transform. Because without power, how is it possible to transform? Just inside the head. But transforming history inside the head is something which exists in the thought of pre-Hegelian philosophers. It does not make sense. Education means a kind of action which on the one hand is explained by the power which constitutes it, on the other hand it works in the direction of preserving the power which constituted it or works against the power which constituted it.

It is impossible to think of transformation, of education for transformation, without thinking how to mobilize and how to organize power—political power. If you want to transform the world, you have to fight power in order to get it. But for me, the question today in the end of this century is not just to get power, but to reinvent power.

QUESTION FROM PARTICIPANT: *I think the American middle class would say that we want everybody to be rich. That's no threat to us. The question is, Is that possible in our world? Is it possible to bring everybody up to an American middle-class standard? I think it is a debatable issue whether the world's resources can sustain that or not. That is a concrete question of socioeconomic power. That's the background out of which I ask the question about the relationship between freedom and richness. Are those necessarily connected to each other? What do we mean by freedom?*

Once again we are dealing with the question of power, political power based on economic power. The ideal obviously would be that riches and resources were socially available and not possessed by individuals. It's the whole privatization of resources and private, individual control over resources in the capitalist system based on individual possession of goods.

QUESTION FROM PARTICIPANT: *Is it that making the poor rich is a threat to the rich? Or is it the threat of the liberation of the poor, not that every poor would become rich?*

COMMENT AND QUESTION FROM PARTICIPANT: *I think that there is a confusion among richness, freedom, and power. If everyone were middle-class, living at a middle-class standard, would we regard everyone as liberated? Would we consider the middle class "free"?*

No, no. Look, the middle class is very interesting. The middle class is something that doesn't exist but its presence is very clear. The so-called middle class does not have control over the means of production of society. In this sense, the middle class is obviously not the dominant class, the dominating class. And for this reason the middle class can go back and forth between the dominant class and the oppressed. And because they have this freedom to make little journeys back and forth, like tourists, then they feel themselves without guilt. And free. And truly, they are not. Intellectuals are always thinking that they're free.

QUESTION FROM PARTICIPANT: *I have experienced on some occasions that there are the rich, or non-poor, who, in those words of the Magnificat, were "sent away empty," and discovered that, at least momentarily, as the gospel. Some things lead them to that, and some things allow them to maintain it, in order that they work for that kind of transformation not just as individuals but as communities. It happens. Not often, because of the power of the ideology. What some of us are struggling with is the question of what factors allow that to happen and be consolidated. It is not simply that all the rich want to keep the poor permanently poor, because they realize that that's not the gospel. Some are actually making significant steps in transformation and trying to discover how to work on the system. That's part of what the gospel is about. If the crack in the system is not big enough for a screwdriver to be pushed in, where are the points where you can get your fingernails in the crack? I think that's what we are trying to discover.*

COMMENT AND QUESTION FROM PARTICIPANT: *I see strong gates in the way. Sometimes the doors are open. In our regular discussion we always are describing the front door: politics, education, organizing. We understand that. But grace is surprising us somewhere and giving us some kind of crack. That's where our theology must contribute. Who knows that something isn't going on at the back door, some significant opportunity for the Magnificat to empower us?*

I am sure it's not even a question of believing. It's a question of being sure that some rich people, that some representatives of the dominant class, can make their conversion to the poor, to the oppressed. And can go beyond, can become strong fighters, but as individuals, not as class.

But I think we must be very clear that when we talk with individuals we are talking with individuals who have a certain position of class, and the position of class comes with us by way of our history, through our history. In my home I have a very good chair. I bought it for studying, writing. The other day I was talking with my son. He came to discuss with me some text by Max Weber. And I said at a certain moment, "Look, my son, I am also this chair. You understand? This chair conditions me." The position of class we have independently of our wish. We were born in a certain family, in a certain class. This is what is difficult for us.

EDITOR: *Later, Paulo shared a pertinent story about how painful it is to learn that lesson about one's position of class.*

I remember I did research about the relationships between parents and children and the question of punishment. The results were very strong. Then after studying the results I began to talk about punishment to all the parents we invited to the schools of this institution. One night I started very seriously, and had begun to talk to the parents about the need to have dialogue with the children. I quoted Piaget about this, about the moral code in childhood, and I said that in a long speech.

When I finished, one of the workers there put up his hand like this. I said, "Okay." And he looked at the colleagues and said, "Doctor, Doctor Paulo (in Brazil everyone who belongs to the ruling class, or is next to it, is 'doctor,' whether he or she is or is not), you said beautiful words now, beautiful words." That man was one of the most important educators I had till today. "Doctor Paulo, I don't know where is your house, but how many children do you have?" I said, "Five." And he said, "How many boys and girls?" I said, "Three daughters and two sons." I was beginning to be afraid. And he said, "Okay. Your house first of all must be free on both sides [a free-standing house]. Secondly, your house must have a garden with grass. You must have a good room for you and your wife and two big rooms for the three daughters and the two boys, at least two. I admit that you don't have five. And your kitchen must be very good with all the equipment, and also a shower, with electric hot water, even in northeast Brazil." And he said, "When you arrive at home, in the end of the day, your children, they are happy, beautiful, with clean clothes. They've had good food. At seven o'clock at night, you don't have any problems; the children will go to bed. You don't need to force them to sleep because they really are sleepy. They are well, they have health, and above all, they ate. Then they sleep. When one of your children has some problem, the doctor comes immediately to see what it is. But, Doctor Paulo, this is not our situation. Our house doesn't have even one bedroom. One room, just one, for all the things or functions of the house. I arrive at home tired. I did not eat well. And my five children did not eat also. They are not clean. We can't be—we don't have water. They are hungry, and they are diabolic. The next day at four o'clock again I must be awake in order to go again to the manufactory. I have to beat them in order for them to sleep because I need to sleep. If I don't sleep, I can't work, and they cannot be alive. Then, Doctor Paulo, don't think that the workers beat the children because they don't love them. We love our children as well as you love yours. The question is that you have different material conditions to love, and we don't have. Then, for you, the fact of beating is as if we did not love them. I would like, Doctor Paulo, to know whether in our situation you would be very dialogical."

I confess to you, I was so impacted. But in order for you to see how difficult it is for us to learn, and how when we are convinced about something, how difficult it is to change, because we need really to be sure in order to change—when I was going back home, I had the strange feeling of somebody who felt he had lost a battle, but felt that he had to keep on fighting. I said to myself, "That was a very interesting man, but it's necessary to insist with him that dialogue really is necessary."

Once again, Elza helped me: "Look, Paulo," she said, "in the last analysis the man is absolutely right." I said, "But Elza, we have to change this country. How is it possible to create a democracy with punishment like this?" My goodness, how naive I was! And she smiled and said, "No, no, it is another question, Paulo." I spent times, many times, a lot of time to learn that so easy lesson which that man gave me that evening. I tell you the story with humility.

How to go beyond our position of class? How to deny it, how to make our Easter, how to die in order to be born again, differently? This is Easter. For me one of the central questions for us as Christians is that we speak about Easter but we never do Easter. But we speak a lot. A lot. We write a lot about Easter. But it is so difficult to make it. Precisely because making Easter is to become committed, completely committed, in history, but committed not to the preservation of the status quo but to the creation of the world, and in favor of the poor people, not of the rich people.

QUESTION FROM PARTICIPANT: *You used the phrase "to reinvent power," and I'm thinking about St. Paul's practical statement that "when we are weak, then we are strong," and the whole theology of the cross. How do we reinvent power in the light of the theology of the cross?*

To "reinvent power": I use the phrase because for me the principal, real transformation, the radical transformation of society in this part of the century demands not properly to get power as it is from those who have it today, or to make some reforms, some changes in it but preserving it as it is now. For me, this is a challenge for the revolutionaries, the socialists, for example. The question, from my point of view, is not for them just to take power but to reinvent power. That is, to create a different kind of power, to deny the need the power has as if it were metaphysics, bureaucratized, anti-democratic. Do you see? This is why I said it is necessary not to take power but to reinvent power.

COMMENT FROM PARTICIPANT: *I'm interested in the cracks and back doors, too. I know the nuclear freeze movement is sometimes criticized for being so middle-class. But for me it is one of the possible cracks. People really almost have to be confronted with their own annihilation before they are really aware of others. I pursue that as a crack in the wall, because I see people who are normally very supportive of the status quo, supportive of the government, who begin to see things that they never saw, that are directly tied into the issues of poverty and justice, almost overnight. But we wouldn't have that otherwise. I really think that's one of the most exciting cracks, and I fear when I hear all the theologians criticizing the freeze as being so middle-class and abandoning it rather than pursuing that crack and trying to use it.*

COMMENT FROM PARTICIPANT: *I'm still worried about our view of class. I think this class analysis needs to be taken much more comprehensively right down to every single level. My experience has been that the little village shopkeeper in the highlands of Central America is doing the same kind of exploitation, exploiting the next poor person, that is happening in Wall Street. It's a tremendous hierarchy which works like a giant escalator: everyone is jumping on and moving up as fast as possible only to be kept in place and to be ideologically justified in that place, that place of exploitation and of being exploited. And another illustration of this problem: when I talked to the Hispanic director in a U.S. theological seminary about the urban situation and asked if there is a common cause with the blacks in the cities, the answer was that there is no greater exploiter than someone who's been exploited. So the whole dichotomy of the poor and the non-poor I think is inadequate. It has to be seen in a million ways in which it carries right down through our society. So many people have bought into this and are scrambling, and the greatest scrambling may be at the very bottom, in which the exploitation is taking place. It's a universal human phenomenon that we're dealing with, and somehow this gospel of a different kind of power has to work if the transformation will ever be really possible.*

EDITOR: *A discussion of fear and hope ensued; it was evoked by the broadcast the previous night of the film* The Day After *(see footnote, p. 223, above). Paulo Freire commented at some length on those topics.*

It's not the ideas that we have about the world, but the world that suggests those ideas to us. If we can get that really fixed in our minds, then I want to comment about the part of this meeting we went through last night, seeing the TV film *The Day After.* A civilization which can create a person, a situation [Freire here is referring to a scene in the film], in which someone who has demonstrated himself to be very capable of love can, at the end of the road when there's nothing more, say "Get out of my house," a civilization that can bring forth that way of being in the world, I'm afraid I almost believe that it will end. I don't say this as a deep and serious pessimist, but really because I'm frightened.

Someone who had heard the comments of children repeated on television this morning told me that some of those children said, "The movie wasn't so bad. It wasn't so scary." They said that has something to do with the kinds of scary films that people see all the time, in which that kind of killing and ending of things and people burning up is nothing new. But something is deeply wrong, and it is a civilization which can't continue this way.

The list of learnings from these case studies has some deep and fundamental things on it. Somewhere at the base of this list is a very fundamental fear, the kind of fear that Erich Fromm identified as the fear of liberty, of freedom. We are talking more about a challenge to the non-poor rather than their education. Our education.

Sometimes we are in despair, but sometimes because of reasons to despair we may get hope. What is so difficult is exactly in this area of power, of what's going on. Sometimes as that situation becomes more depressing, more powerful in its effect on us, then humanity rises up and moves in the other direction and that is indeed reason for hope. The hope comes out of both the nonhope and the promising. I think that perhaps this is one of those times. But this change does not happen by chance. We must do the change. Maybe I'm now very naive, very optimistic, but I hope that it can be done.

The oppressed are not being prevented from being by God. Never in any biblical or doctrinal moment in history did God send some delegate here to oppress the people. Then it's not God. Who, besides those who participate in history, is God's power? Faith in power, some economic power? Then millions don't eat, while some eat. One day, the millions begin to say: This is impossible. Why cannot we eat? When millions ask the first question, the minority begins to be preoccupied, because the millions begin to discover that the minority eat, and eat well. Independent of science or ideology, you want to eat, because your body needs food. Then the masses of the people begin asking more questions. They just would like to have the right to eat. When they sometimes are near to get the right to eat, the minority say no, but these people want to eat. Because of that I always say the violence never was in history initiated by the violated. Never. In some moment the violence, which I don't like, the violence of the violated becomes a legitimate right of self-defense. It's not a question that depends on you and on me, it's a question of the concrete historical situation.

If someone asked me the question would I prefer that change should be made by peaceful means or violent means, obviously I want to say by peaceful means. However, the question is if I could get all the dominant class or oppressors together and say, "Don't do this any more," and it worked, then it would reach the oppression. I think that we must explore every possibility to change reality democratically.

I don't want to say stop working with middle-class people, no, because I think that it's possible. We have to take advantage of the space we have in order to challenge. But it is very important for all of you working in this space to study ideology, in order to understand how ideology has power, how it hides and masks reality, and to understand how people are conditioned. This is why I am sure it is a temptation to understand freedom, liberation, and transformation as strictly subjective. It's ideology. The dominant ideology needs that to continue. And in a society like this, so complex, so difficult, it is important to discover this. You need eventually to challenge the system.

It's very important for those who are going to start getting engaged in this kind of project that their political dream is very clear. I don't think it's possible to get so engaged without a kind of serene confidence that that dream is possible. In fact the personal engagement with this process is dependent on the commitment and belief that that dream can come about, that it is a viable dream. The moment in which you discover or make coherence between your practice and the verbalization of that practice and begin to attempt to justify yourself in terms of the world is when you are dedicating yourself and moving toward realization of the dream. And at that point you discover that in relation to the realization of your dream there aren't little tasks and big tasks, or important ones and less important ones, but just the one task, to work to do it. I think that everything we've heard here has a significance.

WILLIAM BEAN KENNEDY

CHAPTER 10

THE IDEOLOGICAL CAPTIVITY OF THE NON-POOR

To further the dialogue about transformative education, three fundamental questions can be raised from the eight cases:

—*Who* are involved, as learners and leaders?
—*Why* are they involved, against what, for what, and with what motivation?
—*How* are they being educated in the various models?

I. WHO ARE INVOLVED?

A. Who Are the "Non-Poor"?

The term is a problem. Education for liberation of the poor in Latin America can perhaps be related to the various "underclass" people in North America, those living in urban ghettos or rural poverty areas, but even so the transfer is not simple. However, our concern here is with the broad "middle class," those neither radically poor economically nor extremely rich. The non-poor are those with low infant mortality rates and high life expectancy, those above the poverty line, or, more simply, those who are well fed. In the Introduction Alice Frazer Evans, Robert A. Evans, and I discussed the difficulty of precise class analysis in North America and some other parts of the First World. Knowing that the vast majority of people in North American mainline churches and synagogues consider themselves "middle-class," we decided to focus on specific education/action efforts targeted at that broad group. Hence "pedagogies for the non-poor" was used as a working title for this book.

The various models reflect that broad categorization. Some refer directly to the "middle class." Others point to characteristics that are indicative of the category, such as managerial positions in the "Plant Closures" case. Others still contain explicit or implicit references to privilege. More directly related to education is the comment in the "Women's Theological Center" case that by the time women from poor or working-class origins "reached graduate studies, all were middle-class in terms of options, if not income" (p. 116).

In the comments recorded in chapter 9, Freire spoke of the middle class as being like tourists who could move back and forth into lower- and upper-class situations, as for instance in travel seminars. Some models used "immersion" experiences to help participants get to know firsthand some people in conditions of poverty. But because most participants and leaders of the projects identify with the middle class, the entire exercise reflects the ideology and assumptions of that socioeconomic class and its related cultural characteristics.

The ways social location and ideological assumptions of this class affect transformative educational efforts will be discussed more fully below. Here, rather than worry unduly about classification, I concentrate on education/action models that focus on people in this large, vaguely defined group who make up the large majority of persons in U.S. and Canadian societies and in the churches of the two countries. Almost all the participants and leaders in the eight cases are "middle-class" or "non-poor."

B. Who Are the Leaders?

A second part of the "Who?" question concerns leadership. One way to get at the dynamic of education is to study the verbs used to describe what leaders or teachers do—or what they would like to have happen. Notice verbs used at times in the cases: "induce persons to change," "convince . . . make a dent in . . . sensitize," "must be shown . . . be given time . . . be given skills." These verbs, like most of the verbs used to describe educational activity, imply a one-way direction of strong force from teacher or leader toward student or participant. One leader wondered "how forceful to be" in arguing for Sanctuary. In the "Chrysalis" case it was noted that where the pastor was lukewarm, nothing happened. The travel seminar report remarked on the "drivenness" of the leader, while it affirmed his leadership in the quality of instruction, nurture, and demands for accountability. Another leader felt spread too thin, and asked how to get the group to take off on its own. In general the leader was expected to provide charismatic leadership as well as resources for the participants' learning.

Cautions against such assumptions also were stated: "No design can do more than provide the environment that perhaps will enable fundamental change, conversion, to happen" (Hunter commentary, p. 180). The frequent references to the importance of creativity, myth, and ritual, and the emphasis on more aesthetic and holistic approaches warn against overdependence upon rational understanding and the image of leaders as knowledgeable "experts."

Gregory Baum, building on Max Weber, describes the charismatic authority that he believes provides the dynamic element in the history of institutions. His words invite deeper analysis of the type of leadership needed for transformative education:

> The charismatic person has power over people because he touches them where they suffer. The charismatic person is intuitively aware of what disturbs, wounds, and exasperates people in their society. . . . The charismatic person gives voice to the common suffering; he *articulates the alienation* of the community; he speaks with an authority ultimately derived from the misery or unredemption of the many.
>
> The charismatic person senses the hurts of people and *proposes a new imagination* by which this harm can be overcome [*Religion and Alienation: A Theological Reading of Sociology,* New York, Paulist Press, 1975, p.170].

When that approach to leadership is tied to ideological analysis, to the biblical and theological affirmation that God has a bias toward the poor, and to Baum's development of imagination as the key to concrete utopia, it opens up stimulating thinking about how leaders can best operate in this kind of education.

II. WHY? AGAINST WHAT? FOR WHAT? WITH WHAT MOTIVATION?

How does transformative education express its hopes and goals? What do these models *intend?* Freire reminds us that prophetic activity involves both denunciation and annunciation, so the question needs to be posed with both those aspects in mind.

A. The Ideological Context

Ideology has a central place in the following analysis of transformative education. Since its introduction into Western discourse in the period of the French Revolution, "ideology" has been an ambiguous term. It refers to the process by which every human being internalizes a basic understanding of the world from growing up in a particular society. Sociologists call the process "socialization," the social conditioning that gives every person a certain way of looking at reality. Anthroplogists call it "enculturation." The process is largely an unconscious one. Persons "breathe in" the framework by which they interpret their world and their experience. The symbolic structure of the mind is not freely chosen, but is inherited and appropriated through the institutionalization of symbols, as Gregory Baum points out *(Religion,* p. 7). Or, to put it another way, society produces human consciousness.

In that process a distortion occurs. Baum describes it, interpreting Marx:

> In the Marxian terminology, ideology is always something false, a distortion of the truth for the sake of social interest, a symbolic framework of the mind that legitimates the power and privileges of the dominant groups and sanctions the social evils inflicted on the people without access to power [ibid., p. 34].

> What takes place is a distortion of awareness, according to which the present social order becomes the measure of reality. People then generate ideals that protect this falsification of perception [ibid., p. 24].

Ideology, then, is deformation of truth for the sake of social interest. Baum identifies it with the collective blindness, the corrupting religious trends that emerge to protect the community against hostile forces and in defense of its power elites (ibid., pp. 75ff.). These trends "tend to attach people uncritically to their tradition, protect them from coming to self-knowledge, defend the authority of the dominant classes, create a false sense of superiority over others, and produce dreams of victory over outsiders" (ibid., p. 75).

However, despite the distortion that is unconsciously built into all ideology, the term can express both a negative and a positive influence. As Douglas Kellner writes, "The concept commonly refers both to those ideas, images, and theories that mystify social reality and block social change, and to those programs of social reconstruction that mobilize people for social activism" ("Ideology, Marxism, and Advanced Capitalism," *Socialist Review* 8, no. 6, Nov.–Dec. 1978, p. 38). Those "programs" obviously also involve ideas, images, and theories. Kellner therefore distinguishes between "ideology-as-hegemony" and "ideology-as-ism." Gibson Winter writes that:

> Ideology . . . faces in two directions. It is a Januslike phenomenon. Ideology may be primarily oriented to preserving and legitimating the established powers in a society. It may also face primarily toward the future and project a utopian model for a more just society. In either case, ideology draws upon the symbolic powers that generate a people's identity, whether to legitimate powers that be or to authorize proposals for transformation [*Liberating Creation: Foundations of Religious Social Ethics,* New York, Crossroad, 1981, p. 97].

Baum takes the analysis one step further:

> Religion (or any symbolic language) is ideological if it legitimates the existing social order, defends the dominant values, enhances the authority of

the dominant class, and creates an imagination suggesting that society is stable and perdures. By contrast, religion is utopian if it reveals the ills of the present social order, inverts the dominant values of society, undermines the authority of the ruling groups, and makes people expect the downfall of the present system. . . . Utopias envisage a qualitative transformation of the conditions of human life. Such utopias may be revolutionary or evolutionary [*Religion,* pp. 102–3].

What Kellner calls "ideology-as-ism," Baum, following Karl Mannheim, calls "utopian." While the use of the term "ideology" in both the hegemonic and the utopian sense may be confusing, it preserves the awareness of the hidden danger of distortion that is always present. Every ideology, whether dominant or particular, distorts and hides reality and therefore needs to be exposed. The most difficult to recognize and unmask is the ideology of one's own community.

As particular ideologies (ideologies-as-isms) gradually win in historical struggles, they in time become hegemonic ideologies. As the new dominant ideas of the society, they are then used to stabilize and legitimate the new order. As the hegemonic ideology continues to bring together the most widely shared beliefs and attitudes which are incorporated in social practices and institutions, it nevertheless faces competing oppositional ideologies. In fact, by producing alienation in reaction to its control, the dominant system always summons forth countervailing forces. Again, Baum:

The dominant system of society produces not only the dominant consciousness that keeps the system going, but it also produces, by way of critical response and passing through the creativity of certain personalities, the countervailing movements and the emergence of a new consciousness. The critical movements are generated in the womb of the old society [ibid., p. 173].

Transformative education has a special interest in the processes by which that new consciousness and those critical movements are generated and developed.

Henry Giroux develops further a theory based on the dialectic between reproduction and resistance in education *(Theory and Resistance in Education: A Pedagogy for the Opposition,* South Hadley, Mass., Bergin and Garvey Publishers, 1983). The hegemonic ideology works through the major social systems, such as the media or education, to reproduce the prevailing mindset of society. But while those influences affect people very deeply, a recognizable resistance emerges within individuals and groups as they sense that they are being manipulated. Often their cultural identity supports them in their resistance to the predominant set of values and attitudes about reality. Such a theory invites us into further analysis of these eight models, and into analysis of many other efforts at transformative education.

Dominant ideologies must continually be engaged in struggles and negotiations to maintain their sometimes fragile combination of various competing particular ideologies. Kellner continues:

Hegemonic ideologies also incorporate elements of new emerging ideologies, as when liberal-capitalist ideology incorporates state planning and welfare-state notions into its political economy. Hegemonic ideology is thus flexible, adapting to changing historical conditions and oppositional struggles, and is often full of contradictions as it makes concessions to oppositional groups ["Ideology," p. 51].

This analysis of ideology allows us to interpret it as both the repressive, mystifying, cover-up agency of the dominant power structures of society, and also as the cementing bond of a social group or organization as it protests against the hegemonic power and mobilizes its members toward realizing its particular vision. It is the first usage that explains how the non-poor "see" and treat the poor with a "false consciousness," not "seeing" them, or seeing them only through stereotypical filters that falsify the real situation. In North America and the First World in general there is strong control of those prevailing views, continually reinforced by the media and the various social systems, including education and church. Building on that perception, the prevailing analysis in these models and the one I am here developing therefore interpret the dominant or hegemonic ideology as a major obstacle to transformative education.

Most of the problems faced in education for transformation of the non-poor must deal with the ideological blinders within which and the ideological filters through which they perceive and interpret their world and what goes on in it. When non-poor—or poor—persons walk into a church or a classroom, they do not bring a "blank slate" open to all the input and interpretation they may get there. Rather they come with carefully constructed protective cocoons through which any new or different interpretation of reality must pass. Experiences that do not come with great force into and through that screen end up adding more layers to the cocoon. Experiences that have enough depth and duration and intensity to challenge the prevailing interpretation are therefore those that education for transformation seeks to develop.

Such education is therefore "counter-ideological"; that is, it is ideological in centering on its own vision and loyalty to a particular goal for human beings, but that vision and bonding challenge the dominant hegemonic ideology, which is perceived as a powerful enemy. Clarity about the nature and function of the dominant ideology therefore contributes to clarity about what the restless or resistant group believes in and wants. The emphasis on ideology in Freire and others hence calls for better understanding of how ideology as a very powerful educative force preempts or shapes the opportunity for other interpretations of reality to be heard and seen and received. Education for transformation can thus be understood as a consciously counter-ideological effort toward different options for the human situation than those embodied in the status quo.

In his commentary on the "Plant Closure Project" David Frenchak speaks of the need for an "artistic theological process" which avoids the cooption of both "scientific" and "professional" theology by the dominant cultural styles of the intellectual and academic milieu. The point is worth repeating here:

Variety and pluralism are captured in this process with the emphasis not on one correct picture of God in context but on an art gallery featuring not only different pictures but different art forms, colors, styles and characters. The product is neither a dogma nor a trained specialist; it is the awakening of critical consciousness and the freeing of the human spirit to express discovery at risk of rejection. An individual who has experienced this awakening has an involvement with the context and environment that is transactional. Communication with the environment that is both objective and subjective results in a dynamic relationship with both things and people. The process does not take place in an institution or a training program but in the immediate context of life. It is done not by authorities or specialists in the field but by people from all walks of life. It is done by the laity, by lovers, by artists, and it is done in community [pp. 87–88].

In that analysis and the analysis I am developing, which view the particular ideologies of continuing historical communities struggling against the hegemonic ideology and with each other, each person or group involved in educational activity becomes in a sense a microcosmic arena for the struggle. Take Sue, the person in the case "Traveling for Transformation." Her built-in sense of values made her reluctant to go because she sensed that the experience would threaten her relatively harmonious existence and affluent lifestyle. Her immersion in African culture and her learnings on that trip did in fact affect deeply her perspective on life back home, seen now from a new perspective. Upon her return, her new ideological loyalty based on her recent travel experience was in conflict with the ideology of her New England context. As she began to make connections—through an understanding of the global economic system— between her affluence and Tanzania's poverty, she began to sense the contradictions in U. S. policies and rhetoric about trade and aid. One of the critiques noted that the case lacked substantial encouragement for her then to join an organized movement within which she would be nurtured in her newly developing ideology so that it could aid in mobilizing her and others' energy toward changing the unjust system. Resistance to the reproductive continuity of the dominant ideology therefore motivates transformative education.

The following analysis of transformative education, the clues and questions I see emerging from these eight models, fits into the theoretical framework of ideology outlined above. The tremendous power of North America and First World dominant ideology upon the middle class becomes more visible, and the grounds and opportunities for resistance and creative, imaginative use of "free space" become viable options for education for transformation.

B. Against What?

It is in terms of what they are against, what they resist, that these models may differ most clearly from traditional education.

1. The middle-class cocoon. The so-called middle class in North America live in an ideological cocoon of which they are largely unaware. For instance, note these statements and phrases from the cases and commentaries:

— "people are still imprisoned in the analysis that the problems are out there and that we can deal with them by helping the people out there"
— "the class structure of churches in this country"
— "cultural insularity"
— "school settings . . . assumed as benign authorities"
— "come out of a culture which assumes that the United States is the center of the whole world"
— "blaming of the victim by those not involved"
— "engrained assumption . . . that our own children have rights above and beyond the rights of other children"

These statements suggest the ideological captivity of persons in North American society. In his comments Freire returns again and again to ideology as a major barrier to the kind of transformative education sought by those working in the models. The provincialism related to limited experience and inadequate analysis lets people focus on the surface of things rather than on the deeper connections and assumptions. The "Gospel Agenda" case reports a dramatic example when workshop participants identified "community" only with the neighborhood instead of with the whole human population of the globe. Canadian Douglas Hall comments that "the myopia and provincialism of the average North American are truly astonishing" (chap. 8, p. 205).

In *Liberating Creation* Gibson Winter develops a theory of three paradigms to interpret the ideological options most prominent in North American life today. The *mechanistic paradigm* sees development as expansion of human powers of control and exploitation, with progress the primary symbol. The mechanistic interpretations hide their own ideological projections and symbolic foundations, and thus mask "the spirituality of their corporate life" (p. 99) and the loyalties that sustain it. The *organistic paradigm* centers in communities of interrelationships, with bonds among peoples, nature, and the sacred. This overly subjective view builds ideological projections on notions of group self-interest and leads to struggle for power. The third, which Winter advocates, he calls the *artistic paradigm,* which challenges the distorted symbols of progress and power and involves a dialogical process of creation and transformation. This paradigm can be a proposal for an authentic future. His analysis provides further background for understanding the ideological cocoon within which North Americans live and the role of imagination in breaking out of it.

2. Affluence. One feature of the cocoon is the relative affluence of the middle class. The term "non-poor" points to that characteristic. In his commentary on the "Gospel Agenda" case Philip Scharper writes:

> In their eyes they [the non-poor] are members of the great North American middle class, struggling just to get by, "to survive." . . . For this reason, an effective pedagogy for the non-poor arouses fear and defensiveness, even as an effective pedagogy for the poor arouses hope and positive action.
>
> Basic to the pedagogical task, then, is to devise methods to convince the non-poor that by any standard they possess land in abundance compared to the truly poor in North America and throughout the world. . . . [But] the human person . . . is capable of almost infinite self-deception, and creates myths and stereotypes about what it fears or hates. So the non-poor, when forced to recognize the existence of the poor, . . . fall back upon such comforting observations as those they learned at home, at school, or even at church or synagogue: "The poor are poor because they are lazy and lack motivation," "The poor are really happy with their lot," "The poor are ungrateful, despite the foreign aid we lavish upon them and the welfare billions we squander here at home" [p. 213].

To the non-poor the poor are all but invisible. The non-poor live in such isolation from the poor that they easily hide in their cocoon and blame the victims because they neither know their hurts nor understand the causes of such hardships as layoffs and unemployment. In non-poor churches there are no hungry people—or at least no visibly hungry people—so people lack any immediate feeling for the suffering of hunger. A congregation or denomination composed largely of management types has great difficulty dealing with labor issues. Just as superhighways hide the realities of urban poverty from commuters driving by, so does the cocoon of ideology mask the realities of the world beyond the comfortable social location of the non-poor. Gregory Baum comments that "middle class people are vulnerable to false but cheerful consciousness as workers are not" *(Religion,* p. 31). What the cocoon does is cushion the problems and make the sufferings seem remote. It narrows the ideological horizons, circumscribes interpretations, and severely limits imaginations which could envision a better world.

3. Civil religion. Another feature of the cocoon is its use of civil religion. Here the application may fit the United States more than Canada or most other First World nations, but its relevance is not limited to the United States. Kosuke Koyama, in commenting on the "Chrysalis" case from his Asian perspective, writes that the people in that model "come out of a culture which assumes that the United States is the center of the whole world" (p. 161). Another case notes how the initiative of the poor is "perceived by the non-poor as dangerous [and is] often categorized as 'communist' and hence worthy of abhorrence" (p. 192). Baum says civil religion—what Will Herberg calls "the operative faith of the American people"—is

> a vast ideological system, subsuming the inherited biblical religion, that sacralizes the dreams and aspirations of the American middle class, persuades the lower classes to imitate as much as possible the middle class style, blinds people to the actual exclusion of whole sections of the population from the American consensus, breeds intolerance with public critics, and fosters political aggression against nations that have repudiated the American values [*Religion*, p. 135].

Civil religion also has utopian potential. It holds up a vision from residual and seminal values of the society that can keep people critical of how things are at the moment. The cocoon, while a "given" with negative power, can also be analyzed in ways that open up possibilities for transformative education as its features are exposed.

People want to remain in their cocoon or return to it when they feel that its comforts and security are threatened. It is better to live with known hurts than risk unknown wounds! We all know that feeling and are conscious of the defensiveness that accompanies it. When nationalism is suffused with a sacral character, as a dimension of the ideological cocoon, it becomes a primary obstacle in transformative education for the non-poor.

4. The media. A major force that forms and perpetuates the cocoon is the media, which dominate the interpretation of what is happening. The cultural impact of the new media has increased the symbolic control exercised in previous centuries by printed newspapers and journals. The "news" is interpreted very largely with a bias toward the dominant powers of society—in the United States particularly the business establishment with its ownership of the means of production and distribution of information. A favorite ideological trick is to make something appear as "natural" and therefore "given," whereas in reality it is historical, developed by human beings and able to be changed by human agency. The religious structures may contribute to this result by confusing the "will of God" with an acceptance of fatalism. The case on parish peacemaking (chap. 1) refers to Freire's conception of "massification," of how people are "manipulated into an uncritical, manageable 'glob' by the use of myths created by powerful social forces." The case gives examples: "We're going to blow ourselves up and there's absolutely nothing we can do about it," "Military spending is good for the economy," and "Those in government know more than we do" (p. 27). As Freire puts it, "They have a diffuse, magical belief in the invulnerability and power of the oppressor" *(Pedagogy of the Oppressed,* New York, Herder and Herder, 1970, p. 50).

Gibson Winter provides a theoretical context for understanding media as cultural expressions, as patternings of social action or praxis. They are more subject to manipulation and falsification, he believes, than institutional praxis. The people of a society dwell in a symbolic world, and "how a society treats its environment, cares for or neglects its poor, educates its young, copes with mortality, and endures its sufferings says very concretely the kind of symbolic world in which it dwells" (*Liberating Creation*, p. 68). Therefore one of the obstacles to education for transformation is the hegemonic power lodged in the systems of communication which shape the ideological cocoon.

5. *The educational system*. Another obstacle often is the educational system with its various parts. In his critique of "The Chrysalis Program" Colin Greer suggests an analysis of the ideology of schools, which are "assumed as benign authorities":

The idea that academic learning is a form of action is not considered [p. 157].

There are epistemological roots to oppression and liberation [p. 158].

Who can know is limited by defining what knowing is. When what certain people already know is ignored, then even access to conventional knowing is an empty offer because their progress to this route requires acceptance of their own ignorance, dependence on others for a beginning to learning, and readiness to embrace dimensions of learning conventions [p. 158].

Transformative education challenges the education assumption that if one learns in one's head, one's feet will follow—that learning precedes doing. In her commentary on the "Gospel Agenda" case, Mary Elizabeth Moore warns that we must not "assume that knowledge about the oppressive situation and possible steps for action will, in fact, lead to action" (p. 210). The warning applies also to the assumption that one who has had a transformative experience can by telling others about it replicate its value in those who only hear about it. "Telling ain't teaching!" It may help prepare, but more is needed. The processes of "replication" of effective experiences usually are reduced to making speeches about them, whereas the original event involved a much more dramatic holistic type of educational activity.

Only two models, the Chrysalis Program and the Women's Theological Center, are part of formal educational structures. The others are informal, outside of the schooling patterns. But the carry-over of assumptions and expectations from the predominant system occurs. Outside information and some kind of "skill training" in social analysis are necessary in all the models, along with some kind of involvement and action. Henry Giroux's work indicates how the reproductive and imaginative possibilities of the educational system need to be part of the analysis of the obstacles against which liberating education must work.

6. *The family*. Showing how subtle are ideological obstacles, Allen Moore points out the limitations built into the institution of the family in contemporary Western culture:

The family owes its significance in North American society to an economic and social system that depends upon consumption, success, achievement, and competition for the rewards of society [p. 60].

Only as we bring families, including both parents and children, to a critical awareness of their own plight will there be hope for justice for humankind and peace among peoples and nations. As long as our agenda remains the plight of others and we do not perceive the destructive values and assumption that are our own captivity, we will neither be free ourselves nor will we be very effective liberators of others [chap. 2, p. 61].

From this perspective, lifestyle changes such as the use of Jubilee Crafts for holidays still reinforce consumerism. It is understandable why we tend to assume that "our own children have rights above and beyond the rights of other children," or why we have exalted our families above the larger community of humankind or livingkind. Mary Elizabeth Moore points out that in the "Gospel Agenda" case "no clear openings were created to invite people to explore and share their own ideologies and attitudes toward the poor or toward the questions of wealth, power, and land possession" (p. 210).

7. Volunteer organizations. Still another subtle obstacle is pointed out by Joseph Hough in his commentary on the "Bread for the World" case; he notes how the employment of a professional intern threatens the group of volunteers. He refers to the last hundred years in the United States when "in case after case . . . volunteer groups were routinized, nationalized, and turned over to professional leadership. The result was that . . . lay participation was finally reduced to fundraising" (p. 109). The tension between professional leadership and lay participation can get in the way of effective education for transformation.

8. The workplace. The workplace stands alongside other "locations" such as media, schools, and family as a significant ideological force. The clearest reference to this obstacle comes in the commentary by Colin Greer on "The Chrysalis Program," where he says "there is no evidence that the immediate educational context is engaged" (p. 154). He asks, "Can the educator critique the social order without including the educational institutions, and can change be possible without change in these institutions? . . . Can the missionary model be superseded if the postmissionary educator does not engage the home-base institutional turf and authority structure of which he or she is victim and beneficiary?" (p. 155). Although the workplace in the Chrysalis model is an educational institution, Greer's suggestions about this ideological obstacle have implications for broader application.

9. Religious organizations and teachings. Alongside these other contributing factors to the ideological cocoon are religious organizations and religious teachings. Gregory Baum emphasizes the ambiguity of religion and the prophetic teaching against idolatry. There is "no safe language in religion" *(Religion,* p. 72), so like any other language system, it must always be open to ongoing critique. Both he and Gibson Winter believe that ethical reflection must come into play in every ideological critique; this must be done with special care when addressing religious bodies and teachings. Winter brings also into his analysis of symbols the spirituality of the "techno-society" of North America. In addition to espousing a hermeneutic of suspicion about ideologies, he affirms that the special function of theology in the critique of ideology is "the disclosure of the symbolic horizons that control the ideology," and that "religious social ethics is, thus, the disciplined inquiry of a community of those who are committed to the struggle for justice and peace. The critique of ideology is the central task of such a community" *(Liberating Creation,* p. 132).

In the North American scene a demonstrable feature of religious mystification is the *privatization of religion.* This trend, Baum says, "lets society off the hook . . . and hence protects institutional power and privilege" *(Religion,* p. 206). He goes further:

If [Christian teachers] prefer obedience to disobedience, conformity to criticism, modesty to public controversy, patience to impatient longing for justice, then they make the gospel a symbolic language for the defense of the dominant forces in society. . . .

The stress [on] Jesus as personal savior is always linked, therefore, to the defense of the political *status quo.* The individualistic religion of traditional evangelical and fundamentalist Christians legitimates the individualism of our economic system, and while they present their message as nonpolitical, it has significant political consequences. The privatization of sin and conversion, fostered in Catholicism by the confessional practice, is promoted in the Protestant churches by the traditional evangelical stress on personal conversion to Jesus [ibid., pp. 206, 209].

In a following chapter Baum discusses how psychoanalysis has contributed to this privatization by locating the source of human misery in the self and emphasizing adjustment to the social world.

Matthew Lamb discusses these issues as *social sin* and advocates "prophetic" and "political" theology as a means of analyzing and exposing it and working toward social transformation. He writes:

Individuals may have the best will in the world, may be good and upright, and yet by their actions contribute to social and historical processes which oppress and dehumanize. . . .

The social sins—or biases—of economic oppression, racism, ecological pollution, and sexism stain human history with their all too evident horrors. . . .

Poverty is man-made, and its present global intensification results more from stupidity and a shortsighted bias of unenlightened self-interest than it does from a cunningly intelligent greed [*Solidarity with Victims: Toward a*

Theology of Social Transformation, New York, Crossroad, 1982, pp. 3, 4, 5].

In his little book *Sinful Social Structures* (New York, Paulist Press, 1974) Patrick Kerans elaborates in a popular way on the elements involved in social sin. Philip Scharper comments on the "Gospel Agenda" case that

> what concerns prophets principally is not sinful individuals, but sinful structures, sinful institutions, the sinful society. To the degree that we have privatized religion, we have also privatized sin.
> We must learn—and teach—the reality of social sin and sinfulness. Among the "right questions" to be asked are . . . these: "Is my country sinful? . . . Is my church sinful? . . . Is my seminary or Christian university sinful? If so, why? If so, to what degree?" [p. 215].

A story is told in Virginia about old Senator Harry Byrd, the dominant figure in state and sometimes national politics for several decades early in this century. At the annual Apple Festival hosted by the Senator, hundreds of political leaders gathered to celebrate apples, crown a queen, and talk politics. A new young neighborhood pastor was there, and before he left he went up to the old Senator to express his appreciation. He apologized for interrupting a conversation between the host and another Senator, saying that he did not know much about politics. The old Senator harrumphed, "The church is the graduate school of politics!"

The analyses I have been discussing and developing above reveal some of the forces and factors that make it difficult to do systemic analysis and mobilize people for structural change. The ideological cocoon filters alternative interpretations of the world, and blocks the "raising of consciousness" and action to change the system.

C. For What?

All the models aim at both personal and political/structural changes.

1. New Consciousness. The primary goal throughout these models seems to be a new consciousness and understanding about justice issues. For example, the following are some phrases and statements from the cases:

— "seeing things from a new perspective"
— "the way the non-poor see the world *must* change"
— "a new way of perceiving"
— "new feelings"
— "new perspectives arise"
— "it's a different kind of consciousness I bring to the issues"
— "a complete reshaping of the participants' view of themselves and of their world"

—"a radical new reorientation is to result in a reordering of values and new ways of acting out those values in individual behavior and in political and social action for change"

—"a new vulnerability, an openness to questioning impressions previously accepted as 'the way things are.' "

One of the dangers in formal and informal education is emphasis upon "attitude change" and upon the assumption that changing one's attitude will lead to changes in one's behavior. In each case, however, personal attitudinal change is linked to some behavioral change or action. These projects all attempt to keep the personal and the political in dialectical tension, recognizing that one cannot work well without the other. For example, Mary Elizabeth Moore states the following about the Gospel Agenda project:

> The center of power in the Sisters' pedagogy is their own conviction that the way the non-poor see the world *must* change so that their actions *will* change so that the poor *can* change their situation. This power of conviction is like gravity pulling non-poor persons toward the earth for a new look. The gravity defies the forces of fear, comfort, or blindness which propel people up and away from reality. It attempts to ground people so that they will deal with what is on the ground with them [p. 209].

The goal of a new consciousness requires social analysis if the social sin is to be addressed. That involves gaining an understanding of the structures of power in the world, the networks of political, economic, and social forces that influence human life. North American education in general does not develop that kind of awareness and the related ability to contribute to change in an oppressive situation. People need to comprehend their own domestic situations, the different situations of other people around the world and the connections between the two.

This goal is enriched by Frenchak's "artistic theological process" and Winter's emphasis on imagination (see p. 239, above). Baum locates this goal in the important utopian vision that uses imagination to create the future. "Utopian imagination," Baum writes, "makes people sensitive to the breaking points of the present system and nourishes in them a longing for a new kind of society, and as such exercises a significant role in social change" *(Religion,* p. 171). These theoretical approaches try to avoid the polarization between economic determinism and cultural power. As they work toward conscientization with a realistic action/change component, they affirm the important dimension of imagination in transformative education and its contribution to envisioning the new world.

2. Lifestyle change. Another goal of several of the projects is lifestyle change by the participants. In several places there are references to changes in one's pattern of living, and in one's behavior, as a result of the educational experience. Despite the warning about the consumerism compromise, the involvement in Jubilee Crafts may represent a helpful incremental step forward for those involved in the first stages for social change. How can it be used most effectively to lead into further action for transformation in society? Lifestyle change may look like an obvious purpose for participants in transformative education, but it is important and requires careful planning to fit it effectively into the changes desired.

3. Political/social action. All of the models "search for action-oriented pedagogies." Some concentrate on political mobilization of people and groups to struggle against injustice. Still others make a conscious effort to construct and nurture support groups. Many of the groups consciously seek sustained commitment of their members. Because the criteria for selection of the models emphasized action learning, all in different ways exhibit efforts to fulfill that purpose.

4. Conversion. Matthew Lamb writes that "the social sins of racism, sexism, ecological destruction, political and economic oppression . . . require profound conversions of personal, social, economic, and political conduct or praxis" *(Solidarity,* p. 120). Douglas Hall in his commentary frankly states that "the 'repentance' that is required here cannot, in my opinion, be produced by pedagogy" (chap. 8, p. 206). He continues:

> While certain things may and can be taught the non-poor, ignorance is not their fundamental barrier to life. Neither is their problem the lack of courage or assertiveness, though many middle-class persons feel "locked into" the rituals and expectations of their social stratum. The predicament of the non-poor at its most rudimentary theological level of expression is their lack of *caritas*—not "charity," but "suffering love" (agape) [p. 206].
>
> Through contact with the poor in the Third and Fourth worlds; through contextually-conscious biblical study . . .; [and through other types of pedagogy, study, and experience], it is possible to put the non-poor *in the way of the metanoia* that is needed to alter their (our!) condition from one of anxious self-seeking to suffering love for the neighbor. . . . At bottom what is required in the case of the non-poor is *a fundamental and ongoing conversion of the spirit,* namely a "continuing baptism"—the "drowning" of that within all of us which grasps after ultimate *securitas,* and the birth of that "new being" which reaches out to "the other" [p. 207].

The goals and purposes of the eight models reflect the mixture of hope and expectation of most action/reflection educational models.

D. Motivations

What calls or leads people to change? If these models represent struggles between larger social forces with their conflicting ideologies, what are the determining factors in whether or not participants do change, become transformed, and sustain that new commitment?

1. Altruism. One view builds on human altruism and intentional solidarity with those who suffer. The "Plant Closures" case states that staff and volunteers work on the "assumption that Christians do not turn their backs on human suffering; rather, they want to address it. But to do so they need understanding of the causes of injustice and knowledge of specific ways they can address the root causes to bring about change" (p. 66). Once they see that suffering, they will then be able to "let go of the things the poor need in order to survive," as the "Gospel Agenda" case puts it (p. 191). Some transformative educators believe that, whether based on guilt or on more positive motivation, people will voluntarily sacrifice, give up, let go, if and when they see the real situations of oppression and understand how people are being hurt.

Douglas Hall, citing and then expanding upon a quote taken from the "Gospel Agenda" case, writes:

"This model seemed to promise *some reduction of the non-poor's reluctance to let go* of the things the poor need in order to survive." This . . . is what can be reasonably and legitimately aimed at by pedagogy as such: clearing away some of the debris, so to speak, so that the light of the gospel may get in. But if such a goal is what we envisage, then we should not proceed on the assumption that a "conscientization" program for the poor can be applied *mutatis mutandis* to the non-poor. It *is* hard for the rich to enter the Kingdom! Our pedagogy should not assume that it is anything else than hard, terribly hard [p. 207].

2. Self-interest or shared oppression. A second view emphasizes the solidarity of suffering, and the need to help "the group members see themselves as 'oppressed' " (chap. 1, p. 28). One case advocates "objectify[ing] our own present imprisonment by identifying the obstacles to our true freedom" (Hunter commentary, chap. 7, p. 180). If the non-poor realize how the armaments race cuts down or prevents their own fulfillment and how ecological destruction is affecting their own health, then they will be moved out of self-preservation to work for change. In the face of such threats, all persons share a common humanity. Noē Gonzales points out that in the base communities of Latin America the struggle for life, for survival, is obvious, and motivation is therefore lodged in the condition of the participants themselves (chap. 1, p. 36). The self-interest argument holds that middle-class people in various ways face the same questions of survival, of life itself. Their situations pose the options much less dramatically, of course, but the difference is one of degree, not of kind. The intention to join in solidarity with the more drastically oppressed thus comes out of a recognition of a kind of existential solidarity in being dehumanized, though in different ways, by the same mechanisms. It also comes from sharing the potential of our common humanity. The dominant ideological forces have an easier time hiding oppression with the illusions of fulfillment built into consumption of material goods, weekend leisure to hide the unjust conditions of weekday toil, and other substitute satisfactions which mask the reality of life in First World societies today.

3. Local problems. Another element in motivation, and the understanding which fosters it, can be seen in the challenge to deal with the home-base situations as people see the similarity between the mechanisms at work in those situations and in global, overseas contexts. People live locally, but also globally. Therefore transformative education calls for thinking of both and connecting them. The movement of industry overseas obviously sets up human problems with unemployment in California. Nuclear targeting or leakage turns the people affected toward peace activity. Exclusion of women from responsible positions leads to their heightened consciousness and mobilization. Where the personal is touched by oppression, the experience becomes fertile for political mobilization.

Focusing transformative education and action on local problems, however, may arouse intense opposition and even violence. So it is not surprising that for two hundred years churches in the North Atlantic world have found it easier to give to overseas missions to deal with the problems abroad than to address some of the same, related problems at home. Most of the cases in this book attempted to involve participants in some immersion or direct exposure to situations of poverty or oppression in the home community and tried to encourage and develop ongoing involvement in education/action movements in the home country. However, might it not be possible that the emphasis in some models on addressing problems overseas could work against the commitment to more risky, immediate change at home? Because of the greater difficulties in "implementing," replicating, or addressing the problems at home, Hall points out the special importance of the local support group, such as a Christian congregation (see chap. 8, p. 208).

The old story about the revival preacher's answer to the question about whether to try to attract or scare people into salvation illustrates the variety of motivation: "Well," he said, "you got to use both. Sometimes I just talk about the love of God, and woo people into the Kingdom. Other times I rake open their wounds with fire and brimstone preaching, and then spread on the balm of Gilead."

III. HOW? WHAT PROCESSES ARE USED IN THESE MODELS? WHAT CLUES DO THEY SUGGEST? WHAT QUESTIONS DO THEY RAISE?

A. Commitment of Time and Energy

An example of seeking commitment was when the Parish Peacemaking project got started with the distribution to the congregation of the "Call to Faithfulness" in *Sojourners* and then gathered those who signed for their first meeting. Every case shows the importance of some specific commitment, whether the initial involvement or a later more threatening decision, for example to demonstrate or support Sanctuary. Follow-up in the travel seminar case involved a covenant among the members, a procedure found helpful in many adult education ventures. Usually the commitment means giving time and energy. Time, in the world of the non-poor in the West, is a valuable commodity, so to give up other activities for a new commitment involves far more than just intellectual assent to some proposition. Furthermore, energy is often carefully rationed by the non-poor. In the world of two-income families and with human fulfillment tied to "meaningful" (i.e., remunerative) employment, commitment of energy as well as time requires a considerable act of will.

Throughout these cases the non-poor who were seriously involved were into far more than a casual, business-as-usual religious education exercise. Contrasted with the inherited patterns of religious education for lay people, which usually do not expect serious study or commitment of any intense energy or time, this clue seems obvious as one worth noting and developing.

A question emerges, therefore, about whether this is education for a remnant or a vanguard. Is it really a strategy of "cadre formation," of building small groups of the relatively more committed within a vast body politic? If so, questions about how to expand the cadres, how to engage others, and how to recruit from the majority outside the cadres become of great strategic importance. The Women's Theological Center made greater inclusiveness a high priority. The members of the group in "Peacemaking in a Local Parish" frankly stated that their task was "to change the majority, themselves included." Their processes included regular input into weekly worship services and sustained openness to the entire congregation as their program developed.

Just as the question of the role of the leader or the change-agent must be faced, regarding professionals, so must the related question of how a small, committed group relates to the larger constituency of which it is part.

B. Radical Change of Environment

The "shock value" of taking a group of people to another culture and plunging them into a "provocative and contrasting educational setting" is illustrated dramatically in the "Traveling for Transformation" case. The "immersion" on a trip to India energized participants in Chrysalis. The experiential dimension of intensive involvement with the lives of other people in their own environment challenged radically the provincialism and myopia of the visitors. Of course preparatory reading and briefing helped, but actually being there with other human beings opened up new understandings and feelings.

The field trips into nearby poverty neighborhoods, the "Stations of the City" experiences, sought the same educational value, and even though they were of more limited duration, something of the same transformation of perception and awareness took place. What otherwise is "learned" cognitively now comes mediated through real people. Contact with persons and leaders who before had been only abstractions makes a significant difference in how those persons and their situations are perceived. The "Women's Theological Center" case reports a way to develop this clue:

Field-based Critical Action began with student immersion. In the Boston streets and at the placement agencies, students were confronted with sights, sounds, smells, and ideas that often radically undermined their presuppositions. Kate led them to voice and analyze their experience by asking them to look at which factors in those first days were most surprising, most anxiety-provoking, most hopeful, and most revealing about themselves [pp. 122–23].

Granted the value of such radical change of place, people, and culture, yet with all the difficulties of arranging such local "plunges," the expense of overseas travel, and the imposition on the hosts, is it worth it? It is quite possible for such an experience to turn out the opposite way, for it to reinforce negative stereotypes and "blame the victim" ideological opinions that are all too prevalent in the at-home setting of the non-poor. More attention should be paid to the overall process of such an experience: preparation for it; the nature, duration, expense of it; scheduled times for probing into the ideological dimensions of the participants; follow-up investigation of its meaning, as the quotation above indicates; and other aspects of using it effectively, such as how to "learn" from the people there in ways that contribute to overall social analysis of the total situation and the connections between the home and the visited environment.

C. Risk

Closely related to the level of commitment is the factor of risk. One of the limitations of school-type education is that it is carefully controlled by its cognitive emphasis and its avoidance of conflict. In these models, with their goal of conversion or transformation, risk seems to be a necessary aspect of the experience. Without one's adrenalin running it is difficult to be turned around, to be able to challenge the traditional and become open to the new. The admonition from Jesus for Christians to be "born again" suggests the depth of the experience necessary for significant holistic change in people.

Two of the groups in the cases faced in their development new dimensions of risk: the Parenting for Peace and Justice group faced the issue of Sanctuary and civil disobedience, and the Parish Peacemaking group confronted the fears of those for whom a public demonstration would be a new experience. Participants in the Traveling for Transformation model faced internal anxiety about the decision to go. Whether initially, or in the process of incremental growth in understanding and consciousness, risk seems to be an important clue to education for transformation.

Questions therefore need to be raised about when, where, and how to phase this dimension into the planning for pedagogical models for the non-poor. What supports are necessary to free people to take risks? How can the internal barriers to new and "dangerous" experiences be surfaced and dealt with healthily? In what ways can relatively minor "successes" be used to build confidence for more major risks? How can procedural challenges and risky effort be undergirded by theoretical analysis that can help keep tactics from being confused with long-range strategy? How can leaders use effectively the tension betwen patience and "push"?

D. Community of Support

Notice the refrain:

—"the context of a supportive learning community"
—"a small group of ten to fifteen persons [with] enough mutual trust, fellowship, and openness to the Holy Spirit . . . to allow ordinary individuals and churches to take extraordinary steps in action and in faith— even toward something as large and frustrating as nuclear disarmament"
—"we all need continual sustenance and sustaining of the Spirit, and that comes . . . primarily through people of similar commitments who try to work out of their understanding of the gospel in certain visible commitments to social justice, to the poor"
—and there are several references to the base ecclesial communities of Latin America.

The travel group, the volunteer small group in a movement, and the congregation all point to the significance of this clue. Individuals acting alone cannot sustain their commitment in the face of the risks involved. As someone said, "When I get put in jail for this, I don't want to be there alone!"

In his commentary on the "Gospel Agenda" case, Douglas Hall spoke to the support community issue:

It would make much more sense . . . were such a model to be used *within Christian congregations.* Because in that case, besides the influences coming to such a group from the program described in the model itself, there could be many other concomitant contributions to their overall nurture in the faith: the preaching of the gospel, the prayer and spiritual life of the congregation, a wider and longer-range study of the Christian tradition, and so on. These "ordinary" Christian activities, especially if they were sufficiently coordinated with the special pedagogical content of the model, could help to provide opportunities for the non- or trans-pedagogical "possibilities" which, to my mind, are necessary if the "leap of faith" *(metanoia)* . . . is ever to occur. And, of course, it has to occur over and over again—so an ongoing *koinonia* is the *conditio sine qua non* of the deployment of this model [p. 208].

But voluntary communities are not the same as institutionalized organizations when it comes to staying and supporting power. The advantages of the global network of the Sisters of Notre Dame are obvious when they bring into their challenging work in the Boston area stories of oppression from overseas. Lack of an adequate institutional "carrier" seemed to have been among the obstacles facing the Women's Theological Center and Chrysalis, and the relative weakness of support networks handicapped others as well. Even though the tension between the local and the national was a problem for the Bread for the World group, for it and for the Parenting for Peace and Justice group the resource support of a larger community was significant.

The question raised by Joseph Hough deserves careful investigation:

> Like most volunteer organizations, Bread for the World has attempted to preserve a healthy balance by developing a national organization which provides resources which enable local communities to be effective on their own while at the same time attempting to promote a sense of common purpose among all the local groups around the country. In this way, the sense of group cohesiveness and also a sense of significant national achievement serve to keep alive the motivation necessary for broad volunteer participation. The temptation on the part of the national organizational leadership is to move beyond these functions toward routinization of all local groups as "branches" of the organization. When this happens, the motivation for active participation of volunteers subsides, and the local groups respond usually by turning over the movement to professionals who "do the movement" for the members, who in turn pay them. That sort of history was repeated time and again in the late nineteenth century and early twentieth century among lay volunteer groups. In case after case those volunteer groups were routinized, nationalized, and turned over to professional leadership. The result was that lay people began to lose interest and to diminish their active participation in the groups. Finally, the groups became dominated by professional leaders who developed bureaucracies of their own. Lay participation was finally reduced to fundraising [chap. 4, p. 109].

The problem of mobility in Canadian, U.S., and many other First World societies adds to the difficulty of maintaining support groups. A further question leads to the relationship of such movements to the organized church and other religious bodies. Again, those movements which have structural ties to historic religious organizations have relationships of support that the newer movement models do not have. But the reverse of this value may be the inhibiting and controlling power of the traditional structure. Susan's dilemma in regard to the problem she faced in the peacemaking project dramatizes the issue:

> She wondered about the life cycle of small groups . . . and about sustaining not just the action agenda but also the sense of inward journey and excitement about participating in God's peacemaking. "As the church becomes institutionally involved in peacemaking, what is the role of the small Peacemakers group?" she wondered. She knew that even such a small step as bringing to fruition the nuclear freeze would take a long time. Can a church maintain and strengthen its commitment over time? [p. 33].

E. Reflection

Participants in the Traveling for Transformation model realized later that they needed more scheduled time for reflection in order to assimilate and enhance their learning. Many of the models built in Bible study as a specific component and tried to integrate it into the action/reflection rhythm of their work. There are many other hints that those engaged in education for transformation need to develop more thoroughly their efforts to utilize reflection effectively.

The commentary by Mary Elizabeth Moore on the "Gospel Agenda" case raises stimulating questions about how to enhance the value of reflection. In noting how the case did not deal with the fullness of biblical and church teaching, she raised the question "whether the church's tradition might have been engaged more fully and more fruitfully" (p. 212). She asks also about the "hiddenness of transcendence" and the one–sided selection of biblical and church teaching regarding the poor.

Reflection itself can depend too heavily upon experiential learning. For instance, members of a group might focus most of their reflection on their actions in their work for justice while focusing only superficially on biblical texts or church tradition. Mary Elizabeth Moore serves a good purpose when she forces her questions upon the "Gospel Agenda" case. Just what place do Bible study and more traditional "teaching" have in transformative education? Much of the critique in the present chapter has centered on the limitations of traditional pedagogy and its relative inability to transform persons and systems as it educates. The fact that it does reproduce the dominant ideology of the society still leaves open the question about the place of "content" in transformative education. Taking seriously what Frenchak and Winter are saying about artistic process and creative activity should lead to pursuit of new ways for cultural expression to buttress our efforts in transformative education. If the dynamic of creativity is to go into the past in order to envision the future so that the present can be different, then serious delving into and use of the tradition of faith must be undertaken.

A fruitful further exploration would be into the particular ways such models set up and conduct their reflection. What are the ways it can serve transformative education as the hermeneutical nexus between personal experience and religious tradition, between present and past-and-future, between the personal and the societal, between the particular and the hegemonic ideologies?

F. "Data" from Outside

One prominent type of such data came in the form of stories, as mentioned by several of the cases. Stories of oppressed situations around the world obviously contributed to the Gospel Agenda workshop. For the Gospel Agenda and the Parenting for Peace and Justice models, films provided a helpful means of bringing in needed data and interpretation. But again, note

Mary Elizabeth Moore's caution: "The power lies in stories, in direct communication between the poor and non-poor, in the guidance of tradition, and in concrete guides for action. The most fundamental power lies in the people who have lived these stories, shared them, worked together to define and address the issues, and participated in the institute in hopes that they might make a difference" (p. 212).

Even more "remote" is input of statistical and analytical data. The single issue focus of Bread for the World was cited as enabling a simple-to-complex development of the analysis of the global food situation. Douglas Hall affirmed the value of the "interim objectivity" provided the Gospel Agenda workshop by the input of population statistics. So the value of outside data is not in question. The questions are how and when to use outside data and how much of what kind of outside data to use.

More complex is the question of how to help people learn social analysis. The cases underscore the need for persons to get beyond the simplistic, individualistic understanding of how the systems work. That requires careful and sophisticated analysis in order to make the connections between local and global problems, in the face of media limitations and distortions. Here a particular kind of outside data must be carefully brought in and planned to meet the group's readiness for engaging in complex study and reflection.

Does this relatively modest use of such data input represent a clue for further experimenting and theorizing? Or is this reading of the models inadequate on this point? With television and computers increasingly dominant as data-providers and guides to interpretation in our societies, do these models provide further challenge to the drift of epistemological processes away from the experiential and toward the impersonal?

IV. A FINAL CAUTION: PEDAGOGICAL REALISM

From the beginning the people involved in these models recognized the limitations of their efforts. In his classic essay in the Depression years of the 1930s George Counts asked this question: "Dare the schools change the social order?" These models suggest a more modest question: "Can transformative education make a contribution toward changing the social order?" Obviously the large macrostructural context for these efforts at education for transformation threatens to overwhelm the participants because of the ideological conditioning to which they are subjected and the powerful obstacles to change that they face. Why then do they make the effort?

Probably the persons who created these models were themselves beneficiaries of some kind of creative and prophetic learning about the society and of a vision for the society that came from historical and religious traditions. In different ways they became committed to expenditure of time and energy, to some form of exposure to different environments, to risky experiments. They have belonged to and drawn support from groups of kindred spirits, and they have worked hard at reflecting on what their lived experiences have meant for their own lives—and for their contribution to others and to the world. Because of the elusive mixture of experiences that do not neatly fit traditional pedagogical activity, they have become engaged in these efforts to discover how to do better education for transformation. As serious searchers after better ways, they know both the joys of modest achievement and the disappointments of failure. So they keep on searching.

Their pedagogical models for the non-poor are therefore modest but significant. Accepting that, how do such efforts at education for transformation nurture the vision and sustain the restlessness for *shalom* while they seek to provide stimulation and support for movements of action/reflection that point toward a better world?

Obviously these eight models call forth a wide range of analytical reflections on my part and, I hope, on the part of readers. For the commitment of the architects, their colleagues, and their willingness to risk sharing their work with other readers and myself, and for the contributions of the commentators to our understanding, I give my deep appreciation and respect.

ROBERT A. EVANS

CHAPTER 11

EDUCATION FOR EMANCIPATION: MOVEMENT TOWARD TRANSFORMATION

Four years of concentrated research on pedagogies for the non-poor and my experience as architect of one of the eight models examined in this study challenged me as an educator more than any previous experience in my professional career. The dialogue with my partners in this project plus a fresh encounter with a biblical understanding of "transformation" have provoked for me a new perception of transformative education for the non-poor. This has been distressing and exciting.

Critical reflection on pedagogies for the non-poor forced me to explore three themes I had not previously examined and to redesign the Plowshares Institute's Third World cross-cultural immersion model, Traveling for Transformation. The three themes are:

    I. Criteria of Transformation
   II. Dynamic of Transformation
  III. Components of Transformation

Essential to a discussion of these themes is an understanding of the term "transformative" and the vision which informs this approach to education.

What do we mean by the term "transformative" when applied to education? Is it distinguished from "traditional" or "classical" education as well as from "innovative," "renewing," or even "radical" notions? What criteria delineate it? By what goals or standards can one evaluate its progress? This does not imply that there are empirically verifiable behavioral results, about which there would be complete agreement on success or failure. But some general standards by which to judge the adequacy of our own educational endeavors are necessary. At the conclusion of educational experiences that seem to result in significant behavioral changes, on what grounds can we justify the use of the term "transformative"?

THE VISION

This analysis of the eight models identifies the primary problems to be addressed and the vision toward which the transformative educational process moves. M. Scott Peck provides a useful image in *The Road Less Traveled* (New York, Touchstone, 1978) as he discusses the continual need to change the "map of reality" by which individuals "negotiate the terrain of life":

When we are poor, the world looks different from when we are rich. We are daily bombarded with new information as to the nature of reality. If we are to incorporate this information, we must continually revise our maps, and sometimes when enough new information has accumulated, we must make very major revisions. The process of making revisions, particularly major revisions, is painful, sometimes excruciatingly painful [p. 44].

Transformative education goes beyond information in revising our maps of reality. The process, though painful, can be liberating as well. What are the contours of the new map, and what are the dynamics of its revision?

A New Map of Reality

Each of the models carries a vision of a newly-ordered map of reality, explicit or implicit, toward which the transformative process is intended to move. To employ the language of one model, this could be stated as: "a more *just, sustainable, and peaceful* world community." The vision names as its foundational problems: *injustice* and *inequity*, with the gap between poor and non-poor the greatest in the modern era and still growing; and *unsustainability* and *militarism*, which are buttressed by a nuclear threat which has reached new thresholds of potential devastation. Statistical studies supporting this analysis of the present world situation are readily available in the *Global 2000 Report to the President* (vol. 1, Washington, D.C., U.S. Government Printing Office, 1980). The report pictures a world which, if present trends and national policies continue to the year 2000, "will be more crowded, more polluted, less stable ecologically . . ." (p. 1) and perhaps—most frightening of all—will be more vulnerable than ever to disruption by natural and human causes, including a nuclear war.

The models of education for transformation in this study basically concur with this analysis. They also hold up an alternative map of reality which is lodged in a biblical and theological context. This provides further meaning for transformation as a concept. We can identify criteria emerging from that vision which provide data for evaluating transformative education for the non-poor. Before detailing the criteria, however, attention should be directed to the biblical vision from which the models, in part, emerge.

Vision of a Biblical Reversal

"What does the Lord require of you but to do justice . . . ?" (Mic. 6:8). Micah and other prophets call the non-poor to a reversal of their dominant life commitment in their relation to the poor. Jesus draws on the prophet Isaiah for the elements of such a reversal and connects this transformation of priorities with the coming reign of God:

The Spirit of the Lord is upon me,
because God has appointed me to preach good news to the poor.
God has sent me to proclaim release to the captives
and recovery of sight to the blind,
to set at liberty those that are oppressed, to proclaim
the acceptable year of the Lord [Luke 4:18–19].

The transformation Jesus is demanding is what John Howard Yoder in *The Politics of Jesus* (Grand Rapids, Eerdmans, 1972, p. 39) describes as "a visible socio-political-economic restructuring of relations among the people of God." Such reversal implies an accompanying spiritual transformation for the non-poor. Although Christ calls for a new way of understanding and relating to God as well as to the people of God and the world, we need to warn against the danger of language that stresses too much "the poor in spirit" or the "inwardly oppressed" or the "morally blind." This language avoids the ramifications of reversal of societal structures and patterns in the name of justice. As several of the commentators on the models remind us, the transformation calls for nothing less than a *metanoia* or conversion that encompasses the whole person and society. The conversion affects relationships among God's children—the whole of creation. Reversal may not mean that the poor and non-poor immediately change places. However, it is a reversal of the priorities reflected in the status quo. The coming reign of God means modifications of commitments and patterns of living.

Jesus follows the prophetic vision cited above with the shocking announcement: "Today this scripture has been fulfilled in your hearing." This means that in some way the person and presence of Jesus has initiated this social, economic, and political transformation. This paradigmatic biblical account is a foundation for our work on transformative education.

I. CRITERIA OF TRANSFORMATION

The biblical vision of "reversal" or "conversion" involves a realignment or repositioning of the non-poor in relation to the poor and to God. The eight models considered in this project seem to operate on at least three basic levels of change in relation to the meaning of transformation. The first level is *reduction of the resistance to change*, the second, *"letting go" or "relinquishment,"* and the third, *participation* in changing unjust structures. The three belong together, as well as being in some *dialectical* tension. The first level is an important preparatory stage for transformative education. Consequently, I want to urge consideration of criteria of transformative education that are focused on the second and third levels of repositioning by the non-poor.

The standards we set for educational projects for the non-poor will determine in great measure what modifications we make within our educational models. This kind of research has revealed areas of my own work as an educator which should be abandoned and areas where more effort and cooperation are demanded. A more rigorous biblical understanding of transformative education for the non-poor points to three specific criteria for evaluation: (a) sufficiency, (b) solidarity, and (c) emancipation.

A. Sufficiency

The biblical mandate for justice demands basic access to the necessities of life for all human beings. Jesus' parable of the sheep and goats (Matt. 25:31–46) embodies a message that runs from the Old Testament prophets through the Gospels to the Epistles. Sufficiency, as the meeting of basic human needs, is equated with faithfulness to God: "If you have done it to the least of these—you have done it unto me." A contemporary interpretation of this mandate would include food, shelter, access to health care, basic education, and opportunity for emancipation. The basis for action is the sufficiency required for human dignity. Human rights scholar David Hollenbach declares, "Human dignity . . . is more fundamental than any specific human right. . . . Dignity is the norm by which the adequacy of all forms of human behavior . . . [is] to be judged" (*Claims in Conflict*, New York, Paulist Press, 1979, p. 90).

Redistribution and more equitable sharing of the world's resources are imperative if the vision of sufficiency for all is to be realized. The models address in different ways the human suffering and oppression that result from current insufficiency and inequity on a regional and global scale. Forms of injustice may result from: inadequate food or shelter; excessive and inappropriate expenditures of limited resources on attempts to provide false or illusory military or economic security; gross inequity among nations, classes, races, and sexes in access to resources essential for human dignity and survival. This inequality is epitomized by the shocking fact that the United States, with 6 percent of the world's population, consumes approximately 40 percent of the world's resources, and still has 15 percent of its population living below poverty level.

Genuinely transformative education should result in a covenantal commitment to begin and sustain a process of redistribution and sharing of resources by the non-poor. There should be evidence that a "redrawing" of one's map of reality reflects a significant shift in the use of resources that one has control over and/or access to. This requires examination of a transformed commitment at several levels:

1. **Personal:** Assessment of income and resources consumption with regular re-evaluation of movement toward sufficiency for all.

2. **Institutional:** Assessment and advocacy of principles of re-adjustment through sufficiency standards for constituents—with special reference and priority for local congregations and other religious organizations, from judicatories to seminaries.

3. **Systemic:** Assessment and commitment to strategies for political and social change through legislation or modification of structures.

New summative and longitudinal research concretized to suit the focus of particular transformative educational models should help us monitor actual behavioral change. But faithfulness to God or commitment to the liberation of a sister or brother is not reducible to verifiable quantitative measurement. Douglas Hall and Will Kennedy remind us that "conversion" contains an extra-pedagogical element that is not controllable, researchable, or measurable. However, unless we are willing to rely solely on limited individualist and subjective analysis of what constitutes transformative education, then we must try to develop standards by which to judge what is transformative in matters of justice and peace on a personal pilgrimage for one of the non-poor and in society's structures.

No one knows precisely what the turning points for a new map of reality may be. The models suggest many: a letter to a Congressperson, an act of civil disobedience, a restructuring of family and institutional priorities and lifestyles. However, our criteria and guidelines must be seen as tentative and preparatory marks which are often eclipsed by God's gracious intervention in the lives of individuals and communities. Paulo Freire fears the "consultation mentality of the non-poor." We hold another workshop, or course, or project in which the analysis of the problem may be increasingly astute, but no action is ever taken—except to call another consultation. It may assuage guilt, but it does not result in transformation. Sufficiency can be measured. To some degree our personal and political contributions to sufficiency can be monitored.

B. Solidarity

All eight models reveal deep societal divisions based on self-interest: First World against Third World, whites against peoples of color, management against labor, men against women, non-poor against poor. The cases expose the virtual absence of significant solidarity across these divisions. This is in stark contrast to the biblical vision of a creation-wide community, a global family:

> For Christ is our peace, who has made us both one, and has broken down the dividing wall of hostility, by abolishing in Christ's own flesh the law of commandments and ordinances, in order to create in Christ one new humanity in place of the two, so making peace, and in order to reconcile us both to God in one body through the cross, thereby bringing the hostility to an end. And Christ came and preached peace to you who were far off and peace to those who were near; for through Christ we both have access in one Spirit to [God] [Mother and] Father. So then you are no longer strangers and sojourners, but you are citizens together with the saints and members of the household of God [Eph. 2:14–19 (*An Inclusive Language Lectionary: Readings for Year B*, jointly published by John Knox, Pilgrim, and Westminster, 1984, pp. 168–69; see the note on "Addition to the Text" and the appendices on "Metaphor" and "God the Father and Mother")].

These messages from Paul could begin to be heard as "good news" by the poor and the non-poor through a recovery of the vision of community where an experience of our common creaturehood breaks down every barrier. God is seen not only as "liberator" but as "reconcilor," "creator," and "sustainer" of the earth inhabited by the whole human family. If redistribution were imperative under the first criterion—that of sufficiency—then *repositioning* in community is critical to the second criterion—that of solidarity.

Transformative education should result in a covenantal commitment to begin the repositioning of oneself, so that the power of the middle-class cocoon can partially be mitigated by sustained contact with the poor. The eight models reveal that experiential repositioning promotes advocacy beyond narrow self-interest and for the welfare of the wider community. Three areas merit consideration:

1. Personal and familial: Discernment and redesign of contacts with and advocacy for the poor in building a new community through support systems for justice.

2. Institutional and organizational: Evaluation and strategy for consultation of and participation in decision-making processes by persons discriminated against by class, race, sex, or geographic location.

3. Systemic: Assessment of and support for movements or legislation which places the needs and participation of the poor and marginalized above the self-interest of the non-poor.

The power of base communities or convenantal support groups among the poor has been evident. The solidarity of the non-poor with the poor has similar potential for transformation. Again, such commitments should be monitored through research for the sake of both support and accountability. These actions for solidarity not only reflect genuine transformation, but contact with the community sustains the commitment to change.

C. Emancipation

Each model addresses the captivity of the non-poor by dominant ideology. This captivity frustrates those attempting to implement new maps of reality for the non-poor. The pervading power of controlling ideology influences the family, workplace, media, and educational and religious systems. The aim of a pedagogy for the non-poor must therefore be more than to change persons' views of how to alleviate hunger or reduce the nuclear threat; the aim must also be to initiate their emancipation from the controlling ideology.

Paulo Freire has helped me learn to seek root causes. Henry Giroux illumines this process in his introduction to Freire's book *The Politics of Education* (South Hadley, Mass., Bergin and Garvey, 1985). Giroux writes: "Central to Freire's politics and pedagogy is a philosophical vision of a liberated humanity [a vision informed, according to Giroux, by Latin American liberation theology]. . . . By combining a dynamic of critique and collective struggle with a philosophy of hope, Freire has created a language of possibility that is rooted in what he calls a permanent prophetic vision" (p. xvii). Further, Giroux shows that Freire links "critical sensibility," which is an extension of "historical sensibility," to the cultural forms that "give meaning to the way we think, talk, dress, and act. . . . [Critical sensibility] is used to distinguish between the present as given and the present as containing emancipatory possibilities" (p. xxiv). "Emancipate" is a helpful term; its etymology can be traced to ancient Roman law, in which it meant to free property, slaves, children, and women from paternal control. To "emancipate" was to deliver from bondage to participation in society those previously excluded from its benefits. Thus, education for emancipation, in Freire's sense, calls for a holistic, humanizing liberation of the non-poor from often unrecognized bondage. Transformative education is a movement toward emancipation for the non-poor.

To the criteria of redistribution of resources and repositioning within a new community, let us add critical *re-evaluation* of and challenge to the hegemonic ideology which acts to contain any threat to its authority and to insure the continued dominance of the non-poor and the continued subservience of the poor. Therefore, a transformative educational experience should be marked by a critical stance toward economic, political, and social structures which perpetuate the bondage. Transformative education moves toward a sharing in the mobilization of forces to change the structures that deny the poor participation in the decision-making processes which determine their own survival. There should also be signs of the refusal by the non-poor to participate knowingly in the benefits of a society or structure that continues to perpetrate inequity and

resist change. This refusal might take the form of refusing to pay the proportion of one's income tax used for weapons, of refusing to purchase products
advertised through demeaning images of women or minorities, of engaging in
civil disobedience for the sake of opposing unjust intervention in the affairs of
a Latin American or African nation, or of insisting with the Sanctuary Movement that laws governing political asylum be applied consistently to persons
from all foreign nations. Mahatma Gandhi insisted that "non-cooperation
with evil is as important as cooperation with good." The issues may differ, but
critical re-evaluation and rejection or subversion of controlling ideologies for
the sake of emancipation should be evident. Again, this may occur at several
levels:

1. **Personal:** Critical evaluation and participation in collective action for
change in at least one area judged to be unjust—an area where captivating
power provides special benefits or privileges.
2. **Organizational:** Assessment and critical proposals to identify and
modify processes that hamper the free expression of alternative economic,
political, or cultural options.
3. **Systemic:** Explore collective action to challenge legislation and public
or private organizational policies which deny a hearing to concerns of poor
and marginalized people.

Transformative education may only succeed in penetrating a portion of the
non-poor's cocoon. Transformed consciousness, change of lifestyles, or effective political influence for justice and peace requires critical re-evaluation of
the ideological bondage of the non-poor.

II. DYNAMIC OF TRANSFORMATION

"Warning: This seminar may be hazardous to your lifestyle," suggested one
of the participants in the Traveling for Transformation model. Reports by
participants in other models repeatedly match that depth of feeling and tone of
surprise. The lay leader in the Chrysalis Program declared that the visit to India
changed her life. Members of the group in "Peacemaking in a Local Parish"
shared feelings of being overwhelmed by the threat of nuclear destruction.
Family members in "Parenting for Peace and Justice" reacted with renewed
conviction as they faced the poverty of families in Latin America. In each case
persons and communities began to see the world with new eyes and to act
differently. The degree or level of change differed, but by the participants' own
witness those encounters were life-modifying. Their changes were directly
associated with an educational experience that sought to bring about some such
modification of intention and behavior.

Within the eight models there appears to be a consistent and recurring
dynamic or rhythm of transformation. When analyzed in light of the criteria
delineated above and linked with what appear to be critical components in the

transformation process, a pattern begins to emerge. The identification of a pattern results not from a consensus among the dialogue partners in this book, but rather from my reflection on the writing of this volume and on more than a decade of personal experimentation with models of transformative education for peace and justice. During those years some disasters and a few minor miracles connected certain educational processes to sustained and faithful transformation of behavior. Those experiments have been grounded in my biblically-based theological conviction that "to know God is to do justice." The "renewal of our minds" called for in Paul's Letter to the Romans (12:2) involves just such a transforming encounter with God. The power of that encounter continues to call into question the values and criteria of the world to which we have been culturally conformed and socialized. The power which begins to break this captivity is a gift of God which must be constantly rediscovered. The power of God is hidden in the weakness of the cross of Jesus Christ.

In this emerging dynamic of transformation five elements or components consistently appear. The order of the elements is not necessarily sequential, and there is a degree of overlap and interchange. These elements are:

A. Facing the Problem
B. Maintaining the Restlessness
C. Sustaining the Vision
D. Countering Controlling Ideology
E. Reinventing Power

As I describe the components of the dynamic as I have experienced them and been able to observe them in other pedagogical constructs, I invite the reader to compare and contrast my analysis with his or her own experience in order to further the dialogue.

A. Facing the Problem

Facing the problem is, not surprisingly, at the root of an educational process that is often described as "raising awareness." The most effective models, however, seek a particular kind of awareness, a personal confrontation with injustice that demands a response. This encounter must be so convincing that it cannot be denied or rationalized. Group members of the Gospel Agenda seminar saw the plight of persons victimized by inadequate housing in Boston's Columbia Point area; they not only visited the site, but also met with residents and heard their reflections following a film about the housing project. In the "Plant Closures" case, Reverend Ed Harrington's response was directly tied to the personal reflections of workers who had been left powerless by management.

Personal experience with those suffering injustice holds one accountable and demands response. Initial reaction by the non-poor to the plight of the poor or oppressed, when outright denial is no longer possible, often trivializes human suffering. In *The Road Less Traveled*, M. Scott Peck speaks of the drive to avoid pain. Some of us acknowledge the reality of human suffering but then see it as the exception in our experience of the human condition, not the norm. Only when the education process can pierce this armor of rationalization can the problem of injustice be faced. The need is to centralize rather than trivialize the problem. Each of the models seeks such a method to expose and dissolve this protective covering of rationalization.

At other times we privatize the reality of human suffering by acknowledging the problem and then dismissing it from the non-poor's sphere of responsibility because the difficulties have been essentially created by those who are poor or oppressed. We blame the victim. In the "Plant Closures" case the session members cite the "real" problems as the inability of workers to learn new skills, their unwillingness to move families to new locations, and the excessive demands of the union. If we can privatize injustice, we can also relocate it and distance it from basic causes of suffering.

A path is cleared to the dynamic of transformation when we personalize human suffering rather than privatize it. Personalization involves empathizing with the pain of one who is genuinely a victim, not a producer of the suffering. For the non-poor this personalization also means accepting some personal responsibility for continued participation in a system that sustains poverty and dehumanizes. We must attribute accountability primarily to the victimizer, whether a person or a system, rather than to the victim. A significant move is made when the non-poor acknowledge some degree of *mutual* or reciprocal responsibility. This acknowledgment may not always be the first step in the process of transformation; but when it does come, it is almost invariably associated with a profoundly disturbing restlessness.

B. Maintaining the Restlessness

To maintain restlessness is an essential and creative element in the process of transformative education. The models teem with illustrations of restlessness, often expressed as frustration and exasperation. Staff and students at the Women's Theological Center confess that with their history and education they cannot become the poor. Yet they cherish a vision of ministry beyond the bounds of class and race. The Bread for the World group, overwhelmed by the responsibility for the U.S. role in problems of world hunger, is restless about what appropriate action to take in strengthening their lobbying efforts. The families in "Parenting for Peace and Justice" are so distressed by the possibility of moving toward offering sanctuary as an act of civil disobedience that it threatens their continued existence as a group. Such personal and group discomfort is usually seen as a liability to be eliminated or resolved as quickly as possible. On the contrary, such restlessness is a critical element in the dynamic of transformation, both for initiating change and for sustaining the movement toward justice.

This restlessness with the structures of injustice is, I believe, a divine restlessness, a gift of God's grace. For the ancient prophets and contemporary dissidents, the restlessness seems to be stirred by the contrast of the present human condition with the biblical vision of a new order, a new society, a new kingdom. Perhaps Augustine was not only wise but prophetic when he prayed that our souls "are restless til they find their rest in Thee." Maintaining the prophetic restlessness which encourages resistance is crucial to facing the problems that require transformation. The responses of some individuals in the cases reveal a restlessness that sometimes takes the form of resistance to structures of injustice. Those structures are seen as supporting patterns of dehumanization. We should, therefore, celebrate rather than seek to deny or mitigate this restlessness. Without the disquietude of prophetic voices and similar emotions evoked in those who hear those voices, there might be no dynamic of transformation.

C. Sustaining the Vision

This also fits into the dynamic of transformation. The vision of a biblical reversal for the sake of justice fuels the resistance and provides energy for the transformation. Though each model takes a different path, they all are guided, in my judgment, by a vision with common elements. Jesus' announcement of his ministry at the synagogue in Nazareth reaffirms the prophet Isaiah's vision of a just, humane, and whole world (Luke 4:18–19, Isa. 61:1–2), and each of the models shares in Jesus' and Isaiah's vision of a new reality.

The earth's resources are to be shared by all because the land belongs first to God, the Creator. In the Gospel Agenda model, the experience of the Sisters of Notre Dame indicates that participants will not take action toward a more equitable distribution of the world's resources unless they believe in God's ownership of the earth and their stewardship obligations as creatures of God. As the guarantor of security and peace, God provides a vision for the participants in the Peacemaking in a Local Parish model. Confidence in God as one's ultimate security gives the courage to demonstrate and consider civil disobedience. However, the peacemaking group needed constant nurture to sustain the vision and block their inclination to rely on a massive national security system.

The implementation of the vision must have accomplishable stages to sustain the momentum for transformation. If a process for moving toward the realization of the vision cannot be articulated, and if some early minimal successes do not occur, the vision tends to fade and the model loses energy and effectiveness. The Peacemakers group focuses on the nuclear freeze because it is a way to deal concretely with fears, needs, and concern about the future. The freeze is a politically feasible first step, even if difficult, and political victories in churches, villages, and states sustain and renew the ownership of the biblical vision of a peaceable kingdom.

In the "Gospel Agenda" case Sister Marie Augusta Neal points to the first stage of transformation as reducing the resistance of the non-poor when the poor reach out to take what is rightfully theirs. Paulo Freire emphasizes a theme which each model explores: there is no liberation for the poor or the non-poor without political involvement. The vision calls for a change of socio-economic and political structures from the perspective and foundation of faith. One measure of the effectiveness of education for transformation is the degree to which a model sustains the vision for change.

D. Countering Controlling Ideology

Countering controlling ideology is an element of the dynamic of transforma-tion. This observation is undergirded by the insights of Paulo Freire and by Will Kennedy's analysis of the power of ideology. Douglas Kellner calls con-trolling (or hegemonic) ideology "those ideas, images, and theories that mys-tify social reality and block social change" (cited in Kennedy, p. 235, above). *Controlling ideology* can then be contrasted with *liberating ideology*, described by Kellner as "programs of social reconstruction that mobilize people for social activism" (ibid.). Those programs involve images and theories that embody an alternative or liberating ideology. The monitoring power of the current, controlling, unjust ideology must be broken if transformation toward a more just and liberating ideology is to become a possibility.

Controlling ideology can be compared to the water in which fish swim: it is so much a part of our ordering environment that we do not even recognize its existence, to say nothing of its dominating power. This tends to be the case until something counters the foundational assumptions of that ideology. That many people are poor can be an "acceptable reality." Awareness that the suffering of the poor is not only unjust but unjustifiable counters that acceptance. The notion that the privileges of the non-poor not only are unmerited but are acquired through the benefits of a system that exploits the poor threatens the controlling ideology. Even more so does the call for the redistribution of resources held primarily by the non-poor. The call is not for an act of mercy, but rather for an act of justice—demanded by the poor and required by God.

One of the most powerful forces countering the controlling ideology is the exposition of the biblical vision. Paul declared that "worldly standards have ceased to count in our estimate. . . . When anyone is united to Christ, there is a new world; the old order has gone, and the new order has already begun" (2 Cor. 5:16–17). A "new world" involves not only a new way of interpreting the world, but also a new process for ordering our priorities and responding to the pressures of the communities in which we function. In theological terms, what Paul urges when he warns us "not to be conformed to this world" (Rom. 12:2) is not an escapist, otherworldly theology, but rather an acknowledgment of the power of a controlling ideology or worldview. Paul calls us to be transformed by the renewal of our minds. Transforming education can be an important element in that conversion.

Liberating ideology calls for social reconstruction of reality for the sake of justice and contrasts that vision with the current controlling ideology of the non-poor. Walter Wink in his *Transforming Bible Study* (Nashville, Abingdon, 1980) and Robert McAfee Brown in his *Unexpected News: Reading the Bible with Third World Eyes* (Philadelphia, Westminster, 1984) illustrate what Jesus constantly does with the non-poor of his age and ours. Consider Brown's interpretation of the "vision" of Matthew 25 where the sheep are separated from the goats in the final judgment. The criteria are: Did they feed the hungry, welcome strangers, clothe the naked, and visit the sick and those in prison? One could read this passage as a call for individual charity. But Brown reminds us that those called before the throne of judgment are not individuals but *nations*. The terms for those separated for reward and condemnation, in eschatological or ultimate terms, can be more accurately translated as the "just" and the "unjust" rather than the "righteous" and "unrighteous." After interpreting the passage from the eyes of the poor and oppressed of the Third World, Brown applies the above criteria, for example, to the United States and Cuba. With critical analysis one discovers Cuba is one of the few Latin American countries that has addressed the basic problems of hunger, housing, and health for the poorest one-third of its population. One consequence of the U.S. economic embargo of Cuba is not only to fail to assist the poor of that Caribbean nation, but also to frustrate the attempts of their own government to redistribute the limited resources to the poorest people of the island. Thus, shockingly for many North Americans, Cuba lands on the side of the sheep and the good shepherd, and the United States with the goats (see *Unexpected News,* pp. 139–40). This kind of Bible study assaults several foundational presuppositions of the non-poor in North America and challenges a whole ideology which protects our privileged position in the world. Both as a nation and as individual Christians we conform to controlling ideology of inherited power and pride. The vision of judging human and national worth by the degree of service "to the least of these"—our poverty-stricken brothers and sisters in North America and throughout the world—is seen as an affront because it clashes with our ideological self-identity.

It is not surprising that this controlling ideological element in the dynamic of transformation evokes different responses. One response rejects the analysis, as occurs among the session elders in "Plant Closures." Often countering an ideology brings anger, as with the journal editor in "Gospel Agenda." The hidden power of the controlling ideology is so pervasive that it deceives even those seeking liberation. Allen Moore's commentary on "Parenting for Peace and Justice" exposes the ideological power of the model of the nuclear North American family versus the alternative liberating values of an "extended family" model more characteristic of the Third World. Occasionally persons may feel relief when the ideology is exposed, as occurred when several members of the Peacemakers group suspected they, too, were victims of the national security system that actually reduced their real security while diverting funds from the needs of the poor. In some cases the power of the ideology is so substantial that it is virtually impossible to develop an adequate counter-ideological strategy. The Greer commentary (chap. 6), highlighted by Kennedy, sees the structure of the seminary and the authority of the church as part of the controlling ideology from which it is difficult to gain liberation. This is especially true when one is working through those institutional structures.

These multifaceted responses to the controlling ideology are reflected not only in each of the models, but also in the responses of the architects, commentators, and editors. As those who participate in the ideological assumptions characteristic of the non-poor of North America, we are all captives, to some degree, of the assumptions of the society in which we are immersed. Some level of self-deception is characteristic of us all. However, we also know that in Christ's liberation we have been given a new world. It is a world of a liberating ideology.

Freedom, however, is frightening. As Freire reminds us, all of us fear our own liberation because the liberation which results from successfully countering the controlling ideology also brings accountability. The issue is not how to achieve it immediately, but how to make significant progress on the journey toward that vision. For those of us who are caught up in the dynamic of transformation and who believe in a new world, even if we do not know how it will come about, the question is: By what power will this transformation move from a vision toward reality?

E. Reinventing Power

Reinventing power may be the most difficult component of the dynamic of transformation to communicate, but from a theological perspective it may be the most important to understand. Paulo Freire encourages us to think about the relationship between any kind of education and power (see chap. 9, pp. 225–26, above). This relationship is especially critical for transformative education. Freire's notion of "reinventing power" (see chap. 9, p. 229, above) drew me into a new way of thinking theologically about the "underside" of power, much as Bonhoeffer inspired me to think about Christology "from below."

The vision of the biblical reversal discussed earlier is placed disarmingly in the song of a pregnant Jewish peasant girl named Mary who remembers from her Jewish tradition the theme of Hannah, the mother of Samuel (1 Sam. 2:1–10). Mary sings, "My soul magnifies the Lord." She states the implications of another kind of religious reversal when God becomes human to dwell among us. God comes to bear our suffering and humanity as God's own in order to transform it. Mary's Magnificat declares that God *has* (not "will" or "might") "put down the mighty from their thrones, and exalted those of low degree; has filled the hungry with good things, and the rich has sent empty away" (Luke 1:52–53). This stark reversal of the status quo is shown as already having been enacted in this incarnational act by God, who identifies with a poor, humble, working-class Jewish maiden. How could this act possibly have the power to challenge the socioeconomic structure of the world as we know it? This understanding of the incarnation would turn our normal understanding of power upside-down.

Several dialogue partners in the preparation of this book stimulated my reconsideration of the meaning of power. Freire's notion of the reinvention of power opened the door. Two other colleagues, one a biblical scholar and the other an ethicist, contributed to the reflection. Walter Wink not only enriched my approach to biblical exegesis with his *Transforming Bible Study*, but also forced me to rethink the meaning of "powers and principalities" in scripture. He released me from a narrow view of the duality of powers, seen as *either* earthly or heavenly, to a new understanding of powers in the biblical tradition. Wink carefully documents this understanding in *Naming the Powers* (Philadephia, Fortress, 1984). Wink understands powers as the "outer and inner aspects of any given manifestation of power." Powers do not exist independent of the tangible forms that they take in the world: "As the outer aspect they [the powers] are political systems or appointed officials. . . . As the inner aspect they are the spirituality of institutions, . . . the inner spirit or driving force that animates, legitimates, and regulates its [the institution's] physical manifestations in the world." (For a helpful summary of the argument in Wink's book, see *The Auburn News* [Auburn Theological Seminary, New York], Fall 1984.) Powers can be destructive or constructive, demonic or healing. Powers are a dimension of ideology, either a controlling or liberating one, and they do not exist apart from their actual manifestation in the ideology of a political party, economic system, or educational structure. A particular power can become an idol and can function in an idolatrous way to reject God's purposes for the good of the whole. The power of a revolutionary movement which removes unjust structures is in danger of consolidating its own power. In an idolatrous way it may become the new controlling ideology. Or a particular power can promote God's purposes for sufficiency, solidarity, and emancipation as a dimension of a liberating ideology that acknowledges God's comprehensive power. Wink suggests there are ways not only to *name* the powers, but also to *unmask* and *engage* them, processes which he is exploring in a trilogy on the powers. Transformative education for the non-poor is engaged in those tasks. Wink's refusal to accept powers as independently or permanently evil or good opens us to a fresh way of reflecting on power in a biblical context.

The reinvention of power is related to the rediscovery of power as used by Jesus. Larry L. Rasmussen, in "Jesus and Power" (address given at Union Theological Seminary, New York, Sept. 12, 1985), helped me see all power as relational, whether it is gentle persuasion or physical coercion. We anticipate the object of the power to be affected by the subject. Rasmussen reminds us that the dominant understanding of power, parallel in my view to controlling ideology, is "calculatedly nonmutual." In most cirumstances we "seek maximum influence on the other with minimum influence upon ourselves." Power is exercised "competitively and adversarially with the aim of mastery or control." The reinvention or rediscovery of power as observed in the dynamic of transformation poses an alternative view. Power is still relational, but is characterized by mutuality rather than sovereignty. According to Rasmussen, the result is not "mastery" but "meeting," which is marked by a shared understanding of power. There is a reciprocal relationship between two subjects which is not one of "distance and domination, but rather intimacy, vulnerability, and exchange."

Rasmussen's analysis called to my attention that the power we see in Jesus is not "powerlessness" or "weakness." Rather, it is the "power of God" which is "present in weakness" in order "to banish powerlessness." What we see in Jesus as the "great charismatic leader is precisely the one who can enter into the pain of people and articulate it, calling up from the people themselves powers of healing and change they did not know they had." The powers of the weak are real because they are "shared powers." Here is the potential for transformation, for *empowerment*. This is the "weakness of God" which is stronger than the power of human beings, especially when human power is manifested in its nonshared, nonmutual, controlling form. Beyond the historical biblical account, this new sense of power of the weak may also be seen in an act of civil disobedience for a just cause, in an economic boycott, in the voluntary sharing of power that informs the dynamic of transformation initiated in several pedagogies explored in this book. The solidarity and repositioning of the nonpoor with the poor provide the potential for the reinvention and perhaps the reenactment of power from the perspective of a liberating, empowering ideology.

God's incarnation requires a new understanding of power out of weakness, of life out of death, of resurrection out of the cross. As Paul expresses it: "We preach Christ crucified. . . . For the foolishness of God is wiser than human beings and the weakness of God is stronger than human beings" (1 Cor. 1:23–25). Douglas Hall's commentary (chap. 8, above) sees this theology of the cross as the "silent" part of the tradition. We have consistently ignored the people who are the underside of history and the force for conversion that is the underside of power. The historical pattern is clear. When a coup or revolution removes a controlling oppressive government, those who take over the power frequently adopt the former dominating oppressive style. The dynamic has not changed, only those in power, and the new leaders install a new controlling ideology to secure their own privileged position. Though historically this is a normative pattern, it is possible for power to be transformed or reinvented. Liberation requires that the cycle of simply taking over unshared power be broken. The Reign of God is characterized by a new form of power seen in God's incarnation in the person of Christ.

The Reign of God requires a new understanding of power that rests unequivocally on *trust in God*, a total dependence on God's care and mercy as the ultimate foundation, not only of security, but of life itself. Strangely enough, power is rightly exercised only when it empowers others to maximize their humanity. Power is not in holding but in relinquishing. This view of power from below measures its effectiveness in terms of service rendered, not service acquired. This power is shared with love and seeks the wholeness, humanization, and emancipation of the neighbor. Power in this biblical sense is evaluated not in terms of the empowerment of an individual or the development of singular human achievement. Rather, the measure of power from below is the mutual and reciprocal enhancement of the community. As discussed above, one of the criteria for transformation is solidarity, and if it assumes one cannot be fully human alone, unconcerned with the welfare of others, then it follows that neither can one participate in the administration of authority without the benefit of all the people being foremost in one's mind. Complete trust in God and the standards of the new order of the Kingdom of justice are consistent with what Freire calls reinventing power, the rediscovery of the underside of power seen as application of power for transformation. Individuals and movements within nations have advocated, modeled, and initially implemented a new understanding of power. Mahatma Gandhi and Martin Luther King, Jr., in modern times, present two attempts on a nationwide scale, but many of us know groups or persons working against forces of injustice, in solidarity with oppressed persons, and with a rediscovery of shared power. In my experience, examples of those working to "reinvent power" are members of the Witness for Peace community, John Fife and participants of the Sanctuary Movement, and Desmond Tutu and those communities committed to a reconciliation-oriented structuring of a non-racist society in South Africa.

Trust in God literally empowers one to *risk* his or her own life and commitment in a pattern contrary to the conforming pressures of society. Each of the models in this book assumes, at least implicitly, trust in the reinvention of power. Yet the power of the controlling ideology shows in the stubborn tendency pedagogically and pragmatically to hedge our bets. There is a reluctance really to believe that a person must lose his or her life in order to find it. It is appropriate, in Will Kennedy's terms, to be pedagogically modest about our claims. The problem is that we are also often theologically modest; we lack faith in an underside to history or power. Mary Elizabeth Moore (chap. 8) reminds us the issue is not what *we* are doing in the world but what *God* is doing in the world. The concern is what God might ask us to do (or has called us to do) as cocreators of a more just global village. As the Kinsler commentary illustrates (chap. 5), the Women's Theological Center is willing to question and put at risk the whole program for the sake of racial inclusiveness. Confidence in God's trustworthiness allows us to risk for the sake of justice.

The human dimension we have often neglected to trust is the power of our own *woundedness*. Each of the eight models moves participants toward standing with the victims, whether they be victims of a global famine, of fear of nuclear annihilation, or of race or class discrimination. Douglas Hall (chap. 8) calls this movement "suffering love." Joan Petrik in her commentary (chap. 5) highlights struggle *and* vulnerability. The models consistently acknowledge that the non-poor will not easily give up their power and privilege. One way to break into the power structure may be a rediscovered structure of solidarity, a *solidarity of suffering*. Henri Nouwen has captured at the individual level the transformative potential of the "wounded healer," who can identify with the suffering of others through an understanding of her or his own woundedness. Petrik employs Nouwen to define ministry as entering into communion with others via our human brokenness. Reinventing power understands that the solidarity of suffering as a corporate or community experience carries enormous transforming power.

Kosuke Koyama is concerned about idolatry that results in "lack of feeling and inaction in the face of the fundamental need of starving humanity" (chap. 6, p. 161). That response comes from the protected, controlling ideology of the non-poor in North America as representatives of the First World. There appears to be no front door to subverting the dominant notion of power. At the consultation, Koyama proposed that we look for a back door, a crack in the wall. A pedagogy for the non-poor must take seriously the admonition to be as wise as serpents. Thus Koyama declared we need a serpentine strategy. This strategy would seek the crack where charismatic grace breaks through. I am convinced, with Koyama, that this transformation occurs by finding the underside of power. This discovery could be seen as an act of grace. Douglas Hall's commentary (chap. 8) refers to trans-pedagogical factors which contribute to transformation. This process is perhaps what Freire means when he urges Christians not just to talk about Easter but to "do Easter" or "make Easter." There is a noncontrollable, nondescribable process akin to conversion that occurs in the dynamic of transformation. However, some of the principal pedagogical components or factors in the transformative process *can*, I believe, be identified. These are:

A. Encounter with the Poor
B. Experiential Immersion that Challenges Assumptions
C. Openness to Vulnerability
D. Community of Support and Accountability
E. Vision and Values
F. Cycle of Critical Socioeconomic Analysis
G. Commitment, Involvement, and Leadership
H. Symbol, Ritual, and Liturgy

III. COMPONENTS OF TRANSFORMATION

Research on pedagogies for the non-poor confirms that transformative education does occur and can be documented. This knowledge calls for celebration. Reflection on the pedagogies project of the Plowshares Institute has resulted in renewed hope for some educators with special concerns for peace and justice. However, the most significant consequence of the research for me was the identification of components which appear to be critical in the process of transformative education. Dialogue with the architects and critics of the models helped me discern in transformative education these key elements and a recurring pattern. If such components can be identified and replicated, they may influence how we design new educational projects seeking transformation for justice and peace. Clarification of components should also help us to modify current educational endeavors or even to abandon some long-standing projects as lacking appropriate components for transformation.

Let me stress that it is an *initial* identification of critical components that I find personally illuminating and provocative. No claim is made for a causal relationship between the presence of the components and transformative education. However, in educational models where there is evidence that such transformation of intention and behavior has occurred, these components seem to be consistently present in one form or another. This coincidence merits further dialogue, investigation, and research.

The nature of the components and their implications are still in debate. Will Kennedy and I reflect this ongoing dialogue in our articles, and we invite the reader to join us. What Kennedy identifies in the "how" section of his article as the "clues" for transformative education (pp. 249–55, above) are not identical with my "components for transformation." There are stimulating differences, and yet there is also a core of commonality in our analyses.

Is there a necessary sequence or an order of importance for this combination of components in a design for transformative education? I doubt it. However, I shall highlight those components which I believe should be given more attention in many of the models. It has become increasingly clear that certain components are indispensable.

A. Encounter with the Poor

The initial revision of the map of reality for the non-poor requires a *direct* encounter with the poor or oppressed, those persons who suffer as innocent victims of the structure of a society that protects the privileges of the non-poor. The controlling ideology is so powerful and pervasive that it is virtually impossible for the non-poor to educate themselves on issues of peace and justice, to pierce the ideological cocoon, apart from a direct encounter with the poor. Acquaintance with the victims precedes any identification or solidarity with the poor. Dialogues, visits, or immersion experiences in the models in this book provide this component, while preparation for such a direct encounter may come through stories and films. The research confirms the participants' own evaluation that the "turning point" or "conversion" in the transformative dynamic comes with a direct and personal encounter with poor or oppressed persons or groups. "Encounter" should not be confused with a superficial "meeting." Genuine encounter calls forth an acknowledgment of unjust conditions and a demand for action on the part of the non-poor.

The evidence makes me profoundly skeptical that indirect encounters such as stories, case studies, films, or presentations by even the most articulate advocates of the poor or oppressed will succeed in doing any more than providing basic preparation for or reinforcement of a *direct, personal,* and *sustained* encounter. Change is not initiated by indirect or secondary processes of confrontation. Direct encounter exposes the non-poor not only to the consequences of the suffering at some level, but also to the strength, resources, and gifts of the poor as they challenge their own oppression. Participants in the models that incorporate direct encounter declare they have discovered a "richness" of human spirit and community not present in their own more privileged and protected non-poor circles. In addition, a personal encounter is often the only way effectively to challenge the non-poor's stereotype of the poor as "lazy," "undependable," or otherwise responsible for their condition. The conclusion for me is to acknowledge that the poor and oppressed themselves are the indispensable teachers and eventual liberators of the non-poor. Thus every educational model that hopes or claims to be transformative must give priority in time, energy, and resources to direct, personal, and sustained encounters between the poor and non-poor. Many programs fail to recognize sufficiently the teaching and transforming role of the poor.

B. Experiential Immersion that Challenges Assumptions

The language of "conversion" and "reversal," the vision of countering the controlling ideology for the sake of justice, and the discussion of the necessity for adjustments in lifestyle all imply major shifts in perspectives for the non-poor. The research points to the need for an experiential shock that challenges previous assumptions, reduces one's resistance to change, and requires the exploration of alternative patterns of living. For those reasons some type of immersion experience appears indispensable to transformative education. The immersion experience shapes the conditions under which a personal encounter with poor and oppressed people can be fully incorporated. It has an intensity and sustained quality that breaks down the barriers erected by our previous isolation and assumptions.

Will Kennedy describes a parallel component as a "radical change of environment" (see pp. 250–51, above). He warns that some shifts in environment, rather than countering the controlling ideology, may actually reinforce negative stereotypes and confirm assumptions that hold the victims responsible for their poverty and lack of freedom. I grant that in regard to the immersion component the need for more attention to preparation, process, and bridging between the old environment and the new is critical, but I am convinced both by an analysis of the research and by personal experience that transformative education is almost impossible apart from an immersion experience of some type. The location of an immersion may vary from Columbia Point in Boston to Spanish Harlem, from India to Nicaragua. The theme may shift from hunger and housing to racism and sexism. The focus may be a freeze on nuclear weapons or unjust labor practices. However, an immersion experience which forces one to confront the unjust suffering caused by current structures and exposes one to the human courage to combat such injustice seems to be crucial to initiating transformation.

The cost, even the imposition upon the poor, must be assessed, but there is increasing evidence that energy for sustainable change for justice and reconciliation comes from such experiences. If we want our educational models to succeed and wish to enlarge the tiny core of those among the non-poor working for structural change, we must be willing to pay the cost in concentration, time, money, and openness to critique that is necessary to implement viable models of experiential immersion. A middle-class black pastor who participated in two plunges, one in an inner-city in the United States, the other in Africa, made a confession: "What changed my life and the nature of my ministry was not primarily what I learned about Africa or Harlem, but rather what I learned about my own assumptions concerning America and my congregation. I saw in a new way the justice demands of the gospel to change, and we got started."

C. *Openness to Vulnerability*

Vulnerability is impossible to assure in an educational design. Therefore, I have used the idea of openness to vulnerability as a feasible goal. The risk involved in placing oneself in vulnerable situations is an important component of transformation. This is especially true when the situation is likely to require one's temporary dependence on the poor, who are normally perceived as dependent on the charity or generosity of the non-poor. Will Kennedy stresses the dimension of "risk" and the importance of getting the "adrenalin running" in order to be turned around (pp. 251–52, above). In my experience such risk includes for the non-poor a sense of danger, a high level of energy, and a desire to investigate new alternatives. Yet one result which a risk-laden act evokes may be even more determinative for transformation. It is the willingness to be genuinely vulnerable to and dependent on the care and skills of a person in whom one would normally place no trust, especially concerning personal health and safety. Persons voluntarily engaging in a cross-cultural immersion experience, either overseas or in an urban domestic location, usually feel deep anxiety. They then feel deep appreciation for the basic support and human companionship that result from living through an experience and discovering the common bonds of humanity and necessary interdependence between poor and non-poor. In the Traveling for Transformation model, the highest impact rating for influencing how participants viewed justice issues in a North-South perspective went consistently not to presidents, prime ministers, bishops, or scholars with whom the group met but to ordinary village hosts who cared for group members in what was perceived as a vulnerable time and location.

Is it a sign of our lack of experience or trust as educators that we tend to seek ways to reduce rather than heighten the degree of risk and vulnerability for participants when designing educational events? Not only does risk increase the potential for transformative consequences, but it actually makes the educational experience more attractive for many candidates. If isolation from the poor, as Kennedy describes it, was one of the principal problems to be addressed in the first two components of "encounter" and "immersion" with the poor, then protection from risk and consequent vulnerability is the concern in the third component. However, a particular type of "community" undergirds the effectiveness of all three initial components.

D. Community of Support and Accountability

The components of transformative education often function in interdependent and complementary ways. A community of support can provide the foundation for taking the risk to be vulnerable in an immersion encounter with the poor and oppressed. Will Kennedy has documented the critical role of community in the models represented in this study (see pp. 252–53, above). The type of transformative education measured by the criteria set forth here can be initiated and sustained only in an intimate, ongoing community of support and accountability. Often both internal and external conflict are very high for individuals and communities which are exploring action for change in relation to justice and peace. Studies on conflict management make it clear that persons and organizations are best able to hear accurately and receive constructively both critique and suggestions about alternative ways of functioning when they feel good about themselves, when there is a psychological power base. G. Douglass Lewis, in his development of principles of conflict management in a theological context (see *Resolving Church Conflicts*, New York, Harper and Row, 1983), links that power base to an experience of Christian community similar to what I called "shared power" in my discussion of reinventing power. A supportive community, especially a community of faith, allows persons to discern and respond to the demands of a biblical reversal for their own lives and institutions with a degree of honesty and integrity that would be impossible alone. There is little evidence of effective transformative education for individuals unrelated to a community of support.

However, to sustain the transformation the community of support must also be a community of accountability. We are naturally threatened by the modifications of lifestyle and structure demanded by a call for justice. The process of establishing covenants of accountability that set forth achievable goals for moving toward redistribution, repositioning, and reevaluation is essential to sustaining transformation. The ability of the community to acknowledge failure, grant forgiveness, and renegotiate covenants is also critical to the process of transformation. Covenant partners for individuals as well as group contracts have been employed as effective aids in focusing accountability. Disillusionment, self-deception, and burnout often characterize the journey of those seeking to promote a liberating ideology that would transform unjust structures of society. Immediately accessible communities of support such as the Latin American base communities or support networks in North America are again and again cited as being pivotal in the transforming dynamic.

Transformative educational models must give a high priority to establishing and nurturing communities of support and accountability. Community-building is especially critical at the local levels of immediate contact, but it is also important at regional or national levels, through national networks of common concern, and through congregations and denominations in the faith community. There will frequently be resistant and blocking forces within the community at both a local and regional level. However, the aim of "solidarity through a repositioning" with a new community of poor and oppressed also offers an experience of community across the boundaries of class, race, sex, or nation. This solidarity is fragile but profound, and is usually rooted in an immersion encounter. Participants in educational events whose experience of solidarity can be developed into ongoing relationships will continue to find support and accountability for change in the direction of sufficiency and emancipation. The community plays an important role in sustaining the vision and values considered in the next component.

E. Vision and Values

Articulating and sustaining the vision are essential to movements toward change. The vision of a more just, sustainable, and peaceful world, which in the case of most models in this study includes a theological dimension, was developed in an earlier section. The research suggests that transformative education needs the explicit articulation and remembrance of a vision and the constituent values that sustain that vision. Effective resistance to injustice and certainly the energy to act for structural change demand constant clarification of the new map of reality. The implementation of transformative models seems to insist on careful *preparation* before an encounter or immersion experience with the poor. Several of the models have a clear set of expectations, sometimes reinforced with a learning contract, that participants devote specified amounts of time for reading, discussion, and experience-based encounters with victims as part of an educational event. This process requires clear intentionality and high commitment. Transformative models must be clearer about those expectations and more rigorous in their application.

The following relationship is demonstrable: the more demanding the prerequisites, the fewer the number of persons who will be willing to commit themselves to transformative education. Those who do may be described as a vanguard or a remnant. I personally prefer the image of an "anticipatory community of faith." The models in this book are Christian-oriented models of transformation for global justice and peace. The vision and the values reflected in these models are shared neither by the whole human community nor probably by the majority of the Christian community. This means that special concentration must be given to: (a) methods of assisting participants to identify their own values; (b) innovative approaches for the appropriation or reappropriation of the biblical vision; and (c) concretely bridging the gap between values and their application to local issues of injustice and alienation. The models begin that process by illustrating a number of approaches and inviting the readers' scrutiny and adaptation. New approaches to biblical exegesis and application of theological themes to current situations have been exciting areas of exploration and exchange among the models. In the faith community the biblical roots of justice have sometimes been assumed, especially in small groups of Christians committed to a particular cause. The articulation and application of the vision and values need to become more explicit.

F. Cycle of Critical Socioeconomic Analysis: Reflection/Action/Reflection

Neglected components in the transformative educational exchange, I have argued, are the experiential and the dialogical. Control over the non-poor by the dominant ideology is sustained by their experiental isolation from the reality under which the victims of poverty live. The reluctance on the part of the non-poor to trust their intuition and emotions when they are exposed to this reality contributes to that control.

In addition to the need for the emotional, intuitive, and experiential components, there is a need for an analytical and critical element in transformative education. The Introduction to this volume traced the recent polarization of action and reflection. A balance to the rhythm or cycle must be restored. This calls for a dual emphasis on critical, reflective preparation and follow-up plus experiential-based action: that is, a cycle of reflection/action/reflection. Although I believe the pivotal components for transformation in the cycle at this historical moment are encounter and immersion, I am also convinced transformation is unlikely without serious, critical, systemic socioeconomic analysis. Will Kennedy has probed this theme under his hints on "reflection" and "outside data" (pp. 254–55, above). I want to underline the importance of the rhythm between the two which shapes the "praxis of social action," or, in the case of these models, "the praxis of social ministry."

There is a troubling absence of critical social analysis that takes seriously economic and political systems that are alternatives to the dominant North American "democratic-capitalist" ideology. Many of the Third World nations and the marginalized people of First World nations are becoming committed to a "democratic-socialist" model or the exploration of a third alternative between traditional capitalism and traditional socialism. The profound ignorance among the non-poor of North America, Western Europe, and Japan concerning these alternative socioeconomic models calls for more use of credible and reliable socioeconomic data to encourage consideration of these alternatives. Whether the content of the preparation employs government population data or comparative global economic statistics such as those contained in the *Global 2000 Report to the President*, this component is a significant part of the design of an educational project. Reflection on the data alternates with an action-encounter with the victims and then with another reflection or debriefing session in light of the experience.

G. Commitment, Involvement, and Leadership

This cluster of components may appear so necessary to transformative education as to be self-evident. However, it is interesting how often architects, including myself, underestimate the significance of what Will Kennedy calls "learning with your feet." He emphasizes the demands of a self-conscious commitment of precious time and energy on the part of the non-poor in his section on the "how" of transformative education (pp. 249–50). The role of leadership is also explored in his essay (pp. 233–34). I wish to join the two in this component because I think there is a strong connection between expected commitment, empowered involvement, and empowering shared leadership. The latter is facilitated not just by the formally designated leader of an educational event but by the developing and reciprocal leadership of the whole learning community as well.

Each of the models reveals the importance of consolidating one's learnings about injustice and oppression through corporate activity of the community and by means of a specific agenda. Becoming a Sanctuary community, participating in an antinuclear demonstration, lobbying Congressional representatives, modifying a consumer-oriented lifestyle, or positioning oneself as part of a Witness for Peace human shield on the Nicaraguan/Honduran border are examples. The research implies that transformation cannot be sustained without some incorporation of commitment into concrete action. Transformative educational models should seek to be as clear about the involvement anticipated or follow-through obligations as they are about preparatory commitment. While one cannot and ought not determine exactly what one will learn and be committed to do, areas of commitment can be anticipated. Specific learning contracts or covenants, at least on a projected basis, have proved effective. These may cause the project to be more selective by nature. However, the common expression of commitment formed by an anticipatory covenant tends to build community and increase involvement.

Educators of all persuasions have stressed the importance of *modeling* in the learning process. The sharing of leadership and power reflects a reciprocal style of leadership that has an impact not only on non-poor participants but also in encounters between the poor and the non-poor. Gregory Baum, notes Kennedy (see p. 234, above), states that charismatic authority is characterized by the ability "to give voice to the common suffering" experienced by all. This understanding can be merged, I think, with Larry Rasmussen's sense of "shared power," where the charismatic leadership of Jesus models entering into the pain of others and calls forth powers of healing and change people did not realize they had. Effective leadership in transformative education appears to highlight a kind of charismatic authority that by its own commitment, involvement, and mutuality is empowering for change.

There are marks of leadership for all participants in models of transformative education: (a) lifestyles tested against the criteria for transformation; (b) styles of learning and teaching that are mutual; (c) ability to learn from and honor the gifts of the poor; (d) skills in articulating common alienation; and (e) sensitivity to empowering others.

Those who design transformative educational events need to focus on the composition of the group and on clarifying the nature and extent of expectations for participants. The emphasis needs to be placed on the quality of the relationship between the participants and their leaders or teachers. *"With whom* we learn" is often as important as "what we learn." I have become aware through my research that, as educators, we sometimes are not sufficiently convinced of the power of change through relationships with colearners. Many educators fail to give priority to recruiting, funding, and creating a learning community that is genuinely diverse in terms of class, race, and sex. The composition of the learning community in projects of transformative education is a key factor in empowering commitment as well as in challenging presuppositions.

H. Symbol, Ritual, and Liturgy

Douglas Hall, in his commentary on the "Gospel Agenda" case, compares transformation to a "leap of faith." Communities, especially Christian congregations, could provide, Hall recommends, opportunities for "non- or trans-pedagogical possibilities" which, he believes, are necessary for transformation (see pp. 207–8, above). Some of the elements of this component exist in each of the models. They are trans-pedagogical in that they go beyond what could be perceived in educational terms alone. There is often an interconnection between symbol and ritual that appears in the transformative experience. In the Christian community the liturgy or worship experience frequently becomes the event in which the symbols of the community and the ritual that dramatizes those symbols is lived out. Transformation of consciousness by experience or reflection is enhanced by receiving and participating in illuminating and transforming symbols. This is especially true of the faith community. Rollo May supports this assertion about religious symbols in noting their two psychological functions. First, they are a way of seeing one's life, self-image, and relation with the world. Second, symbols embody "the vital meaning of . . . experience" (*Symbolism in Religion and Literature*, New York, Braziller, 1959, p. 34). In the process of transformation the vision of a new reality contains the symbolic declaration of the meaning and direction of human life. Thus the images, slogans, songs, and so on that symbolically bind the members of a community together are a means of embodying the transformation toward which they are striving. The symbols are then combined in ritual activities, that, according to anthropologist Monica Wilson, "reveal values at their deepest level" ("Symbol and Ritual," *American Anthropologist* 56, no. 2, p. 241). In the study of transformative education we must acknowledge the critical influence of symbol, ritual, and liturgy and thus the trans-pedagogical dimension of the process. Worship is essential to transformative education in a community of faith. The models in this study reflect the crucial nature of worship, prayer, and Bible study. "Peacemaking in a Local Parish" highlights the necessary connection between the inward journey of spiritual nurture and the outward journey of action for justice. Research on some models indicates that "deepening spirituality" parallels behavioral change.

The models in this study consistently return to the symbolic resources of the

Judeo-Christian tradition, particularly the biblical symbols, as resources for the educational dynamic. Yet given our preoccupation with models of traditional schooling, even in theological education, we are still in danger of giving inadequate attention to these trans-pedagogical components. The idea of re-inventing power with the cross as the symbol of suffering love has not been a major feature in the restructuring of theological education around the images of sufficiency, solidarity, and emancipation. The artistic imagination that David Frenchak evokes (chap. 3) will demand special concern in the predominantly non-poor seminaries and congregations where the implementation of a liberating ideology has not yet been systematically pursued.

PERSONAL POSTSCRIPT

A discussion and listing of components may appear to imply that it is only a matter of "plugging in the right elements" to achieve transformation. Nothing could be further from my understanding of transformative education. The preceding analysis is constructive if it helps educators examine those factors which assist in removing the obstacles or clearing the ground for transformation to occur. Yet transformation is like an experience of genuine community or *communitas* (explicated by R. A. Evans in "The Quest for Community," *Union Seminary Quarterly Review* 30, 1975, pp. 188ff.). Transformation can never be simply created because transformation is not a possession. Transformation is a gift which can be celebrated and cared for by stewards. Transformation is not hierarchical or authoritarian; it is egalitarian and reciprocal. It requires the support of a community. The process of transformation retains an element of mystery that is beyond our control and beyond our complete comprehension. Even those of us who have experienced and continue to re-experience transformative encounters for the sake of justice and peace are unable adequately to articulate and analyze what has occurred to us and our communities. We can only rejoice (although frequently we also complain) that the divine restlessness is maintained and the vision for ourselves and God's global village is sustained and revitalized. We are not altogether sure how this occurs.

Transformation is a quality of relationship among the persons in community who are radically open to the Transcendent. Transformation is the transpersonal embodiment of God's grace that seeks justice and reconciliation for all. The experience of transformation is not segmented; it is holistic. There is a periodic demand that new experiences of transformation be reintegrated into our maps of reality. Thus there must be an adjustment in the priorities and lifestyles of our communities of support and accountability. We frequently resist these changes or ignore threatening new information because it is too painful and difficult to face. But the demand persists, and new transformative educational experiences help prepare us to face the next round of creative change. Such a preparation and renewal period was connected to the research done for this book on pedagogies for the non-poor. It emerged as we developed the models in case form and particularly when my wife Alice and I renewed our relationship to friends in South Africa and Central America.

If we are dealing with a "continual conversion of the spirit," then why struggle to discern and articulate the criteria, dynamic, and especially the components of transformation? I acknowledge the limits of the models and analytic efforts in this book, as does Will Kennedy in his section on "pedagogical realism" (pp. 255–56, above). Yet I also believe passionately that the ultimate goal of liberating education is transformation. The call of the Christian gospel is epitomized by Romans 12:2: "Do not be conformed to this world but be transformed by the renewal of your mind. . . ." Therefore, educators for transformation can and should use the criteria of transformation as new standards, the dynamic of transformation as a suggested rhythm, and the components of transformation as guidelines. The guidelines provide a provocative checklist as we design, critique, and redesign the educational events which we lead and in which we participate. The prospect of that challenge is both distressing and exciting. Fortunately, it is more exciting than distressing, thanks in good measure to the dialogue partners in this book and especially to my coeditors. These colleagues have become a community of learning and faith which Martin Buber described so instructively and eloquently:

> Community is being no longer side by side (and, one might add, above and below) but *with* one another of a multitude of persons. And this multitude, though it moves toward one goal, experiences everywhere a turning to, a dynamic facing of, a flowing from I to Thou. Community is where community happens [*Between Man and Man*, London, Fontana, 1961, p. 61].

It is our "I/Thouness," our common humanity, that stands beneath our ideologically imprisoned selves. This foundational bond of humanity is what the gospel addresses as it calls for our transformation. Despite all our ideological conditioning, by God's grace the non-poor, including ourselves, can and do respond to the call to transformative educational experiences and to committed action for justice and peace.

CONTRIBUTORS

Sydney Brown, Staff Associate, Interfaith Council on Economic Justice and Work, Oakland, CA; and Lecturer in Religion and Society, Pacific School of Religion, Berkeley, CA

Richard D. N. Dickinson, Dean, Christian Theological Seminary, Indianapolis, IN

Alice Frazer Evans, Director of Writing and Research, Plowshares Institute, Simsbury, CT

Robert A. Evans, Executive Director, Plowshares Institute, Simsbury, CT

Candace Fair, Family Therapist and active member of Bread for the World, Hyattsville, MD

Daniel L. Force, Office on Global Education, Church World Service, Baltimore, MD

Paulo Freire, Professor of Education, Pontifícia Universidade Católica de São Paulo, Brazil

David J. Frenchak, Director, Seminary Consortium for Urban Pastoral Education, Chicago, IL

Cheryl A. Giles, Program Coordinator, Women's Theological Center, Boston, MA

Noë Gonzales, Associate General Secretary, Board of Discipleship, The United Methodist Church, Nashville, TN

Colin Greer, Executive Director, New World Foundation, New York, NY

Nancy C. Hajek, Administrative Director, Plowshares Institute, Simsbury, CT

Douglas John Hall, Professor of Christian Theology, McGill University, Montreal, Québec, Canada

Joseph C. Hough, Jr., Dean and Professor of Christian Ethics, School of Theology, Claremont, CA

Thomas Hunsdorfer, Assistant Director, Chrysalis Program, Christian Theological Seminary, Indianapolis, IN

Carman St. J. Hunter, Technical Specialist, World Education, Inc., Brooklyn, NY

Frances H. Kennedy, Consultant, Church Women United, New York, NY

William Bean Kennedy, Skinner and McAlpin Professor of Practical Theology, Union Theological Seminary, New York, NY

F. Ross Kinsler, Director, Southern California Extension Center, San Francisco Theological Seminary, Inglewood, CA

Kosuke Koyama, Professor of Ecumenics and World Christianity, Union Theological Seminary, New York, NY

G. Douglass Lewis, President, Wesley Theological Seminary, Washington, DC

James B. McGinnis, Director, Institute for Peace and Justice; and Co-National Coordinator, Parenting for Peace and Justice Network, St. Louis, MO

Allen J. Moore, Professor of Religion and Personality and Education, Claremont School of Theology, Claremont, CA

Mary Elizabeth Moore, Associate Professor of Christian Education and Theology, Claremont School of Theology, Claremont, CA

Marie Augusta Neal, S.N.D., Professor of Sociology, Emmanuel College, Boston, MA

Jan Orr-Harter, Associate Pastor, West-Park Presbyterian Church, New York, NY

Joan Petrik, M.M., Maryknoll Sisters World Awareness Team, Maryknoll Sisters, Maryknoll, NY

John Quinn, Religious Education Consultant, Hamilton-Wentworth Catholic School Board, Hamilton, Ontario, Canada

Nancy D. Richardson, Co-Director, Women's Theological Center, Boston, MA

Philip J. Scharper, the late Editor-in-Chief and General Manager, Orbis Books, Maryknoll, NY

Grant S. Shockley, The Divinity School, Duke University, Durham, NC

Adele Smith-Pennington, Faculty, Women's Theological Center, Boston, MA

Suzanne C. Toton, Associate Professor of Christian Living and Religious Education, Villanova University, Villanova, PA

Jane K. Vella, Director of Training, Save the Children Federation, Westport, CT

Other Orbis Titles . . .

HUMAN RIGHTS
A Dialogue Between the First and Third Worlds
by Robert and Alice Evans

A collection of eight case studies of Christians faced with dilemmas involving the violation and/or preservation of basic human rights. The dilemmas involve a variety of issues such as racism, foreign investments by multinational corporations, migrant rights, and housing. Each case study is supplemented by a "teaching note" and by two or three commentaries by well known theologians including Rubem Alves, John Mbiti, Jürgen Moltmann, and Kosuke Koyama.

no. 194-2   236pp. pbk. $9.95

CONVICTIONS
Political Prisoners—Their Stories
by Arthur Dobrin, Lyn Dobrin, and Thomas F. Liotti

The vivid accounts of the experiences of political prisoners in nine different countries— Argentina, Uganda, Rhodesia/Zimbabwe, Cambodia/Kampuchea, the United States, Poland, the Soviet Union, the Philippines, and Chile.

"Torture, unjust imprisonment, and political repression seem almost commonplace today. In this book the true stories of persons who have gone through such fires remind us of brutal facts that must never be commonplace to any of us. If God is on the side of the oppressed and the sinned against we must listen carefully to their experience—as we can in this little volume—not to recoil in horror but to commit ourselves in solidarity to the many who even now anonymously suffer these same indignities." *Eugene L. Stockwell,*
Associate General Secretary, National Council of Churches

no. 089-X   100pp. pbk. $5.95

THE STRUGGLE FOR HUMANITY
Agents of Nonviolent Change in a Violent World
by Marjorie Hope and James Young

A series of portraits of leaders in the nonviolent struggle for social and political change.

". . . an immensely helpful and valuable book . . . the authors have combined an unmistakable admiration for and appreciation of these leaders with a perceptive and judicious criticism of them." *Occasional Bulletin of Missionary Research*

no. 469-0   305pp. pbk. $6.95

JUSTICE AND PEACE EDUCATION
Models for College and University Faculty
edited by David M. Johnson

A collection of models for integrating justice and peace concerns into courses in various disciplines ranging from the humanities, the social sciences, and interdisciplinary studies to business, management, and engineering. Based on the practical educational and research experience of professors in U.S. Catholic colleges and universities, each model includes a course syllabus, a list of required texts for students, and suggested readings for faculty. The result is an intelligent, pragmatic manual for educators seeking to promote a more just and peaceful world. Contributors include Monika Hellwig, William Byron, David O'Brien, Marie Augusta Neal, Thomas Shannon, and Suzanne Toton.

"A remarkable array of authors and a really sophisticated approach in which peace and justice themes are introduced without despoiling the inner integrity of the various disciplines."
Padraic O'Hare,
Boston College

no. 247-7   256pp. pbk. $16.95

PARENTING FOR PEACE AND JUSTICE
by Kathleen and James McGinnis

How do parents act for justice without sacrificing their own children? How do they build family community without isolating themselves from the world? In this practical and insightful volume, Kathleen and James McGinnis address these and many other problems families may encounter in their effort to integrate social and family ministry. Topics discussed include stewardship, nonviolence both in and outside the family, promoting sexual equality in the family, multiculturalizing family life, and inviting children to participate in social action.

"The guide is filled with exercises, readings, and worksheets to supplement the reading of the book and make its contents all the more real in our lives. This combination is indispensable for educators and families alike."
Religious Education

no. 376-1   143pp. pbk. $6.95

WORLD HUNGER
The Responsibility of Christian Education
by Suzanne Toton

"I believe this is the one best book available for serious analysis and action on world hunger. It brings together effectively the dimensions of the problem that must be considered as a whole: emergency food relief, aid and trade, multinational structures, and analysis of 'root causes' as well as practical suggestions for study and action."
William B. Kennedy,
Union Theological Seminary

no. 716-9   224pp. pbk. $7.95